ENCYCLOPEDIA OF
FAMILY HEALTH

ENCYCLOPEDIA OF
FAMILY HEALTH

CONSULTANT
DAVID B. JACOBY, MD
JOHNS HOPKINS SCHOOL OF MEDICINE

VOLUME
16

TYPHOID AND PARATYPHOID—ZEST

MARSHALL CAVENDISH
NEW YORK · LONDON · TORONTO · SYDNEY

Marshall Cavendish Corporation

99 White Plains Road

Tarrytown, New York 10591-9001

© Marshall Cavendish Corporation, 1998

© Marshall Cavendish Limited 1998, 1991, 1988, 1986, 1983, 1982, 1971

Update by Brown Partworks

The material in this set was first published in the English language by

Marshall Cavendish Limited of 119 Wardour Street, London W1V 3TD, England.

Printed and bound in Italy

Library of Congress Cataloging-in-Publication Data

Encyclopedia of family health
17v. cm.
Includes index
1. Medicine, Popular–Encyclopedias. 2. Health–Encyclopedias. I. Marshall Cavendish Corporation.
RC81.A2M336 1998   96-49537
610'.3-dc21   CIP
ISBN 0-7614-0625-5 (set)
ISBN 0-7614-0641-7 (v.16)

INTRODUCTION

We Americans live under a constant bombardment of information (and misinformation) about the latest supposed threats to our health. We are taught to believe that disease is the result of not taking care of ourselves. Death becomes optional. Preventive medicine becomes a moral crusade, illness the punishment for the foolish excesses of the American lifestyle. It is not the intent of the authors of this encyclopedia to contribute to this atmosphere. While it is undoubtedly true that Americans could improve their health by smoking less, exercising more, and controlling their weight, this is already widely understood.

As Mencken put it, "It is not the aim of medicine to make men virtuous. The physician should not preach salvation, he should offer absolution." The aims of this encyclopedia are to present a summary of human biology, anatomy, and physiology, to outline the more common diseases, and to discuss, in a general way, the diagnosis and treatment of these diseases. This is not a do-it-yourself book. It will not be possible to treat most conditions based on the information presented here. But it will be possible to understand most diseases and their treatments. Informed in this way, you will be able to discuss your condition and its treatment with your physician. It is also hoped that this will alleviate some of the fears associated with diseases, doctors, and hospitals.

The authors of this encyclopedia have also attempted to present, in an open-minded way, alternative therapies. There is undoubtedly value to some of these. However, when dealing with serious diseases, they should not be viewed as a substitute for conventional treatment. The reason that conventional treatment is accepted is that it has been systematically tested, and because scientific evidence backs it up. It would be a tragedy to miss the opportunity for effective treatment while pursuing an ineffective alternative therapy.

Finally, it should be remembered that the word *doctor* is originally from the Latin word for "teacher." Applied to medicine, this should remind us that the doctor's duty is not only to diagnose and treat disease, but to help the patient to understand. If this encyclopedia can aid in this process, its authors will be gratified.

DAVID B. JACOBY, MD
JOHNS HOPKINS SCHOOL OF MEDICINE

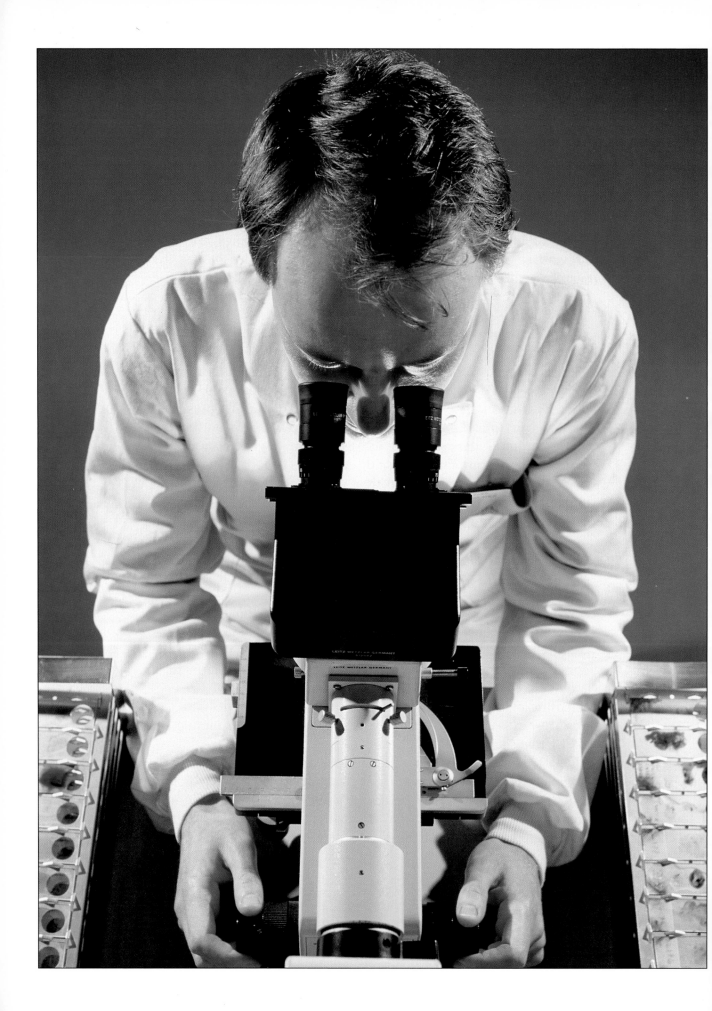

CONTENTS

Typhoid and paratyphoid	2054	Vitamin D	2125
Typhus	2058	Vitamin E	2127
Ulcers	2060	Vitamin K	2130
Ultrasound	2065	Vitamins	2132
Unconsciousness	2068	Vitiligo	2133
Uremia	2072	Vocal cords	2134
Urethra	2073	Vomiting	2135
Uterus	2074	Vulva	2137
Vaccinations	2078	Warts	2139
Vagina	2080	Wax in ear	2142
Vaginal discharge	2083	Wellness	2144
Vagotomy	2087	Wheezing	2148
Valves	2088	Whiplash injury	2150
Varicose veins	2090	Whitlow	2152
Vasectomy	2094	Whooping cough	2153
Vegetarianism	2098	Withdrawal symptoms	2158
Veins	2102	Worms	2161
Ventricular fibrillation	2104	Wounds	2164
Verruca	2106	Wrinkles	2170
Vertigo	2109	Wrist	2172
Virginity	2112	X rays	2174
Viruses	2114	Yeast infections	2180
Vitamin A	2118	Yellow fever	2183
Vitamin B	2120	Yoga	2184
Vitamin C	2123	Zest	2190

Typhoid and paratyphoid

Q I have heard that typhoid is worse if you have gallstones. Is this true?

A No. If you have gallstones you are much more likely to become a carrier of the disease. The organism seems to be particularly disposed to settle in the gallbladder, and the presence of gallstones makes this easier.

Q Are children likely to catch typhoid?

A Yes. However, the illness in children can be difficult for a doctor to recognize. The disease usually lasts for a shorter period and may seem to be primarily a respiratory illness.

Q Can typhoid be treated with antibiotics?

A Yes. Chloramphenicol is used to treat typhoid and has made a great impact on mortality from the disease. Typhoid can still be fatal but usually the illness responds well to treatment, and the fever settles within about five days instead of persisting for three weeks. Chloramphenicol has the serious disadvantage that in a tiny proportion of patients it leads to suppression of the bone marrow, so that blood cells are no longer produced. This is a fatal condition in itself, but the risk of this happening is much smaller than the risk of dying from untreated typhoid. Chloramphenicol is less effective in clearing up carrier states. Ampicillin is used successfully for this.

Q Can you catch typhoid from corned beef?

A There was a famous outbreak of typhoid in Aberdeen in Scotland in 1964. It seems that some contaminated water was sucked into a can of corned beef through a tiny crack during the cooling period after the canning process. This was indirectly a waterborne infection; water contaminated with sewage is a common cause of typhoid outbreaks. However, canned foods are usually safe.

Typhoid is still one of the most serious infectious fevers, but antibiotics and modern sanitation have gone a long way toward controlling it. Paratyphoid, as the name suggests, is a similar but less severe illness.

The serious infectious fevers typhus and typhoid have been recognized for centuries, but until the middle of the last century no distinction was made between them and they were both called typhus (see Typhus). In reality, the two diseases are quite distinct in their effects. Although typhoid, which affects the intestines in particular, was gradually recognized as a separate disease, its association with typhus remained since the name *typhoid* simply means "typhus-like." Paratyphoid is a disease very like typhoid but is considerably less severe.

Causes
Typhoid is caused by one of the salmonella organisms (see Salmonella), which

Typhoid in the small intestine

A serious complication of typhoid occurs in the small intestine, where the organism infects lymphatic tissue called Peyer's *patches. These become inflamed and ulcerate, causing perforation of the intestinal wall (insets).*

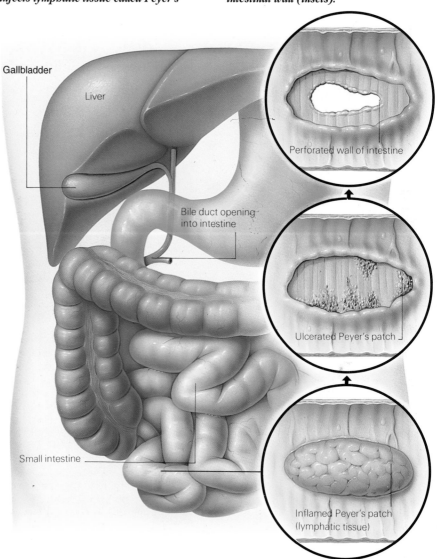

Gallbladder

Liver

Bile duct opening into intestine

Small intestine

Perforated wall of intestine

Ulcerated Peyer's patch

Inflamed Peyer's patch (lymphatic tissue)

The typhoid organism is carried in human feces, which can contaminate food and water in unsanitary surroundings, like this street market in Bangladesh. A major reason for the far fewer epidemics in the West are the higher standards of hygiene that prevail there.

are spread by contaminated food and water and therefore give rise to food poisoning. *Salmonella typhi* (the typhoid organism) has developed in such a way as to cause a generalized illness only in humans. There are three different types of paratyphoid caused by the organisms *Salmonella paratyphi* A, B, and C. In the West, paratyphoid B is the only one of any real importance.

How infection is spread

Salmonella typhi survives so successfully because some infected people continue to pass the organism in their feces, yet remain quite fit and symptom free. Such people are called carriers, and are obviously ideal hosts for the organism, which tends to settle in the gallbladder and can remain there for years while new organisms are excreted into the intestine via the bile duct.

In the past, food and water became readily contaminated with human feces, and this enabled typhoid to become very widespread. It is perhaps this disease more than any other that owes its successful eradication in the 20th-century West to modern techniques of hygiene and sanitation (see Public health).

Another reason why the organism is so well adapted to infect humans is that it survives well in fresh water; indeed, many of the serious epidemics have been waterborne. Organisms can, however, only survive for any length of time in water if there is decaying organic matter present for them to feed on. If water is simply stored in a clean reservoir the number of organisms will be reduced.

Salmonella typhi do not survive well in seawater, so there is little risk of catching typhoid by sunbathing on a polluted beach, even though it may be very undesirable for coastal towns to discharge raw sewage into the sea. However, shellfish filter gallons of water to extract their food, and sewage may certainly contaminate seafood.

Dairy produce is a fairly common source of infection since it provides an excellent medium for the bacteria to grow in. Infected milk almost always occurs through a human carrier, and less often by contamination with sewage. Typhoid can of course be spread by any food, although the organism is destroyed by thorough cooking (see Food poisoning). A carrier who works with food is especially dangerous, since there is a very high risk of fecal contamination of the hands. The most famous carrier of all was an American cook who was known as Typhoid Mary.

Symptoms

Typhoid has an incubation period of between 10 and 14 days. It begins as an illness resembling influenza, with a headache, muscle pains, and abdominal discomfort. Initially, constipation (see Constipation) is common and diarrhea (see Diarrhea) occurs occasionally.

The fever rises slowly over the course of a week or so, in a classic stepladder pattern (see Fever, and Temperature). The temperature is always raised in the evening, but has fallen slightly by the following morning until it finally reaches 104°F (40°C) by the end of a week.

By the end of the first week, the patient obviously has a serious disease and is in a poor general condition with a severe headache. At this stage, chest symptoms are very common and sometimes pneumonia develops (see Pneumonia). The abdomen is distended, and two of the most significant symptoms will be present: the spleen can be felt in the top left-hand corner of the abdomen, and a few pale pink patches appear on the skin.

The organism can be grown in cultures of the blood during the course of the first week, and this is often how the diagnosis is made. The organisms are so widespread after about a week that they can also be grown in culture from a specimen of skin containing a rose-red spot.

Alan Hutchison Library

Q When I went to Greece last summer, I had the most dreadful bout of diarrhea. Could it have been typhoid?

A No, it is most unlikely. The main point about typhoid is that it is a generalized disease affecting the whole body. If you do get diarrhea, it comes on late in the illness, after about two weeks. It is certainly possible that the illness you had was caused by one of the salmonella organisms (as typhoid is) since these cause acute gastroenteritis. Paratyphoid can give you an illness similar to typhoid, but sometimes it just causes an attack of gastroenteritis.

Q Is it possible to catch typhoid from animals?

A No. Typhoid seems to be an exclusively human disease, with the one exception of fruit-eating bats in Madagascar! If you do catch the disease, therefore, you must have caught it from someone else, although you would do so via fecal contamination of food or water. It is unusual for it to spread directly from person to person. On the other hand, paratyphoid seems to be less specialized and it can attack other animals. There is at least one outbreak on record where cattle were the source of the infection.

Q I have heard the term *typhoid carrier,* but what exactly does it mean?

A Typhoid carriers are the main source of the infection. Once someone has been infected, and has recovered from the acute stage of the illness, the typhoid organisms may settle in the body and be excreted in the feces or urine without causing any serious symptoms. It is quite normal for people who have had the disease to excrete the organisms for about three months, but if this continues then they are called carriers. It is unusual for anyone under the age of 20 to become a carrier. The state is most likely to occur in middle-aged women. There are known cases of people carrying the organism for 50 years or possibly even longer.

During the second week of the disease, patients become progressively sicker, with particular deterioration in their mental function and withdrawal from what is happening around them. Throughout the first two weeks the organism is passing from the blood into various organs of the body, but it is in the intestines that serious complications can occur. At intervals down the length of the small intestine there are collections of lymphatic tissue called Peyer's patches. Typhoid tends to infect these in particular, and their surfaces may ulcerate to cause severe intestinal bleeding.

By the third week an untreated patient is extremely ill, with a swollen abdomen and a stupor that almost amounts to a coma. Diarrhea occurs at this stage since the intestines become involved, but more serious than this is the risk that the walls of the intestine might perforate, particularly around the Peyer's patches. If this does not happen, then the fever begins to settle after three or four weeks, although there is a high risk of a possibly serious relapse.

The carrier state
It is normal for the salmonella organisms to persist in the patient's stools for as long as three months, and they have to be investigated regularly for this reason. Obviously patients who are still excreting the organisms have to take special precautions. In some patients, the carrier state persists, although this is uncommon in anyone under the age of 20. Middle-aged women are, in fact, most likely to become carriers, with the ratio of male to female carriers being roughly 1 to 3.

Anybody who has recovered from typhoid should always be extremely careful about hygiene. Washing the hands after going to the bathroom is a basic precaution that will prevent the spread of a debilitating disease (see Hygiene).

Treatment
A diagnosis is made either by developing a culture of the typhoid bacteria from specimens of the patient's blood, feces, or urine (see Specimens), or by means of a blood test that reveals the presence of antibodies to the bacteria. The antibiotic chloramphenicol has made a great difference to the treatment of the disease, and once it is started the illness should settle within about five days. Unfortunately the drug can cause fatal depression of the bone marrow so that no blood cells are produced. Although this is very rare, it means that this antibiotic has to be reserved for potentially fatal illnesses like typhoid. A newer drug, septrin, is also being used and seems to be nearly as effective as chloramphenicol without the same side effects.

Occasionally, in extremely severe cases, patients may require supplementary treatment with corticosteroid drugs, which reduce inflammation in the intestine. Surgery may also be required if the

The effects of typhoid on the body

Organ/system	Effects
Blood	Typhoid spreads into the bloodstream immediately after infection
Intestine	Organisms spread from the blood back into the wall of the intestine and may cause ulcers and bleeding, or lead to rupture of the intestinal wall
Skin	The typical typhoid rash takes the form of a few rose-red spots
Gallbladder	Typhoid is particularly likely to infect the gallbladder, and it is the site of infection in carriers
Kidneys	The kidneys are also infected, and are another possible site of infection in carriers, who then pass infected urine
Lungs	A cough is common in the early stages, and pneumonia may occur; lung problems are common in children
Heart	The heart is involved in 5 to 10 percent of cases. This can lead to heart failure and can certainly be a cause of death
Nervous system and psychiatric symptoms	The disease starts with a headache and patients become dull and confused. During the second week they become totally withdrawn until they are effectively in a coma—the "coma vigil." Sometimes there is an initial episode of severe psychiatric disturbance, and there can also be cases of meningitis, though these are rare
Bones and joints	Abscesses can form under the periosteum (lining membrane) of bones after the acute stage of the disease. Joints can also be affected

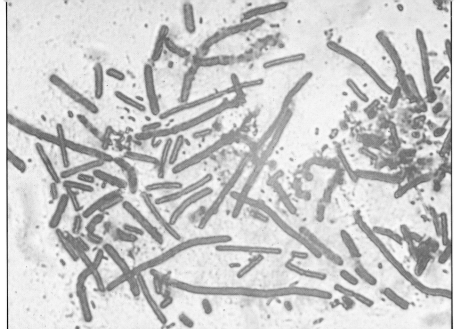

patient suffers widespread peritonitis or severe bleeding.

Prevention

Typhoid is mainly prevented by the control of sewage disposal and the provision of clean water supplies.

A useful and reliable vaccine against typhoid is available, and is worth having if you are traveling to a country where the standards of hygiene are low. It is called TAB, meaning "Typhoid and paratyphoid A and B," and is about 70 percent effective at preventing typhoid if you are infected. A booster is needed after about three years.

Paratyphoid

Paratyphoid closely resembles typhoid in many respects, but it is caused by a different bacterium called *Salmonella paratyphi.* Carriers of paratyphoid exist, but are not responsible for all outbreaks of the disease. The incubation period is shorter, and it is not as infectious as typhoid. This means that you will not necessarily get the disease if you have contracted the organism. Paratyphoid causes symptoms resembling both typhoid and salmonella poisoning. There is an acute phase of gastroenteritis (see Gastroenteritis) but no generalized disease develops, and only in very rare cases does paratyphoid prove to be fatal.

Outlook

Typhoid may well be largely a problem of the past in the West, but elsewhere in the world, usually wherever sanitation is poor, typhoid epidemics are, tragically, a regular feature of life. The vast majority of the cases that occur in the United States are contracted abroad.

However, prompt diagnosis and treatment of the disease generally insure an excellent outlook for patients.

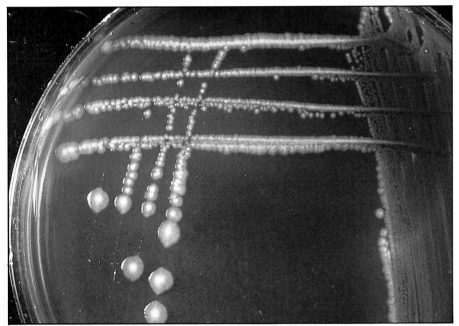

The typhoid bacillus (top) and the less virulent paratyphoid strain are just two of a large group of organisms called the salmonellae. Typhoid and paratyphoid mainly infect humans and have a tendency to remain in the body in a carrier state. Diagnosis of the disease can be made in the first week if a culture of the blood is taken and colonies of the bacillus are found (above). Classic symptoms of the disease are a distended abdomen and the appearance of rose-red spots—pale pink patches on the skin. When someone is suspected of having typhoid or of being a carrier, his or her feces are investigated since these may be contaminated with the organism. A specimen is placed on a culture plate and examined under a microscope (right). The organisms may persist in the patient's stools for as long as three months after the disease has run its course; in rare cases, for much longer.

C. James Webb

Typhus

Q My father died of typhus after he went in to liberate a concentration camp at the end of World War II. I have been told that typhus was common in the camps. Why was this?

A Typhus is found where normal social organization has broken down. The disease depends upon the louse for transmission from human to human, and this means that it only occurs in circumstances where hygiene is poor. Also, typhus is a disease that actually seems to have a preference for cold conditions, and the concentration camps would have favored its spread as a result.

Q Is it true that typhus can cause gangrene?

A Yes. In severe cases of the disease there may be gangrene of the extremities, such as the fingers and toes, ears, and genitals.

Q How do lice spread typhus? Do they inject it on biting?

A When a louse bites in order to eat blood, it defecates at the same time, and louse feces contain the infection. On scratching the bite, the infection contained in the feces is rubbed into the skin and the disease starts. The infection seems to be able to survive in louse feces for a long time, so the dust from the clothes of a person who is louse-ridden can be very infective. The disease also causes the death of infected lice, and their corpses also provide a source of infection in dust from clothing.

Q Does epidemic typhus infect any animals other than man?

A Curiously enough, it infects only one other species so far as we know, and that is the flying squirrel of North America. However, murine typhus seems to be primarily a disease of rats and it occurs where rats are common, for example in seaports. Murine typhus causes a similar but less severe disease in man; but it can still be serious.

Typhus is one of those diseases that waits in the wings to strike at humanity when social breakdown occurs. If normal hygiene measures fall by the wayside, this louse-borne illness spreads rapidly from person to person.

There are actually a number of typhus illnesses, all caused by the same sort of organisms—the rickettsiae (see Rickets). Rickettsiae are spread from human to human by bloodsucking insects.

The most serious form of typhus is called epidemic typhus, and it often occurs in the social breakdown that can follow such disasters as war, famine, floods, and earthquakes. A less serious disease is murine typhus. This is basically a disease of rats, and it spreads to humans via the rat flea. Finally, there is a disease of the Orient called scrub typhus or tsutsugamushi fever.

Causes of epidemic typhus

The organism of epidemic typhus is called *Rickettsia prowazekii* and the infection passes from human to human via infected body lice; it cannot be caught directly from another human. A louse becomes infected by sucking an infected person's blood, but another human has to be very close for the louse to transfer.

Once a louse is infected, the rickettsiae grow in its intestine and are passed out in the feces. Invariably, the louse defecates as it eats, leading to transfer of infection, since the human host will scratch the irritating bite and rub the feces into the wound. Rickettsiae live for a long time in louse feces, and the dust from infected clothing can be very infectious.

Symptoms and treatment

The incubation period for epidemic typhus is about 10 days. The disease starts very suddenly with a high fever and the patient feels ill, with muscular aches and pains; there is also a headache.

A rash appears after three or four days: it begins gradually and can simply be mistaken for the flush of a fever. It consists of small red flat spots, but after about a week or so it gets darker, and the spots

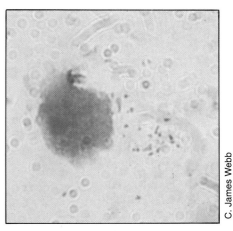

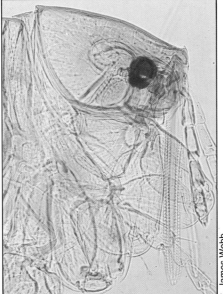

Rickettsiae (right) are the organisms that cause typhus. They are carried by blood-sucking insects such as the chigger (below), which causes scrub typhus. The rat flea, which is carried by the black rat (left), causes murine typhus. This typhus, which is less deadly than epidemic typhus, is often endemic in rat-infested areas—for example, in seaports and food stores.

may start to look like little bruises. The most serious stage of the disease occurs as the rash gets more obvious. The patient sinks into a stupor and, although awake, is often impossible to communicate with. At this point the deterioration can be very alarming: the kidneys start to fail; a cough develops; and the rash may actually progress to gangrene in the fingers, toes, and genitals. In untreated infections, somewhere between 20 and 50 percent of patients will die at this stage.

Those who are going to recover lose their fever in the third week and their brains start working normally very quickly. However, they will need a very long period of convalescence.

The condition responds to treatment with certain antibiotics. The most likely drugs to be successful in controlling the infection are tetracycline and chloramphenicol. But often, in the squalid circumstances where lice spread, antibiotics are not readily available (see Antibiotics).

Murine and scrub typhus

Murine typhus is less severe than epidemic typhus and the death rate without treatment is probably around the 2 percent mark. Murine typhus is a disease that is found in circumstances where humans are is in quite close contact with rats. It is often endemic in rat-infested areas such as ports and food stores.

The characteristic feature of scrub typhus is that 60 percent of infected people develop a hard scar at the site of the infecting bite within about five days. This scar is called an eschar. The disease then goes on in a very similar way to epidemic typhus. The illness exists in a large number of animals and is spread by a bloodsucking mite or chigger. As the name suggests, scrub typhus is a disease that occurs in scrubland when the free-living chiggers leave the scrubby undergrowth to bite and infect.

Prevention

Vaccine against typhus does exist, and it provides good protection. It is also possible to take tetracycline when traveling in an infected area (see Vaccinations).

However, the most important means of prevention is to control the fleas and lice that carry the disease. In the case of epidemic typhus this is not too difficult, since the louse is fairly easy to deal with. In areas with murine typhus the thing to do is to try and eradicate the rats; this can be quite an undertaking.

The most serious control problem is that of scrub typhus. This is found in rural areas, and the disease has many small animals in which it can survive; in fact, humans are probably an unusual host.

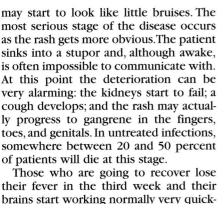

Survivors of a cyclonic flood in India. In the emergency camps set up after such a disaster, people live close together, often in unhygienic conditions where body lice flourish and typhus can spread quickly.

Ulcers

Although commonly associated with gastric problems, ulcers also occur elsewhere on the body. Caused by a variety of factors, from disease to injury, they can range from a mild irritation to a serious condition.

Q My teenage daughter keeps on getting ulcers on her forearm, but our doctor says that he cannot do anything about it since she is inflicting the injuries on herself. How can this be?

A The doctor probably suspects that your daughter is suffering from hysteria. This condition is uncommon nowadays, but one of the symptoms may be self-inflicted injury, performed perhaps to gain attention or avoid some anxiety-producing situation at home or school. If your daughter is suffering from hysteria, she may be unaware that she is injuring herself. Perhaps you might discuss with your doctor the possibility of taking her along to have psychiatric counseling.

Q I have an embarrassing ulcer in my groin region. What could this be due to?

A There are a number of possible causes of an ulcer in the groin, ranging from mild irritation or even injury, to more serious sexually transmitted diseases. You should see your doctor as soon as possible to have the cause of the ulcer diagnosed.

Q My father is bedridden and suffers from bedsores. How can these be prevented?

A A special air mattress will help considerably. This has sections that can be alternately inflated and deflated to change the pressure-bearing areas while the patient lies still. Rubbing a barrier cream into the likely spots will also help to alleviate the bedsores.

Q Is it true that ulcers in the mouth mean that one is run-down or unhealthy?

A Not necessarily. Mouth ulcers can be caused by a number of different factors that have nothing to do with being run-down. However, recurrent ulcers caused by herpes are particularly common and often appear following any emotional stress or during illness. Mouth ulcers may also be a symptom of anemia, and, if this is the case, one would feel run-down.

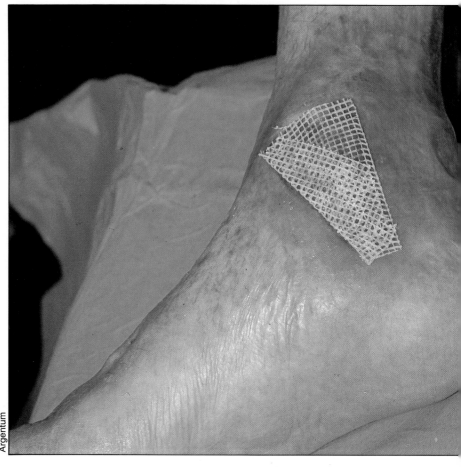

Argentum

An ulcer is a localized area of loss of tissue on the surface of the skin or on any other surface in the body, such as the wet lining of the digestive tract and other internal surfaces. The result of such loss is an open sore (see Sores). An ulcer heals slowly because its edges are separated, and healing can occur only by growth of tissue in from the edges. Ulcers are usually associated with inflammation (see Inflammation). Loss of surface tissue as a result of a wound from injury (see Wounds) is not primarily an ulcer, but if infection occurs such a wound may become ulcerated.

Ulcers are often circular or oval in shape and sometimes irregular in outline. Ulcers on the surface of the body vary considerably in their depth, some involving skin loss only, but others extending deep into the muscle or bone beneath the skin. The causes of ulcers are numerous and range from a mild irritation or injury to a serious disease.

Mouth and lip ulcers

Mouth ulcers are a common problem, and occur either as a one-time condition or as a recurrent disease. Almost everyone has at some time or other suffered the discomfort of the nonrecurrent type of mouth ulcer. They are brought on by a variety of factors, but are usually due to some identifiable physical, chemical, or biological cause, or are a symptom of some underlying condition (see also Mouth).

Physical causes of mouth ulceration include irritation from jagged teeth (see Teeth and teething), compulsive cheek-chewing, too vigorous use of a toothbrush, or burning from hot foods or drinks (see Burns). Chemical causes include caustic drugs, tablets, or sweets that are allowed to dissolve in the mouth, strong antiseptics, and mouthwashes and chemicals used in dental treatment. Ulcers due to physical or chemical causes tend to clear up quickly of their own accord.

A leg ulcer is first cleaned, covered with a sterile gauze pad cut to fit, padded for protection, and then bandaged so that even pressure is applied to the wound. The aphthous ulcer (seen here on the tongue) is the most common of all single mouth ulcers and can be caused by broken teeth or sharp, spicy food (right).

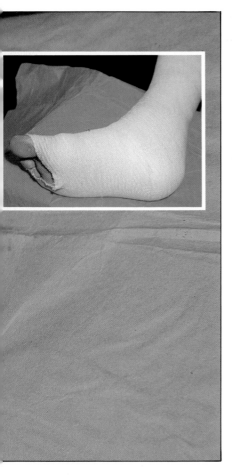

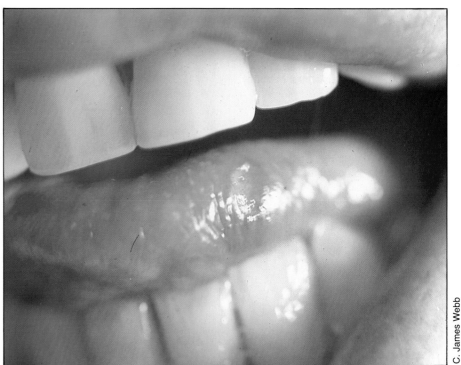

C. James Webb

of the lip, though uncommon, often makes its first appearance as an ulcer.

Aphthous ulcers

Aphthous ulcer is the medical term given to a condition of mouth inflammation featuring intermittent episodes of painful mouth ulcers on the internal mucous membrane. They are also known as canker sores, aphthous stomatitis, or ulcerative stomatitis. These ulcers are covered with a grayish discharge. They are surrounded by a red halo, and occur singly or in groups. Even without treatment aphthous ulcers will heal spontaneously in one to two weeks.

Recurrent mouth ulcers affect about one person in three. They usually consist of numerous small, painful ulcers on or inside the lips, on the tongue, throat, or roof of the mouth, and may persist for a week or two, disappear, and then appear again some weeks or months later. The causes of recurrent mouth ulcers are not so well understood, but it is known that those confined to the lips are nearly always due to the herpes simplex virus. Those inside the mouth may also be caused by herpes, but are more likely due to an allergy (see Allergies), a nutritional deficiency (see Vitamins), anemia (see Anemia), or celiac disease (see Celiac disease).

Biological causes of ulcers include the syphilis bacterium (see Syphilis), various fungi, and the herpes simplex virus (see Herpes). A syphilitic chancre in the mouth is rare but very serious. It is sexually acquired (see Sexually transmitted diseases), consisting of a single round, button-sized, painless ulcer on the lip or tongue (see Tongue).

On the other hand, an acute herpes infection in the mouth consists of numerous smaller, painful ulcers on the gums (see Gums and gum diseases), tongue, and membranes that line the inside of the cheeks or the inside of the lips.

Nonrecurrent, but persistent, mouth ulcers may also be a symptom of diabetes (see Diabetes), blood diseases (see Blood), or tuberculosis (see Tuberculosis). Cancer

Habitual cheek-biting can become so self-destructive as to cause a line of tissue breakdown that soon leads to an ulcer.

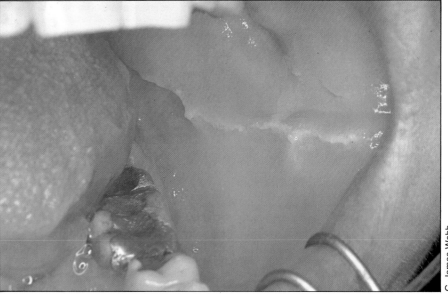

C. James Webb

Q My mother has a leg ulcer, and the doctor has told her that she should sleep with the foot of her bed raised up. Why is this necessary?

A Your mother is almost certainly suffering from a type of leg ulcer that develops from varicose veins. In this condition blood tends to pool in the lower legs. Fluid collects and eventually the skin in the area becomes thinned and breaks down to form an ulcer. During treatment it helps for the person to keep the leg raised above the body during sleep or rest, thereby encouraging normal blood circulation.

Q Is it possible to have a stomach ulcer without knowing it?

A Certainly. Many people accept that a small amount of indigestion is normal. A fair proportion of these people would be found to have an active ulcer, or the signs of an old ulcer, if they had a gastroscopy. If the ulcer is asymptomatic (without any symptoms) and does not have any complications then it really doesn't matter a great deal.

Q I've been told that I have to eat frequently because of a stomach ulcer. Now I'm putting on a lot of weight. What can I do about this?

A The trick is to eat frequent *small* meals. The idea is that frequent small meals do not allow the level of acid to build up, since the acid is continually being neutralized by the food. Obviously you do risk putting on weight, and you should aim to eat a normal amount of food, but split it into a greater number of smaller meals.

Q Does surgery for an ulcer leave a huge, ugly scar?

A The sort of scar that you will be left with will be about six inches long, running up and down the top of your abdomen. Although this sounds very big, the scars often fade away leaving no more than a thin line, so you needn't be too worried about it.

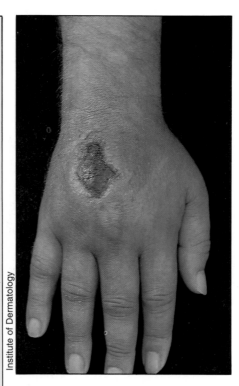

Institute of Dermatology

A faulty drip attached to the hand caused this ulcer. The anticancer drug used accidentally leaked out onto the skin.

Mouth ulcers and general disease

Mouth ulcers may provide clues to the presence of many other general diseases (see Diagnosis). They are, for instance, regular features of several important and potentially dangerous disorders such as ulcerative colitis, Behçet's disease, and Reiter's syndrome.

Ulcerative colitis is an inflammatory disease of unknown cause affecting the lower part of the large intestine (see Colon and colitis) and the rectum (see Rectum). It features extensive ulceration of the inner lining of the intestine, leading to the passage of blood and mucus in the stools (see Feces) and episodes of constipation.

Behçet's disease is characterized by recurrent simultaneous or successive attacks of mouth and genital ulcers and an internal and inflammatory disorder of the eyes known as uveitis. The disease affects men more often than women, and occurs most often in adolescence. The uveitis is by far the more serious aspect of the disorder. This calls for skilled opthalmic management if permanent impairment to the eyesight (see Eyes and eyesight) is to be avoided.

Reiter's syndrome is also associated with internal eye inflammation. The syndrome consists of mouth and genital ulcers, inflammation of the urine outlet tube (see Urethra) with discharge, uveitis, and joint inflammation (see Arthritis). Many cases may also involve

persistent diarrhea (see Diarrhea). These different elements may occur together or separately at intervals of months or years, but once the arthritis is established it is often continuously present.

The treatment of any mouth ulcer depends greatly on the cause; for example, dental therapy for jagged or decayed teeth, surgery for lip cancer, and a gluten-free diet for celiac disease. In many cases of recurrent ulceration, where the exact cause cannot be found, mouthwashes, tablets, and analgesic creams and jellies are often prescribed by the doctor to help soothe the pain. Most herpetic ulcers are usually treated by frequent applications of a substance called idoxuridine, although this is not normally used in the mouth.

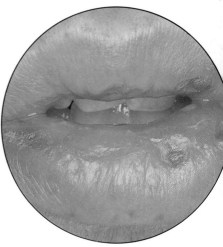

Herpes is often the cause of clusters of small ulcers on the lips, a condition that is also known as gingivostomatitis.

When an ulcer becomes persistent, or when there are repeated bouts of ulcers, it is extremely important that you visit your doctor to have the cause diagnosed. A strong mouthwash or gargle may sound the most likely method of treating a mouth ulcer, but the solution of the mouthwash may be strong enough to aggravate the condition. In addition, the underlying cause will remain untreated. So it is essential that you seek medical advice immediately.

Leg ulcers

Like mouth ulcers, leg ulcers are quite common and have a number of different causes: injury, infection, blood disease (such as sickle-cell anemia), and cancer (see Cancer) are frequent causes. The most common cause, however, is disease of the blood vessels in the legs.

Blocked or narrow arteries (see Arteries and artery disease) diminish the blood supply to the tissues, causing the

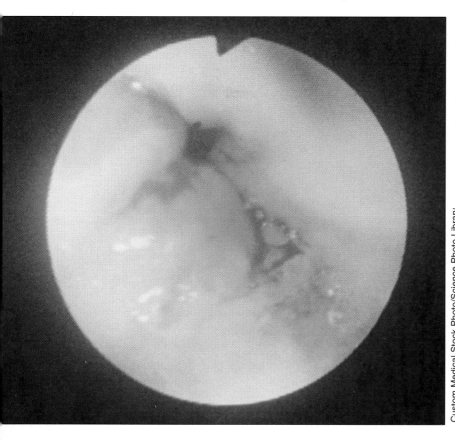

Custom Medical Stock Photo/Science Photo Library

are protected by mucus and by neutralizing bicarbonbate of soda that is secreted by the lining cells.

Various factors interfere with the ability of the lining to resist digestion. These include the taking of certain drugs, especially aspirin and alcohol (see Side effects), the reflux of bile (see Bile), and secretions from the duodenum into the stomach. In recent years it has become apparent that the germ *Helicobacter pylori* is also important in bringing about peptic ulceration. Severe head injury (see Head and head injuries), burns (see Burns), major surgery (see Surgery), and severe infections can also promote peptic ulcers. Ulceration of the lower esophagus occurs when there is considerable upward reflux of acid and pepsin from the stomach.

Duodenal ulcers

The duodenum is the C-shaped first part of the small intestine. The name comes from its dimensions, said to be equal to the breadth of 12 fingers. Because the stomach contents empty directly into the duodenum, the first inch or so takes the brunt of this highly irritating mixture, and it is here that duodenal ulcers occur. Fortunately the acid is quickly neutralized by the alkaline digestive juices secreted by the pancreas, the duct of which enters the duodenum at about its midpoint. Duodenal ulcers are local areas in which the intestine wall is being digested by the acid and the pepsin. They do not occur in people who do not secrete stomach acid.

Duodenal ulcers are usually single, but two or more may occur simultaneously. Those that occur on areas of the intestine wall in contact are called kissing ulcers. They are usually about half an inch in diameter and penetrate the mucous membrane to erode the muscular coat immediately under the lining. In severe cases both gastric and duodenal ulcers may pass right through. These are called perforating ulcers and they leave a hole through which the contents of the intestine can escape into the sterile peritoneal cavity of the abdomen surrounding the intestine. This causes the serious condition of peritonitis (see Peritonitis). Another serious complication of peptic ulceration is severe bleeding caused by the digestion of an artery in the wall of the intestine.

As in gastric ulceration, causal factors of duodenal ulceration include the amount of acid secreted, the efficiency of the mucus secreted by the lining in protecting its own surface from digestion, and the presence of *Helicobacter pylori*. To what extent, and by what means, these and other factors are influenced by the

Endoscope image of a small stomach ulcer. The ulcer is seen as the dark pit that may be due to clotted blood. Causes of gastric ulcers are related to diet, alcohol consumption, stress, and certain drugs. Symptoms are usually alleviated by antacid drugs.

tissues to die and break down, so producing an ulcer. Ulcers of this type tend to occur on the lower leg or foot (see Feet), and have a regular appearance. They may be several inches wide, quite deep, and are extremely painful.

Defective valves in the veins (see Veins) not only cause varicose veins (see Varicose veins), but can also bring about ulcers in the legs through the slow circulation of blood (see Circulatory system). In this case the tissues break down to form large, shallow ulcers over the inside of the lower leg and ankle. The ulcers are not particularly painful but may ache considerably.

The immediate treatment for leg ulcers is aimed at keeping the area as free from infection as possible. This includes frequent cleaning, the use of antiseptic ointments or soaks, the application of a sterile foam pad, and bandaging. Painkilling drugs may also be prescribed. Long-term treatment is also necessary to tackle the underlying cause. This may range from antibiotic therapy to surgery to remove or to seal off the defective veins.

Peptic ulcers

The term *peptic* refers to ulcers of the lining of the stomach (see Stomach) and of the first part of the small intestine

called the duodenum. These are known, respectively, as gastric and duodenal ulcers, the latter being the more common. Peptic ulceration also includes ulcers forming at the lower end of the esophagus (gullet). The whole of the intestine is lined with a wet membrane called a mucous membrane, and peptic ulcers involve local loss of this membrane, with some penetration into the underlying muscular layer of the big intestine. The condition is common, affecting about 10 percent of all adult males and 2 to 5 percent of women. Cigarette smoking interferes with the healing of ulcers and contributes to their causation (see Smoking).

Some of the cells of the stomach lining secrete a powerful hydrochloric acid. This is necessary to help to break down food as a preliminary to digestion and to activate an enzyme called pepsin that digests proteins. Ulcers result when the mechanisms that protect the stomach lining from its own juices have become ineffective and when stomach acid is ejected into the duodenum. In effect, a peptic ulcer is a local partial digestion of the inside of the intestine wall. Normally this does not occur because the acid and pepsin are present in insufficient quantity and because the linings

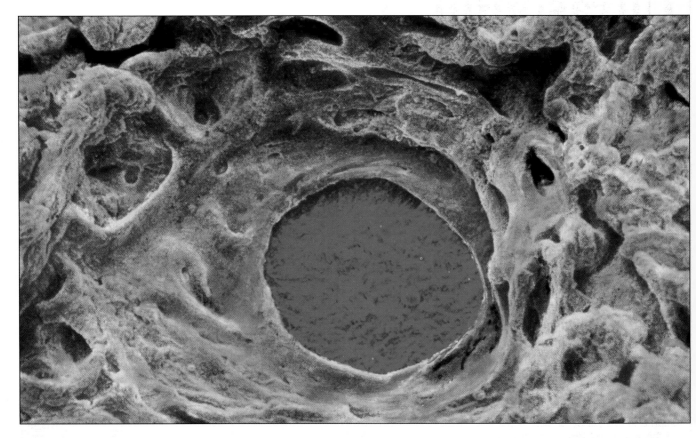

Micrograph of a gastric ulcer. The round, granular wound is surrounded by a smooth border of cells—the body's attempt to repair the injury—and then the rough texture of healthy gastric mucosa.

psychological (see Psychology) or emotional state of the affected person, or by stress (see Stress), is not entirely clear, but it is common experience that some forms of stress make symptoms worse.

Symptoms of peptic ulcers

Peptic ulceration causes a burning, gnawing pain high in the abdomen (see Abdomen), in the angle between the ribs. The pain usually comes on about two hours after a meal.

Duodenal ulcer pain is characteristically relieved by taking a small amount of food. This causes the stomach outlet to close, temporarily, so that the new food can be retained for digestion. The pain is not present on waking but tends to come on around the middle of the morning. It is also common for duodenal ulcer pain to wake the sufferer two or three hours after falling asleep. The diagnosis is often apparent from the history but may be confirmed by barium meal X ray or by direct examination through a flexible illuminating and viewing tube (see Endoscopy).

The great majority of gastric and duodenal ulcers heal in four to six weeks.

Treatment of peptic ulcer

A wide range of treatments is used. Antibiotics (see Antibiotics) are used to eradicate *Helicobacter pylori* organisms, and bismuth antacid drugs to neutralize stomach acid. Histamine H-2 blockers are used to reduce acid secretion, while proton pump inhibitor drugs such as omeprazole (Losec) interfere directly with the chemical mechanism by which the acid is formed. Other drugs are used to form a protective coating on the base of the ulcer and promote healing (see Healing). Prostaglandin drugs are also used since they have a wide range of actions on cells, some of which can be exploited to cut acid secretion.

In some cases, surgical treatment, such as bypassing the duodenum (gastroenterostomy), reshaping the stomach outlet (pyloroplasty), removing an affected part of the stomach (partial gastrectomy), or cutting some of the nerves to the stomach that promote acid secretion (selective or truncal vagotomy) may be helpful. In addition, treatment with tranquilizing drugs (see Tranquilizers) may help by relieving anxiety or depression (see Depression).

Unfortunately, in spite of treatment, chronic peptic ulceration often persists for life, with relapses every two years or so. Relapses are less common if *Helicobacter pylori* organisms are eliminated. In all cases the outlook will be greatly improved if the sufferer quits smoking, stops taking aspirin tablets, drinks alcohol only in moderation and in reasonable dilution, and reduces dietary intake (see Diet). Strict diets are not required, only commonsense avoidance of items known to cause symptoms.

Other ulcers

Pressure sores (which are known medically as decubitus ulcers) commonly affect older, bedridden, and long-term patients. These are caused by constant pressure impairing the blood circulation through an area of skin and underlying tissue, and commonly occur on the hips (see Hip), heels, and the base of the spine (see Bedsores).

The rodent ulcer is a particularly nasty ulcer that occurs on the face. This is actually a type of skin cancer, starting as a red lump that grows and breaks down to form a circular ulcer. Without treatment this continues to grow and spread, but surgical removal or radiation therapy can result in a complete cure.

Ulcers that occur in the groin region can appear for a variety of reasons, including sexually acquired herpes or syphilis. Any ulcer in the groin area should be investigated immediately by your doctor as there is a chance that it may be due to syphilis—a very serious disease if left untreated.

Any persistent, suspicious, or spreading ulcer should always be brought to the attention of your doctor.

Ultrasound

Q Our doctor says that my father needs ultrasound treatment for his shoulder, which is stiff and painful. Will he have to have a scan?

A No. Ultrasound has many other uses in medicine besides scanning. In physical therapy, powerful ultrasound beams provide deep heat and promote healing of inflamed tissues, especially around joints.

Q My sister is 12 weeks pregnant and has just had an ultrasound scan. Before the scan was performed, she was told to sit in the waiting room and drink plenty of water. Why was this necessary?

A Ultrasound examinations in pregnancy are always performed with the bladder as full as possible because this lifts the uterus into the correct position for a scan and pushes other organs out of the way. In addition, the urine in the bladder transmits ultrasound well, and greatly improves the quality of the image attained.

Q Someone told me that it is possible to tell the sex of an unborn baby by ultrasound scanning. Is this true?

A It is only true in a minority of cases when the baby's genital organs can be seen in late pregnancy. But it should not be relied upon too heavily since the appearance is often confusing.

Q My best friend had a kidney transplant last year and has had a number of ultrasound scans. What could all of these scans show?

A Ultrasonography is a good way of following the progress of patients like your friend because it is harmless and gives a clear view of the transplant. There are two important complications that can be detected with ultrasound: any rejection or obstruction of the kidney. Without ultrasound, frequent X-ray examinations would have to be made, which carry a much greater risk.

One of modern medicine's recent innovations is the use of very high-pitched sound to investigate the interior of the body. Ultrasound has added a wonderfully effective weapon to the doctor's diagnostic armory.

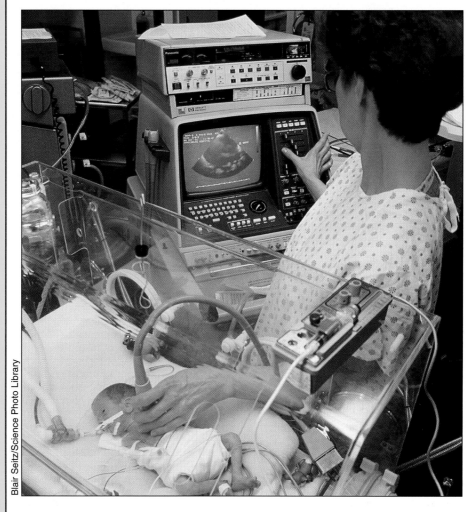

Blair Seitz/Science Photo Library

An echocardiogram is being performed on a premature baby in an incubator. This technique gives a clear picture of the heart and is an invaluable aid when diagnosing suspected heart problems.

Ultrasound technology is not entirely new. Over eighty years ago it was used to probe the North Atlantic in the hunt for the wreck of the *Titanic*. Over fifty years ago its use in sonar equipment was of strategic importance during World War II. Today ultrasound technology is used in most branches of industry and science, and its impact on medical diagnosis has been far-reaching, especially in obstetrics, where its safety and the information it provides about the fetus has made great advances possible (see Obstetrics).

How ultrasound works
Ultrasound consists of sound waves that vibrate at frequencies beyond the range of human hearing. In medical ultrasonography (or echography), a beam of tiny bursts or pulses of ultrasound is generated by a small probe that is moved over the surface of the body. What happens to each pulse of ultrasound depends upon the structure and characteristics of the tissues and organs through which it passes; it may be transmitted, reflected, or absorbed.

The probe produces 1000 pulses of ultrasound per second, and each pulse is so brief in duration, lasting a mere millionth of a second, that there is a relatively long interval between pulses. During these intervals, the probe picks up any echoes

Q This is my first pregnancy, and my baby is due in four weeks' time. I have now had five ultrasound scans because the obstetrician was worried about the position of the placenta. Now he says that everything is fine, but I am terribly worried that so many scans may have harmed the baby in some way. Could anything have happened?

A Doctors have enormous experience with ultrasound in pregnancy, and careful research all over the world has failed to show any evidence of harmful effects. The possible risks and benefits of every procedure used in medicine require consideration. In your case the risk was negligible, and the benefit great. So, don't worry at all.

Q My wife is now 28 weeks pregnant, and so far all seems well. But shouldn't she have had an ultrasound scan to make sure that everything is all right with the baby?

A Ultrasonography requires expensive equipment as well as expertise and both are in short supply. Even if all practical problems could be overcome, routine ultrasound monitoring of every pregnancy is almost certainly not necessary. First, although ultrasonography is reliable, it is not infallible, and a normal scan cannot guarantee that all will be well. Second, tests and technology are no substitute for the experience and specialist skills of the obstetrician. Provided that your wife's obstetrician is happy that all is going well, there really is no need for an ultrasound scan.

Q Last time my sister-in-law went to the prenatal clinic, the doctor used a special instrument to let her hear the baby's heartbeat. Was this an ultrasound machine?

A Yes, it was. Blood flowing through the fetal heart reflects ultrasound in a characteristic way; and numerous devices are available that process echoes returning from the heart into an audible sound, usually a loud whooshing noise.

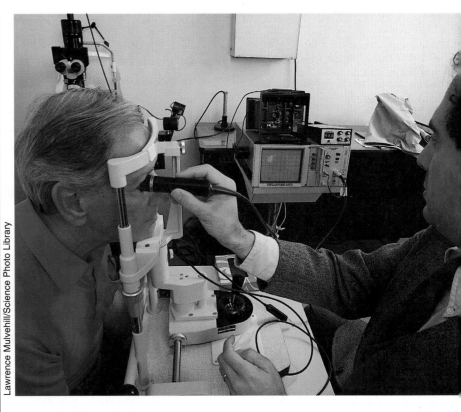

Lawrence Mulvehill/Science Photo Library

reflected from the tissues within the body. Analysis of the echo pattern is a complex process that requires a computer, but the final result is usually an image on a monitor screen that represents a cross section or slice through the body along the path of the probe.

One further property of ultrasound is of importance: the doses of ultrasound needed to form images are so tiny that there is virtually no possibility of any harmful effect. This is one major advantage that ultrasound has over X rays (see X rays).

Having an ultrasound scan

An ultrasound scan is an entirely painless procedure performed by a doctor or technician with special training. After an initial explanation, the patient is asked to undress to expose the region to be examined. He or she then lies down on a couch. A thin layer of oil or gel is applied to the skin to facilitate contact with the probe and improve the quality of the image. The lights are dimmed during the procedure so that the image on the screen may be viewed to best advantage and the probe is passed gently to and fro over the area under examination.

There is no special preparation needed for an ultrasound scan and the patient to be scanned does not need to stay in the hospital either before or after the procedure unless the scan reveals something that needs treatment.

Different types of ultrasound equipment produce different types of images, such as

This patient is undergoing an ultrasound examination of the eye. The probe emits high frequency sound waves and is hand-held by a technician, while an image is built up on the monitor screen in the background.

moving pictures or a sequence of still pictures, both of which can be recorded for further analysis and review.

Ultrasound in pregnancy

Perhaps the most important use of the ultrasound technique is in pregnancy. Here it yields a wealth of information about the fetus, with no risk and at an important early stage. The information gained can have a crucial bearing upon the outcome of the pregnancy for mother and fetus that is not easily obtained by any other method of examination.

Ultrasonography is used to detect multiple pregnancies, and to determine the position of the fetus and precise location of the placenta. It may be used to screen for fetal abnormalities such as spina bifida, and it also assists with the detection of other problems when used as a guide in amniocentesis (see Amniocentesis).

Accurate measurements of the fetus may be taken throughout pregnancy and are used to monitor fetal growth or to predict the date of delivery. Even the beating heart of the fetus can be detected by ultrasound, giving rapid and efficient confirmation that all is well. X rays are still needed during pregnancy in certain circumstances, usually in situations when accurate measure-

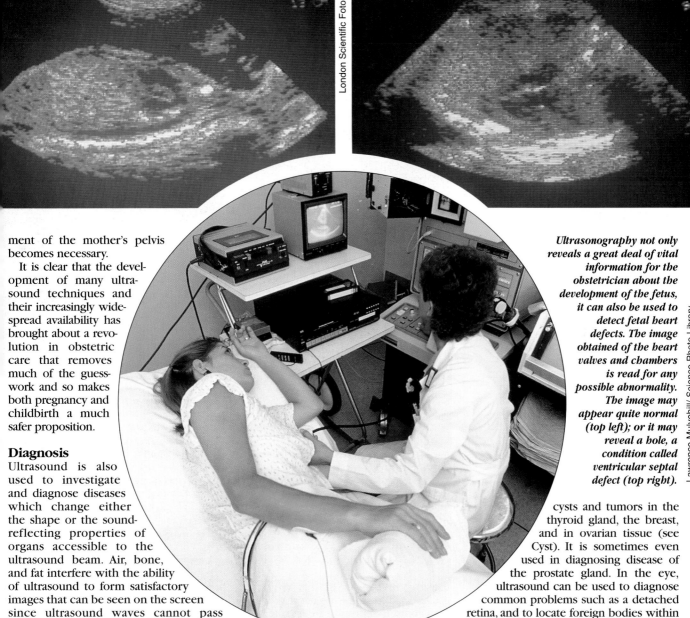

London Scientific Fotos

Lawrence Mulvehill/ Science Photo Library

This young woman is undergoing an ultrasound scan, or echocardiography. The scan gives a clear picture of the patient's heart, which is reflected as an image on the monitor screen in the background.

Ultrasonography not only reveals a great deal of vital information for the obstetrician about the development of the fetus, it can also be used to detect fetal heart defects. The image obtained of the heart valves and chambers is read for any possible abnormality. The image may appear quite normal (top left); or it may reveal a hole, a condition called ventricular septal defect (top right).

ment of the mother's pelvis becomes necessary.

It is clear that the development of many ultrasound techniques and their increasingly widespread availability has brought about a revolution in obstetric care that removes much of the guesswork and so makes both pregnancy and childbirth a much safer proposition.

Diagnosis

Ultrasound is also used to investigate and diagnose diseases which change either the shape or the sound-reflecting properties of organs accessible to the ultrasound beam. Air, bone, and fat interfere with the ability of ultrasound to form satisfactory images that can be seen on the screen since ultrasound waves cannot pass through bone or gas. Organs such as the lungs, the intestines, and the brain are unsuitable for examination.

Ultrasound pictures of the heart have brought about almost as great a revolution as those of the growing fetus. Here, a probe is pointed between the ribs and excellent pictures of the movement of heart valves and of the chambers of the heart can be obtained. This is especially useful in the investigation of heart problems in children and some progress is being made in diagnosing the heart problems of babies in the womb.

The abdomen, liver, gallbladder, spleen, pancreas, and kidneys can be seen clearly on an ultrasound scan. Cysts, tumors, abscesses, and stones, together with many other types of abnormality, can also be detected in these organs by means of ultra-

sonography. Obstruction in the bile duct or in the kidneys can be shown, and ultrasound also provides valuable information about the extent of cancer spread. The major blood vessels in the abdomen are very easily identified, and abnormalities can be detected by the technique.

Ultrasound can also be used for difficult biopsy procedures, thereby reducing the hazard to the patient (see Biopsy).

Another useful application for ultrasound is its ability to distinguish between cysts and tumors in the thyroid gland, the breast, and in ovarian tissue (see Cyst). It is sometimes even used in diagnosing disease of the prostate gland. In the eye, ultrasound can be used to diagnose common problems such as a detached retina, and to locate foreign bodies within the eyeball following injury.

Outlook

The technique of ultrasonography is still under development and more applications are being constantly considered. Techniques now being developed include the use of ultrasound to make precise measurements of bodily functions, such as blood flow rates to different organs. A newer application of the technique is to use it to treat soft-tissue injuries.

Intensive research in ultrasound technology continues to gain momentum, and we will all benefit from its results over the decades to come. The ability to see inside the human body without causing any disturbance or harm will continue to be of extreme importance in the constant battle against disease and illness.

Unconsciousness

Slipping into the dark world of oblivion can be dangerous. Brought on by a variety of causes, unconsciousness can range in severity from a fleeting faint to a life-threatening or permanent coma.

Q While playing rugby, I was kicked on the head and lost consciousness. I was kept in the hospital overnight and told that for a time I should not read or go back to work if I had to concentrate hard. Why was this?

A Concussion has degrees of severity, and, although a patient will often feel all right, the effects can last for up to two weeks. A person who has suffered a concussion may continue to have recurrent bouts of severe headaches and nausea, but these symptoms gradually disappear. However, it has been found that reading, bright lights, and deep concentration can delay recovery and may aggravate the situation.

Q What is the difference between fainting and being unconscious?

A Fainting is a very light form of unconsciousness brought on simply by a lack of oxygen reaching the brain. The person quickly comes around when normal blood circulation is restored. However, a person who is unconscious cannot be roused with ease, and may show signs of confusion, forgetfulness, and even stupor when he or she finally comes around. The condition is more serious than a simple faint: it can be brought on by a variety of causes that threaten health.

Q If you get knocked out, is your brain going to be permanently damaged?

A This depends on the severity of the blow. There may be bruising of the brain and very small hemorrhages in the tissues. In the majority of cases there is no need to worry, but if you have had a number of knockouts, or you find that you lose consciousness easily, then you must be examined by your doctor. It could be that there is some lasting damage from an earlier concussion that needs treatment. Boxers can suffer from their brain cells becoming permanently damaged, known as punch-drunk, but few of us are likely to suffer from this condition.

Neil Leifer/Sports Illustrated/Colorific!

Cleveland Williams lies prostrate in the ring after being knocked unconscious by Mohammed Ali in Houston, Texas, in 1966.

Normal consciousness may be defined as the state in which a person is awake, alert, and aware of the surrounding environment. Unconsciousness is a sleeplike state, but much deeper, with the person having no awareness of the surroundings and showing no response to any stimuli. This condition can vary in severity, ranging from a transient faint to a prolonged coma. Whatever its immediate cause, the condition only arises because of important changes in the brain (see Brain).

Mechanisms in the brain

Exactly how the brain functions in consciousness and unconsciousness is not yet fully understood. However, there are a number of critical areas in the brain that are deeply involved in maintaining consciousness. These are the cerebral cortex, the thalamus, the brain stem, and, in particular, a group of cells within the brain stem called the reticular formation.

The cerebral cortex receives sensory inputs from the main sensory nerves and also from the reticular formation. Nerve routes from around the body branch out to the reticular formation and feed it a constant stream of electrical signals. This action, in turn, causes the reticular formation to fire off signals to targets all around the brain, to the appropriate centers that

Sleep versus unconsciousness

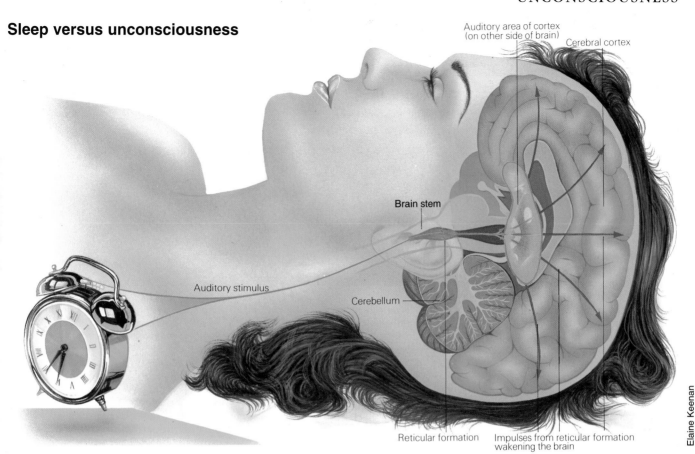

Auditory area of cortex (on other side of brain)

Cerebral cortex

Brain stem

Auditory stimulus

Cerebellum

Reticular formation

Impulses from reticular formation wakening the brain

Elaine Keenan

gather, collate, and act upon the signals. If this driving force slows down, or is prevented from occurring, the cerebral cortex becomes sleepy, and as a result we become unconscious.

The brain stem is also important in that it is responsible for keeping our essential body mechanisms, such as heartbeat, blood pressure, and breathing, running smoothly without our consciously having to think about it.

It appears that when a person becomes unconscious, for whatever reason, the brain concentrates itself on keeping the body ticking over by using all its available energy to maintain normal brain stem function. Damage is thereby confined to what are regarded as the nonessential parts of the brain.

Degrees of unconsciousness

The brain's activity can be measured as electrical impulses on a machine called an electroencephalograph, or EEG (see Electroencephalogram). The impulses of the brain are presented as a pattern of electrical waves. This pattern varies according to the degree of alertness or unconsciousness, thus providing a clue to the severity of the unconscious state a person may be in. For instance, during unconsciousness, the pattern of waves is slow and large, usually about three waves present each second. When someone is

coming around from unconsciousness or waking from sleep, the waves come at about six to eight a second, and increase in frequency until, at full consciousness, the pattern of waves is rapid and jagged, showing increased electrical activity.

The machine is used to determine whether the brain has been severely damaged or even died. If the EEG shows no electrical activity, then the person has almost certainly suffered brain death.

Causes

Unconsciousness can be caused by a variety of factors, ranging from shock to poisoning. The most likely cause that we are likely to come across is syncope, known as fainting (see Fainting).

Fainting can be brought on by anything from excessive heat to standing still for long periods, conditions that result in a temporary lack of blood supply to the brain. The resultant lack of oxygen forces the brain to shut down for a brief spell until the oxygen supply is restored to normal levels. If, for some reason, the blood supply to the brain is not fully and

A boy having an electroencephalograph (EEG) examination. Electrodes are attached to the head and face to record electrical activity in parts of the brain. This is used to form a map or image of the brain that can be compared with a normal control subject.

The sound of the alarm enters the brain through the ear, but the sleeper reacts only when the reticular formation awakens the brain by sending signals to the appropriate area of the cerebral cortex. If someone is unconscious, for whatever reason, the reticular formation is not functioning, so although sensory information arrives at the cortex the person remains unaware of it.

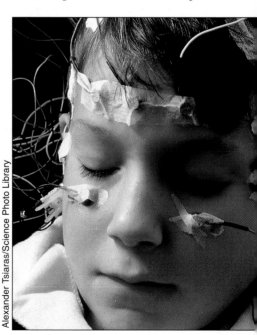

Alexander Tsiaras/Science Photo Library

Q My young daughter often gets into tempers and then passes out. Is there any chance that she is epileptic?

A If you suspect your daughter is suffering from epilepsy, then you should consult your doctor as soon as possible. But what you describe could be a condition known as breath-holding. This can resemble an epileptic attack but it usually only occurs in children of between one and four years of age and during a severe temper or crying fit. Usually they let out a cry before turning blue in the face and passing out. This may be accompanied by small convulsions. Although these attacks can be frightening for parents, they are not serious, and a child will grow out of them. But it is important to have the condition properly diagnosed.

Q Why is it that pilots ejecting from a crashing plane sometimes black out?

A This kind of blackout generally occurs when there is rapid acceleration of the body and blood is suddenly drained away from the head. Momentary unconsciousness then occurs as the brain is briefly starved of oxygen.

Q A friend of mine did not become unconscious when hit on the head, but lapsed into unconsciousness a good while later. How can this happen?

A This emphasizes the serious nature of any blow on the head. Even a minor blow can have a serious, delayed effect in that unconsciousness can follow some time later. This may often be preceded by vomiting and violent headaches, and indicates that there has been possible brain damage brought on by internal bleeding. As soon as someone who has had a blow on the head starts to complain that they are beginning to feel unwell, take them to the hospital immediately, or call the doctor. If you are not aware that the person suffering from these symptoms has had a blow on the head in the recent past, then make sure that it is one of the first questions you ask him or her.

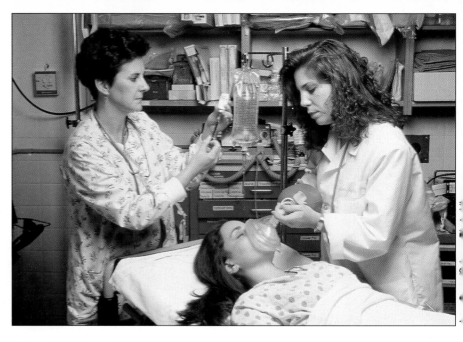

An unconscious woman is given care in the hospital emergency room. Routinely oxygen is given through a respirator.

quickly restored the person may enter a deeper state of unconsciousness.

Symptoms of fainting include dizziness (see Dizziness), light-headedness, and a lack of color in the face. Someone who has fainted should remain lying down for a few minutes until a full recovery has been made. Allowing a person who has fainted to get up too soon, or pulling him or her to their feet, could result in a more serious unconscious state.

Poisoning due to fumes, chemicals, or drugs can also cause unconsciousness, though by different means. For instance, barbiturates (see Barbiturates) depress the central nervous system, in which case the brain stem may be affected, necessitating emergency measures to insure the maintenance of the life-support systems.

Stimulants will be given to treat this form of poisoning when it has led to an unconscious state. Carbon monoxide poisoning, however, replaces the oxygen in the blood and leads to an oxygen deficiency in the brain. Immediate treatment consists of removing the person from the source of the gas, followed by artificial respiration (see Poisoning).

Shock can bring on unconsciousness through a collapse of the circulatory system. Once the circulatory system fails to maintain an adequate supply of blood to the brain, the collection of symptoms known as shock syndrome becomes apparent. This includes sweating, blurred vision, shallow, rapid breathing, and faintness that can lead to unconsciousness.

Shock like this can be brought on by either extensive internal or external bleeding, heart attacks, and loss of body fluid due to various illnesses. In cholera the body becomes so dehydrated that the sufferer actually dies of shock rather than of the bacterium (see Shock).

Treatment of shock varies according to the cause. Replacing lost fluid and raising

the blood pressure are measures taken in the hospital, but it is important to stop heavy bleeding as soon as possible. If the patient becomes unconscious, turn them to one side and make sure he or she can breathe properly. If breathing stops, then artificial respiration must be given.

Head injuries are a common cause of unconsciousness and they occur in many sports such as football, baseball, and boxing. Unconsciousness may be brought on either through direct injury to brain tissue or through a temporary contraction of blood vessels, which impairs brain function. This condition is known as concussion, and varies considerably in the degree of severity.

A return to consciousness may be accompanied by headache, nausea, and difficulty in focusing the eyes. Loss of memory of events that happened prior to the injury also occurs, and is one of the main symptoms of concussion. Anyone who has been knocked out should see the doctor as soon as possible since there may be damage to the skull or internal bleeding.

Epilepsy can also lead to unconsciousness and is usually accompanied by convulsions of differing severity. Why the fit takes place is not fully understood, but it is known that it is brought on by an uncontrollable discharge of electricity by the brain (see Epilepsy).

Coma

A coma is the most extreme form of unconsciousness, a state that is very serious and often long lasting. Unlike when sleeping, the activity of the brain is depressed, and even reflex actions such as coughing, corneal reflexes, and tendon reflexes are absent. In the very deepest

Some common causes of unconsciousness

Type	Cause	Action
Fainting (syncope)	Lack of blood supplying the brain	Lay the patient flat. Cold water or smelling salts may help
Concussion	Blow to the head. Blood vessels contract and starve the brain of blood	Keep patient in quiet and darkened room until he or she comes around. Up to two weeks in bed. No stimulant drugs at all but maybe painkillers to ease headache. Visit doctor's office for checkup
Electric shock	Faulty wiring, lightning. Paralysis of breathing centers in brain	Turn off the power source. Give mouth-to-mouth resuscitation and heart massage, if necessary. Keep it up until medical help arrives (even for hours)
Stroke	Collapse of blood vessel in the brain or blockage by blood clot	Call paramedics immediately. Leave victim alone but place something under his or her head
Poisoning	A variety of poisons have a number of effects	Call doctor, give mouth-to-mouth resuscitation if the victim is not breathing; if poison in mouth give mouth-to-nose. If victim is breathing, place in the recovery position. Do not leave victim alone
Infections such as malaria, cholera, meningitis, etc.	Invading organisms	The illness must be treated by a doctor. Where a patient slips into unconsciousness, make sure they can breathe easily, then inform the doctor immediately
Hypoglycemia	Too much insulin or too little carbohydrate	Give sugar drink and call paramedics
Diabetic coma	Too little insulin or too much carbohydrate in the diet	Call doctor to give insulin and sugar
Epilepsy	Cause unknown but spontaneous dysfunction of the brain	Lay the victim down away from anything that may cause injury. Turn him or her on one side and make sure air passages are clear. Place rolled-up handkerchief, or something similar, between the teeth if possible. This prevents tongue biting. Call paramedics
Shock	Severe bleeding	Call paramedics. Stop bleeding if possible
	Allergic shock reaction to injection. Rarely, bee stings Internal injuries Heart and circulatory problems	Keep victim cool. Reassure and keep him or her calm

A doctor prepares a patient for an EEG. This procedure is a useful diagnostic tool. Wave forms indicate conditions such as epilepsy, dementia, and drug disturbances.

coma, the person may not respond even to the most painful stimuli (see Coma).

The usual causes of coma are injury to the brain (such as bleeding or tumor), severe shock, and blood poisoning (such as urea). Damage to the thalamus may initiate a permanently comatose state.

Both diabetes (see Diabetes) and hypoglycemia (see Hypoglycemia) are also common causes of a coma, but thankfully these conditions can be controlled.

Previously any kind of coma that lasted for more than 24 hours usually resulted in permanent brain damage, but modern treatment and nursing has done much to change this. However, the longer a coma lasts, the less likelihood there is that a perfect recovery can be made.

In all cases of unconsciousness, treatment depends on the underlying cause, and may range from simple rest and recuperation to surgery. A comatose patient will require long-term care.

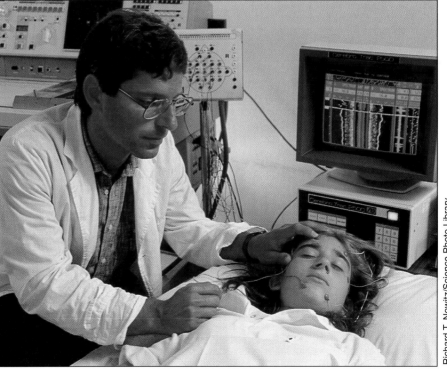

Richard T. Nowitz/Science Photo Library

Uremia

Q If uremia is diagnosed, will the patient have to be put on a kidney machine or have a transplant?

A If someone has a high level of breakdown products, such as urea, in the blood, then he or she is said to be uremic. There may be several causes for this, but one of the most common is that the kidneys no longer have the capacity to cope with the demands made on them. This condition is called chronic renal failure. In these circumstances an alternative method of clearing waste products from the blood will have to be used. A transplant or some form of dialysis are the usual treatments.

Q My grandfather went into the hospital to have prostate surgery and the doctors discovered that he was uremic. Is this common?

A Elderly patients often suffer from prostate difficulties, and this leads to obstruction of the flow of urine from the bladder. If this persists, pressure builds up on the kidneys, leading to uremia.

Q Can uremia be controlled through diet?

A Yes. Before substitutes for kidney function were developed, dietary restrictions were necessary to save the lives of people with chronic renal failure. Excessive urea accumulates from deficient metabolism of protein by the kidneys and the basis of all dietary treatment for uremia is to reduce the amount of protein.

Q If a patient is uremic does it inevitably mean that he or she has serious kidney trouble?

A No. It is not uncommon for elderly patients to have a raised level of urea in the blood without serious consequences. This means simply that the kidneys are growing old and working less efficiently. It is possible for dehydration to produce high levels of urea even in fit people, but this form of uremia will respond simply to taking in a lot of liquid.

This condition generally, but not always, develops as a result of kidney malfunction. Treatment through dialysis or kidney transplant is strikingly effective.

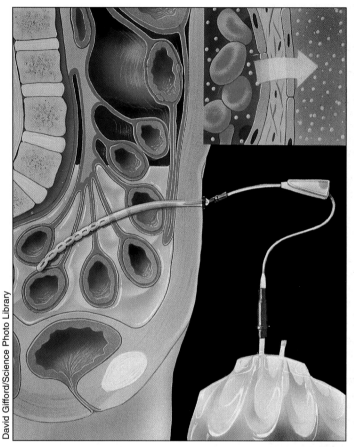

David Gifford/Science Photo Library

This illustration of a section through the human abdomen shows the technique of peritoneal dialysis. This is the infusion of dialysis fluid from a plastic bag directly into the peritoneal cavity via a plastic catheter. The process removes waste products from body fluids of an individual whose kidneys do not function properly. The principle of dialysis is that waste products in blood diffuse across a semipermeable membrane, in this case the peritoneal membrane, toward the lower solute concentrations of the dialysis fluid.

Many kidney diseases involve an accumulation of waste products in the body. Urea is the major waste product and a high level causes uremia to develop.

Causes

The kidney's main function is to filter urea, creatinine, and uric acid from the blood. Kidney problems start if between half and three-quarters of the individual kidney tubules or nephrons stop working (see Kidneys and kidney diseases), leading to a buildup of urea in the blood, and chronic renal failure results.

However, a diseased kidney is not the only cause of uremia. If the blood supply to the kidney is interrupted, urine is no longer produced due to shock (see Shock) and the blood pressure drops for a period of time. This will damage the kidneys and they can take days or even weeks to recover.

Uremia may develop if the flow of urine is impeded, as with an obstruction of the prostate gland (see Prostate gland).

Symptoms and treatment

Over a long period a patient may develop fairly severe degrees of uremia without actually realizing that there is anything seriously wrong. The major symptoms of the disease are a general feeling of ill health and lack of energy. Uremia also affects the way that the bone marrow makes blood, and as a result anemia may complicate the patient's condition.

The brain may be affected as the uremia worsens: the patient may be sleepy and confused until he or she loses consciousness. The skin is dry and turns sallow. Some of the waste products normally excreted through the kidney are lost in sweat, resulting in severe itching.

When uremia is due to chronic renal failure, treatment is by dialysis or a kidney transplant. Dialysis uses a machine to wash urea from the blood. Another form of dialysis uses fluid flowing in and out of the peritoneal cavity. Urea passes across the peritoneum from the blood into the fluid, which is then drained.

Urethra

The channel along which urine passes from the body—the urethra—is a common site of an infection that can be very painful and always needs medical attention.

Q Is urethritis always caused by a sexually transmitted disease?

A No, not always, but a sexually transmitted infection is by far the most common cause. This is not surprising since the penis in men, and the area around the vagina that includes the opening of the urethra in women, are the parts of the body that are usually in closest contact during intercourse. Women may also get urethritis as a result of contamination from the anus. To avoid this women should always wipe themselves after going to the bathroom, or dry themselves after bathing, from the front toward the back, never the opposite.

Q Can urethritis always be completely cured?

A Yes, almost always, though this depends on doing tests to identify the precise cause so that appropriate treatment, usually an antibiotic, can be given. But just taking the antibiotic may be insufficient to produce a cure since, like any other infected area of the body, the urethra needs a period of rest for full recovery. New lining tissue has to become established and replace that which has been destroyed by the inflammation. Thus it is usually necessary to refrain from intercourse for about two weeks. Otherwise the mechanical stress and friction on the urethra will damage the new lining tissue before it has had a chance to settle down. A further attack of urethritis is then likely.

Q A friend told me that her little boy had hypospadias. What on earth does that mean?

A Hypospadias is an unusual abnormality in the development of the penis. This occurs before birth and results in the opening, or meatus, being on the underside of the penis rather than at the tip. In most cases there is no difficulty in passing urine, having intercourse, or fathering children, and no treatment is necessary. In the few cases where there is a problem it can be corrected with minor surgery.

The urethra is the duct that extends from the bladder to an opening on the outside of the body (see Bladder and bladder control). In both sexes its function is to discharge urine. In men, the urethra is also the channel through which semen is ejaculated.

The male urethra

The mature male urethra averages 8 in (about 20 cm) in length and consists of three sections. The first, or prostatic section is about 1 in (2.5 cm) long and passes from the sphincter, or valve, at the outlet of the bladder through the middle of the prostate gland (see Prostrate gland).

The middle part of the urethra is only about 0.5 in (12 mm) long and is often called the membranous urethra.

The final—and, at over 6 in (15 cm), the longest—section is called the spongy or cavernous urethra. This section is within the penis and opens at the slit in the tip, the urethral meatus (see Penis).

The female urethra

In women the urethra is very much shorter and its only function is to be a channel for the disposal of urine. It is about 0.5 in (1.3 cm) in diameter and is surrounded by mucous glands (see Mucus). The fact that it is so short and opens into a relatively exposed, contaminated area, explains why women frequently get urinary infections.

Urethritis

Inflammation of the urethra, called urethritis, is the most common urethral disorder and it can have many causes. The most common are infections acquired as a result of sexual intercourse with an infected partner (see Intercourse).

The symptoms in the male are development of a discharge that leaks out from the urethral meatus, and increasing pain on urinating. In addition, there is a desire to urinate frequently. In women it is usually only the pain (dysuria) and the frequency of urination that are present. These symptoms are often attributed to cystitis or inflammation of the bladder, but it is more commonly the urethra that is involved (see Cystitis).

It is most important that all cases of urethritis are fully investigated and treated, otherwise permanent damage can be done both to the urethra itself and to the reproductive organs.

Cross section of the urethra

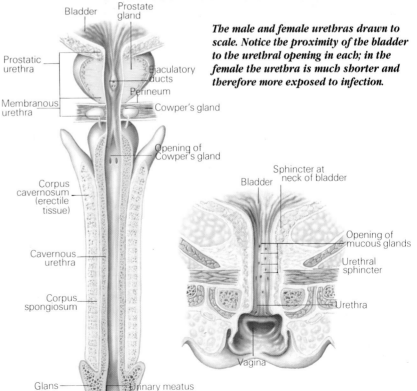

The male and female urethras drawn to scale. Notice the proximity of the bladder to the urethral opening in each; in the female the urethra is much shorter and therefore more exposed to infection.

Bladder
Prostate gland
Prostatic urethra
Ejaculatory ducts
Perineum
Membranous urethra
Cowper's gland
Opening of Cowper's gland
Corpus cavernosum (erectile tissue)
Cavernous urethra
Corpus spongiosum
Glans
Urinary meatus

Sphincter at neck of bladder
Bladder
Opening of mucous glands
Urethral sphincter
Urethra
Vagina

Frank Kennard

Uterus

Q Does the Pill have any effect on the uterus?

A Yes. There are several types of contraceptive pill, and they all contain a synthetic form of the hormone progesterone in levels that make the endometrium, or lining of the uterus, unsuitable for the implantation and growth of a fertilized egg. The Pill also affects the secretions from the cervix to prevent sperm swimming through the cervix to fertilize the egg. Many contraceptive pills also contain a synthetic estrogen. This helps to prevent pregnancy by inhibiting the release of eggs from the ovary.

Q Is it true that some women may go into premature labor because the neck of the womb is too weak to remain closed until the baby is mature?

A Unfortunately doctors often are unable to tell a woman why she had her baby prematurely, which of course makes both the woman and the obstetrician anxious about any subsequent pregnancies she may have. Occasionally a woman is found to have an abnormal cervix that can be stretched open too easily. This can usually be successfully treated in a future pregnancy by putting a purse-string type of suture into the neck of the womb to keep it closed. This is done under anesthesia, and is removed when the woman is in the 38th week of pregnancy.

Q Why do women stop having periods at menopause?

A When a woman has a period she sheds the fleshy lining to the womb, called the endometrium. The endometrium is stimulated to grow by the two hormones produced by the ovary, estrogen and progesterone. At menopause the ovaries are no longer capable of secreting these hormones, so the endometrium no longer regrows and the woman will have no more periods. The onset of menopause is usually between ages 45 and 55. If periods become heavier or more frequent during the middle years, a doctor should be consulted.

Even today, the workings of the uterus remain something of a medical mystery. What is undeniable, however, is that it is supremely well adapted for the protection and nurturing of the unborn child.

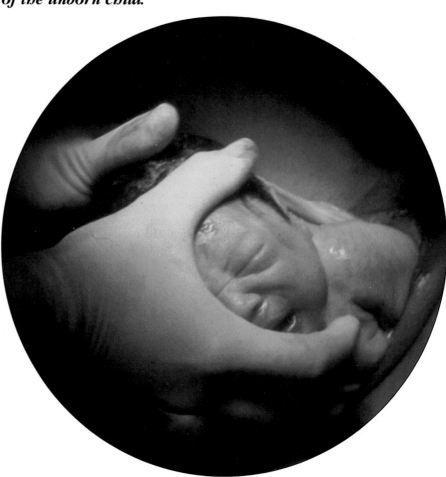

In the past, the uterus has been blamed for almost every mental and physical ailment women suffer. Today we have a more rational, though still incomplete, understanding of this vital organ.

Function

The uterus is composed of two main parts; the corpus or body of the organ, and its cervix or neck (see Cervix and cervical smears). It is capable of undergoing major changes during a woman's reproductive life.

From puberty to menopause, the lining of the womb (endometrium) develops each month under the influence of hormones to provide nutrition for a fertilized egg (see Menopause, and Puberty). If the egg is not fertilized the endometrium is shed during menstruation, and is slowly replaced in the course of the next menstrual cycle (see Menstruation).

Pain, joy, and wonder combine in this unique moment, as a new baby safely completes the journey from the protection of the womb into the outside world.

During pregnancy the uterus expands, allowing the fetus to grow and providing it with protection and nutrition (see Pregnancy). Simultaneously, contraction of the large muscle fibers is prevented.

The uterus suddenly changes its role when the fetus is mature, and begins to contract in order to open the cervix and allow both the baby and the placenta to pass through (see Placenta). It then contracts tightly to close off the large blood vessels that have been supplying the placenta. After the birth the uterus rapidly returns to its prepregnant state, ready to accept another fertilized egg. Reportedly, this is known to have happened as early as 36 days after a delivery.

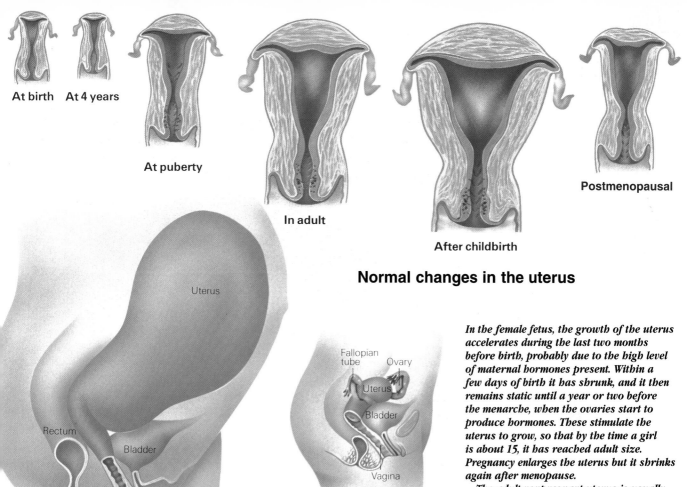

At birth At 4 years

At puberty

In adult

After childbirth

Postmenopausal

Normal changes in the uterus

Uterus

Rectum

Bladder

Uterus in full-term pregnancy

Fallopian tube

Ovary

Uterus

Bladder

Vagina

Uterus in adult

In the female fetus, the growth of the uterus accelerates during the last two months before birth, probably due to the high level of maternal hormones present. Within a few days of birth it has shrunk, and it then remains static until a year or two before the menarche, when the ovaries start to produce hormones. These stimulate the uterus to grow, so that by the time a girl is about 15, it has reached adult size. Pregnancy enlarges the uterus but it shrinks again after menopause.

The adult nonpregnant uterus is usually tilted forward at an angle of about 90° to the vagina; its muscular walls are thick and its cavity a mere slit. In pregnancy, the walls expand dramatically to accommodate the fetus and the amniotic sac.

Mick Saunders

It is astonishing that a baby of 8 lb (3.5 kg) or more could grow inside this organ, which is normally about 3 in (7.5 cm) long.

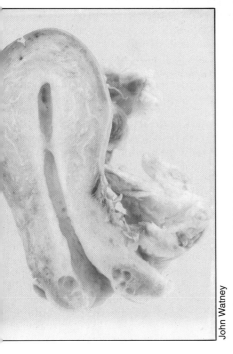

John Watney

The uterus seems to have almost no function prior to puberty and after menopause, when it would obviously be unsuitable, both mentally and physically, for a woman to have a baby.

All these changes in the functioning of the uterus are caused by hormones released from the pituitary gland, the ovaries, and by similar substances called prostaglandins, released by the uterine tissue (see Hormones, Ovaries, and Pituitary gland). How these substances interact is still not fully understood.

Position

In an adult woman the uterus is a hollow organ approximately the size and shape of a small pear. It lies inside the girdle of pelvic bones. The narrow end of the pear is equivalent to the cervix, which protrudes into the vagina; the remainder forms the body of the uterus. This is connected to the two fallopian tubes that carry the monthly egg from the ovaries. In this way the uterus forms part of a channel between the abdominal cavity and the outside world.

Special mechanisms exist to prevent the spread of infection via this route into the abdominal cavity. Thus the lining of the uterus is shed when a woman menstruates, the cervix secretes antibodies, and the acidity of the vagina inhibits the growth of bacteria.

The front of the uterus sits on the bladder and the back lies near the rectum. The uterus is normally supported inside the pelvis by muscles called the pelvic floor muscles, and by bands of connective tissue and blood vessels from the side wall of the pelvis, which are attached to the cervix (see Pelvis).

During pregnancy the uterus enlarges so that by the 12th week it can just be felt inside the abdominal cavity above the pubic bone. At about 38 weeks it usually reaches the lower end of the rib cage, and about two weeks after the baby is born the uterus can normally no longer be felt in the abdomen. After menopause, the uterus shrinks in size.

These size variations are controlled by the sex hormones, which also govern the nature of the glandular tissue lining the uterus (the endometrium). During the first half of the menstrual cycle, the endometrium increases in thickness until the egg is released. It then stops growing

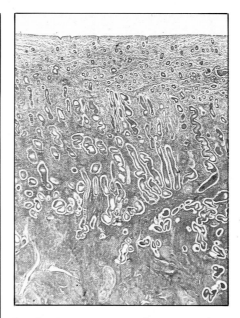

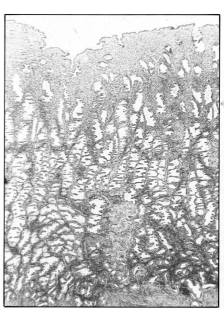

Q I have a retroverted uterus. Can I still get pregnant?

A A retroverted uterus tilts backward from its attachment at the top of the vagina instead of forward (an anteverted uterus). This is quite normal and occurs in about 20 percent of women with no ill effect. There is certainly no evidence that you will be less fertile. Rarely, however, a disease process such as endometriosis or pelvic infection will cause a normal anteverted uterus to become stuck backward, or retroverted. These diseases can cause a decrease in a woman's fertility and, since they are associated with a retroverted uterus, it is sometimes said that retroversion of the uterus causes infertility. A problem like endometriosis can be treated by surgery or hormone therapy, which does not always cure the retroversion but will improve the woman's chances of conceiving.

Q Is it true that some women have two wombs?

A During the development of the womb in the fetus, two ducts, called the Müllerian ducts, fuse. This happens about the 65th day of pregnancy, and the fused portion forms the womb. Occasionally the fusion of the ducts is incomplete, and the woman may have any abnormality from a dimple at the top of the uterus to two entirely separate uteri, which is very rare. Women with this problem seldom have difficulty in becoming pregnant, but they are slightly more likely to have miscarriages or go into premature labor.

Q Is it possible for a baby girl to have a period?

A The hormones estrogen and progesterone can cross the placenta from the mother to stimulate the growth of the lining of the uterus in the developing fetus. Once the baby is born the levels of these hormones in the baby's blood rapidly fall, and she sheds this lining, which is noticed as a pink stain in the diaper a few days after the birth. This loss does not, of course, occur again until the girl reaches puberty.

but begins to secrete substances rich in nutrients to allow growth of the egg if it is fertilized; if it is not, the endometrium is shed during menstruation.

Congenital variations

During the development of the female reproductive organs in the fetus, two tubes of tissue, called Müllerian ducts, grow from the side wall of the abdominal cavity and meet centrally. These tubes continue to grow downward until they fuse with tissue that will later form the lower vagina. The upper portions of these tubes become the fallopian tubes, and the lower central portions fuse to form the uterus and upper vagina (see Vagina).

Very rarely, both the Müllerian ducts fail to form, with the result that the adult woman will have a short vagina but no uterus or fallopian tubes. Nothing can be done to cure this condition, although sometimes plastic surgery is performed to lengthen the vagina. Such women are infertile and do not menstruate.

If only one of the Müllerian ducts develops, the woman will have a uterus and vagina but only one fallopian tube. This does not cause any major problems.

Another rare occurrence during fetal development is incomplete fusion of the Müllerian ducts. This may result in any abnormality from a double uterus to a small dimple at the top of the uterus. If such abnormalities create difficulties for the woman in carrying a pregnancy to term, plastic surgery can be performed to reform the uterus into a single cavity.

Problems with the uterus

Considering the complex mechanism that governs the normal functioning of the uterus, it is remarkable how few women have any problems.

During the menstrual cycle, the lining of the uterus thickens and becomes rich in nutrients (left). It disintegrates and sloughs off during menstruation (right).

Several different conditions can give rise to the same symptoms as menstruation. For example, bleeding from the vagina between periods or after intercourse is often due to a minor condition such as a polyp, which can be easily cured (see Polyps). However, such symptoms are sometimes caused by uterine cancer. This can be completely cured if it is detected early enough, so it is very important for any woman who has these symptoms to seek her gynecologist's advice.

Treatment

Uterine cavity abnormalities are difficult to diagnose because this area cannot be examined directly; a woman may need to have a dilatation and curettage (or D&C) just to diagnose the cause of a menstrual problem or vaginal bleeding after menopause (see Dilatation and curettage). Once the correct diagnosis has been made, however, the doctor can then prescribe the appropriate antibiotic drugs or hormones.

Unfortunately doctors are not always able to control all abnormal menstrual symptoms in this way. In such cases both the patient and the doctor may feel that the only cure is a hysterectomy (see Hysterectomy). This will stop a woman from having any more periods, and will also make her infertile, but should not otherwise alter her life. However, modern medical therapies are improving and this operation is being performed less frequently. It is hoped that in the future most problems of the uterus will be treated simply with medication.

Problems of the uterus

Part of the uterus affected	Name of condition	Possible symptoms	Treatment
Entire uterus	Absent	No periods, infertile	None
	Congenital malformation (double uterus or abnormal division in the cavity of the uterus)	Often no symptoms (when pregnant, a woman may go into premature labor)	Very rarely it may be necessary to do plastic surgery to make the uterus a normal shape
	Prolapse	No symptoms or the sensation of "a lump coming down into the vagina"	Special pelvic floor exercises, avoidance of constipation, weight loss if necessary. Sometimes surgery
Endometrium (lining of the cavity of the uterus)	Endometrial polyps	Bleeding from the vagina between periods or after menopause	Dilatation and curettage (D&C)
	Endometrial hyperplasia (overgrowth of the lining of the uterus)	Heavy irregular periods, usually as a woman approaches menopause	Diagnosis by D&C followed by a course of hormone pills
	Endometritis (inflammation of the lining of the uterus)	Lower abdominal pain and heavy periods	Diagnosis by D&C followed by a course of antibiotics
	Endometrial carcinoma	Bleeding from the vagina after menopause or between periods	Hysterectomy and possible radiotherapy and/or hormones
	Trophoblastic disease (formation of placenta in the uterus with no fetus present)	A feeling of pregnancy and irregular bleeding from the vagina	D&C, avoidance of pregnancy until the condition is cured, drugs if the placental tissue spreads outside the uterus
	Dysfunctional (abnormal) uterine bleeding	Heavy and/or frequent periods with no obvious physical abnormality of the uterus	Diagnosis by D&C, hormone treatment followed by hysterectomy if hormones unsuccessful
Myometrium (muscular wall of the uterus)	Fibroids	Often no symptoms—possibly heavy periods and enlarged uterus	If they cause a problem, fibroids may be surgically removed (myomectomy) or a hysterectomy may be performed
	Sarcoma (cancerous form of fibroid)	Often no symptoms—sometimes the uterus becomes enlarged	Hysterectomy and radiotherapy
	Adenomyosis (endometrial tissue deposited inside the muscular layers of the uterus)	Painful, heavy periods	May be treated by hormonal therapy but often only diagnosed by a hysterectomy
Cervix	Polyp	Often no symptoms—sometimes vaginal bleeding after sexual intercourse or between periods	D&C and removal of polyp
	Erosion or ectropion (cells which normally line the cervix begin to grow on the outside)	Often no symptoms—sometimes a watery discharge	No treatment needed, but the area may be burned so that new cells form (cautery)
	Cervical dysplasia (abnormal cells which may revert to normal or become cancerous)	Abnormal cervical smear	Repeated cervical smears, colposcopy, and occasionally removal of the area of abnormal cells
	Cancer of the cervix	Bleeding from the vagina after sexual intercourse and between periods	Radiotherapy and sometimes hysterectomy

Vaccinations

Q My son got a rash and a mild cold a week after he was given his measles shot. I was told this is what happens with measles itself. Is this true?

A Yes. The measles vaccine, like many of the really successful vaccines, consists of an attenuated (weakened) strain of the virus itself, which is given as an injection of live virus. This is likely to produce the minor reaction that your son had; a mini-attack of the disease. Anyone who has seen the misery of a young child with full-blown measles would be the first to agree that the mild reaction to a measles shot is preferable to suffering the disease itself.

Q When my daughter became due for her TB shot, the hospital ran a test on her and said that she didn't need the vaccine at all. Why was this?

A Tuberculosis is an unusual infection. It is common for people to acquire the illness in the latter years of childhood. When this happens a child may suffer no symptoms at all, and build up an immunity that keeps the disease in check. A child in this situation will not need the immunizing injection, since he or she already has immunity. The original test injection is an extract of the cell wall of the bacteria, and it is read two days later. A red welt on the site of the injection is evidence of a previous tuberculosis infection.

Q How is a vaccine weakened so that the germs build up immunity and yet do not cause the disease?

A It is really the antivirus vaccines that are used in the live form. This means that living viruses are injected into the patient, so they must belong to a strain that is going to introduce immunity without causing serious disease. These strains are produced by growing repeated cultures of the original virus on a suitable medium or by infecting and reinfecting a series of animals such as mice. This continues until the virus has lost its virulence.

Like so many medical advances, vaccination developed almost by accident—when doctors discovered that inoculation with cowpox virus prevented smallpox. Now vaccines offer complete protection against many diseases.

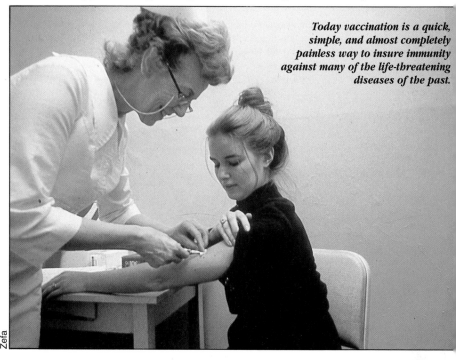

Today vaccination is a quick, simple, and almost completely painless way to insure immunity against many of the life-threatening diseases of the past.

Zefa

The development and use of vaccines has revolutionized treatment of many serious diseases. For example, with the help of an effective vaccine one killer disease—smallpox—has been eradicated from the face of the earth, while another potentially fatal disease, diphtheria, has all but disappeared from developed areas of the world (see Diphtheria, and Smallpox).

The body's defense system

The body's first line of defense is the skin, which cannot be crossed unless it is broken. The lining membrane of the gut and the lungs are also constantly assaulted by organisms, and their main protection lies in the mucus-secreting glands (see Glands, and Mucus). The final line of defense is the complex, blood-based immune system, which comes into action if the skin or a mucous membrane is breached by a foreign organism (see Immune system).

One of the main features of the immune system is the activity of antibodies, which are protein molecules that are carried in a dissolved form in the blood (see Blood). Their function is to help to control and bind infecting organisms, which can then be attacked by phagocytes. Lymphocytes also play a role: these white blood cells are involved in making antibodies and include cells that attack organisms directly, giving rise to what is called cellular immunity (see Cells and chromosomes).

Cellular immunity is an important process for dealing with organisms that are capable of infiltrating the cells themselves; one example of such an organism is the tuberculosis bacillus.

Vaccines work by introducing the immune system to an infecting organism in such a way that the body's defenses are prepared for an actual attack by the disease. Generally vaccines are better at building up antibodies than at establishing cellular immunity.

The origin of vaccination

Like many of the great advances of medicine, vaccination was an accepted technique before its theoretical basis was understood. In the late 1700s English surgeon Edward Jenner heard that milkmaids who had cowpox seemed to have a degree of immunity against smallpox, and he reasoned correctly that this might point to a way of preventing the dreaded disease. He proceeded to inject the fluid from the pustules of cowpox into people at risk from smallpox, with good results. (Cowpox is called vaccinia, hence "vaccination.") The reason the cowpox fluid worked was because the vaccinia virus is so similar to the smallpox virus that it creates effective antibodies to smallpox without giving rise to serious disease. This all happened long before anyone knew what an antibody was.

Live vaccines

The vaccinia virus is alive, and in certain conditions it may cause serious disease. For example, people with eczema may contract a fatal infection from vaccinia if they have been vaccinated. In most cases, however, vaccinia is a virus that is attenuated for the average individual; this means that it does not normally cause serious disease. In order to provide adequate protection in other diseases such as polio, rubella, yellow fever, and the like, the original virulent (disease-producing) virus has to be treated in the laboratory to reduce its virulence, while its capacity to create immunity is preserved. This is done by growing generations of viruses until they lose their capacity to cause serious disease.

Killed vaccines

In some cases, particularly with bacterial infections, it is not possible to produce live vaccines—dead bacteria extracts are

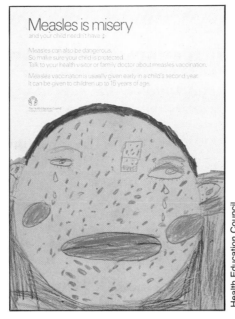

Measles is misery
and your child needn't have it.

Measles can also be dangerous.
So make sure your child is protected.
Talk to your health visitor or family doctor about measles vaccination.

Measles vaccination is usually given early in a child's second year.
It can be given to children up to 15 years of age.

Health Education Council

Variations on the theme of public health: the poster (above) is part of a campaign to persuade parents to have their children inoculated against measles. A medical team vaccinates villagers in Zaire (below) in an attempt to control diseases endemic in that part of the world.

used instead. The vaccines against whooping cough and cholera are examples of killed vaccines.

Generally, however, live vaccines are superior to using extracts of killed organisms. In addition, a vaccine like the polio vaccine can be administered by mouth, so that it goes straight to the normal port of entry of the disease—the intestine. This means that local defenses with antibodies can be built up in the intestinal wall.

Vaccines in common use

In most developed countries preschool children are offered protection against tetanus, diphtheria, and whooping cough in the form of a combined vaccine called a triple vaccine. Oral polio vaccine is also given at this time. Measles vaccine may be given in the second year of life, and rubella vaccine (see Rubella, and Pregnancy) is given to teenage girls to guard against the disease in future pregnancy.

Travelers may be offered a variety of other vaccines to prevent yellow fever, typhoid, and cholera (see Infection and infectious diseases). In fact some countries require certificates of immunization against these diseases: check with the relevant consulate or a travel agent before you travel (see Immunization).

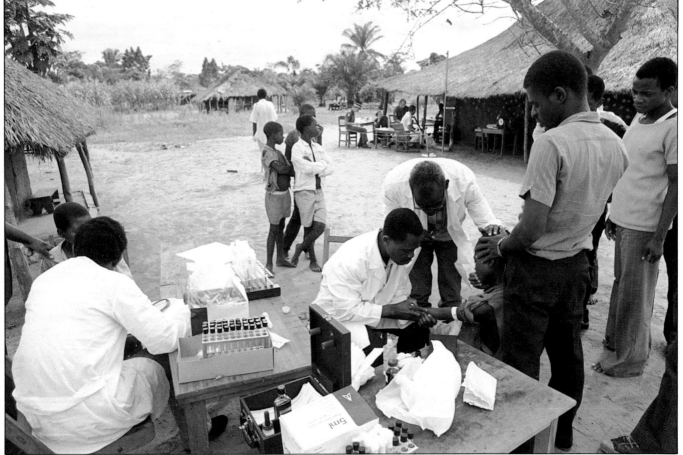

Vagina

The passage for the creation of life, for giving birth, and for sexual pleasure—these are the functions of the vagina. Unfortunately the vagina is prone to minor disorders that require medical treatment.

The structure of the vagina

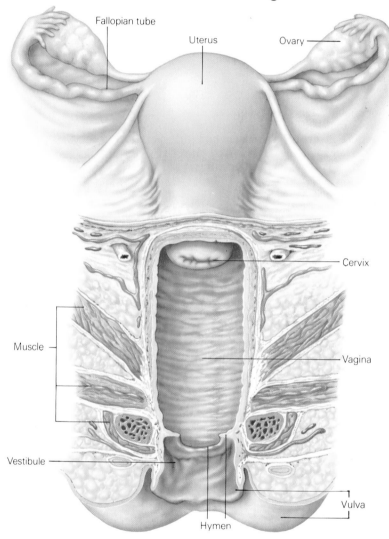

Fallopian tube

Uterus

Ovary

Cervix

Muscle

Vagina

Vestibule

Vulva

Hymen

The vagina is the channel that leads from the vulva to the uterus. During a woman's life the vagina undergoes several changes. A child's vagina is obviously smaller than that of a mature woman. The lining of the wall of the vagina is thinner in a child or postmenopausal woman (see Menopause) than that of a woman in the reproductive years of her life. These changes are largely influenced by a group of hormones released by the ovary; these are called estrogens (see Hormones).

The vagina plays an important role during intercourse and childbirth. The role

The vagina is a tough muscular canal situated between the uterus and the vulva. Its corrugated structure is specifically designed to give it the amazing elasticity needed for the birth of a baby.

during childbirth is relatively passive when the vagina forms the lower portion of the birth canal and is capable of opening sufficiently to allow the birth of the baby. We have only relatively recently begun to understand some of the changes that occur in the vagina during intercourse (see Intercourse).

Vaginal disorders and treatment

Age	Symptom	Cause	Treatment
Infancy and childhood	Vaginal discharge	Nonspecific bacterial infection	Hygiene and estrogen cream
Puberty	Failure to menstruate and have regular monthly periods	Hematocolpos (transverse membrane at the entrance to the vagina that prevents menstrual loss, so the blood is trapped in the vagina)	Minor surgery to incise the membrane
	Failure to menstruate in an otherwise normal female due to absent vagina	Failure of vagina to form in the embryo; usually uterus is also absent	Plastic surgery to make artificial vagina. Patient very unlikely to be fertile or menstruate
Reproductive years	Vaginismus	Psychological cause or physical causes mentioned below	Psychosexual counseling
	Vaginal discharge	Physiologically normal	No treatment
		Foreign body in the vagina such as forgotten tampon or diaphragm	Removal of foreign body
		Vaginal infection with *Candida albicans* or *Trichomonas vaginalis*	Treatment of patient by uterine creams or pills; also treat patient's partner
	Cyst to one or other side of entrance to the vagina	Bartholin's cyst (drainage duct from this cyst has become blocked)	Minor surgery to remove top of cyst and allow it to drain (marsupialization)
	Abscess (tender red swelling at entrance to vagina)	Bartholin's abscess	Minor surgery to open and drain abscess. Antibiotics are sometimes prescribed at the same time
	"Lump coming down in the vagina" or incontinence of urine when laughing or talking	Vaginal wall prolapse	Weight loss and pelvic floor exercises. Fit patients, surgical operation; unfit patients, vaginal ring insert
	Bloodstained loss from vaginal wall	A very rare cause is carcinoma of the vagina	Surgical removal of tumor
Menopause	"Lump coming down in the vagina"	Vaginal wall prolapse	Weight loss and pelvic floor exercises. Surgery or vaginal ring insert
	Sore vagina, pink-stained vaginal discharge	Atrophic vaginitis (infection due to nonspecific bacteria)	Mildly acidic jelly or estrogen creams inserted into the vagina to inhibit bacteria
	Pain during coitus due to dry vagina	Lack of estrogen in the woman's circulation	Use of lubricating jelly or estrogen cream in the vagina, or hormone replacement
	Pain during coitus due to narrow vagina	See above	May respond to application of estrogen cream to the vagina

Structure

The vagina is a canal 2.75 in (7 cm) to 3.5 in (9 cm) long. It is surrounded by fibrous and muscular tissue, and is lined with a layer of cells called squamous epithelium (see Cells and chromosomes, and Muscles). The walls of the canal are normally collapsed and folded onto one another. These properties make it easy for the vagina to be distended during intercourse or childbirth. The urethra lies on the front wall of the vagina and the rectum lies on the upper third of the back of the vagina. The anus is separated from the vagina by a fibromuscular tissue called the perineal body (see Anus). The ducts from two glands called Bartholin's glands enter on either side of the outer end of the vagina, while the cervix protrudes into the top of the vagina.

During a woman's reproductive years the vaginal secretions are slightly acidic. This tends to inhibit the growth of harmful bacteria in the vagina (see Bacteria), but during the prepubertal and postmenopausal years the vagina becomes mildly alkaline. In these years the bacteria can thrive and occasionally make the vagina rather sore and uncomfortable, a condition called atrophic vaginitis.

The walls of the vagina are well lubricated with secretions from the cervical canal and Bartholin's glands. During intercourse, secretions also seep through the vaginal epithelium into the vaginal canal. A certain amount of discharge from the vagina is normal in all women. The amount increases during ovulation and sexual arousal (see Vaginal discharge).

Q Is it true that a woman's vagina becomes smaller after menopause, and can this prevent her from enjoying sex?

A After menopause the vagina ceases to have a high estrogen level, the hormone that seems to be responsible for its elastic properties and the thickness of the lining wall. This may cause the vagina to become narrower and more rigid, especially if the woman ceases to have intercourse, but it is seldom a problem if she continues to have regular coitus.

Q How long should you wait after you give birth to have a diaphragm fitted?

A It takes approximately six weeks after the birth of a baby for the birth canal, including the vagina, to return to its normal prepregnancy state. A diaphragm cannot be fitted until after this time.

Q Are vaginal deodorants really necessary, and can they be harmful?

A Simple practices such as regular showers and changes of underwear are adequate hygiene measures. Some women who use vaginal deodorants can develop a reaction to them, which tends to give the woman a heavier and more unpleasant vaginal discharge than normal. If a woman suffers from an unpleasant, foul-smelling vaginal discharge she should consult her gynecologist, rather than using a deodorant.

Q Can gonorrhea or syphilis give a woman an abnormal vaginal discharge?

A Discharge is a common symptom in the early stages of gonorrhea. It must not be ignored since a reduction in the discharge commonly means that the infection is spreading to other organs of the pelvis to produce the persistent condition of pelvic inflammatory disease. Syphilis does not cause a discharge and may be undetected since the initial symptom is painless ulcers on the genitalia. Most women only learn they have it when their partners are diagnosed.

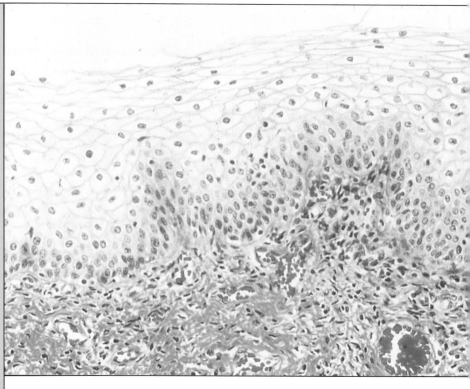

Biophoto Associates

The vagina is lined with a layer of cells called squamous epithelium. During sexual intercourse, it is lubricated by secretions seeping through these cells.

Function

During sexual arousal, a woman's genital organs, especially the labia minora and lower vagina, become engorged with blood, and the amount of vaginal secretion increases. During an orgasm the muscles of the pelvis, including those surrounding the vagina, contract involuntarily (see Orgasm).

If a woman is particularly tense or anxious during intercourse, the muscles surrounding the vagina will go into spasm (see Anxiety, and Tension). This makes the vagina narrower and makes sex painful (see Sex). This condition is called vaginismus. It can be cured by help from a psychosexual counselor, but it may take many months before the woman can fully enjoy sex.

Disorders

Some women find it very embarrassing to consult their gynecologist about problems to do with the genitalia (see Gynecology). However, because most of the problems are relatively minor (see chart) and respond to simple forms of treatment it is worth seeking medical advice early before complications occur.

Probably one of the most common problems is an irritating vaginal discharge called yeast, which is caused by the *Candida albicans* fungus (see Yeast infections). This can be easily treated with vaginal pessaries. Unfortunately it is easy to become reinfected with this fungus. It is possible to guard against this by treating the woman's partner at the same time

and warning her to be particularly careful that towels and underwear are laundered very thoroughly since the spores of this fungus can lodge in these articles.

Another common problem is atrophic vaginitis. This condition often affects women in their mid 60s. It tends to make the vagina sore and uncomfortable. This occurs because these women no longer have high enough levels of estrogen in their circulation to stimulate the growth of the vaginal epithelium. The vagina then loses its acidity, which favors the growth of the bacteria. The condition can be easily treated with estrogen creams or a slightly acidic jelly that is inserted into the vagina.

- Take a bath or shower every day
- Change your underwear daily
- Wear only briefs with cotton linings
- Never wear nylon panty hose directly against your skin
- Avoid tight pants and jeans
- After urinating, wipe yourself from front to back
- Never use douches or vaginal deodorants
- See your gynecologist if you have an unpleasant vaginal discharge

Vaginal discharge

Q My doctor says it is normal to have some vaginal discharge. Is this true?

A Your doctor is right. A small amount of vaginal discharge is normal. It is merely the secretion of some of the mucus glands in the cervix, together with cells cast off by the lining of the vagina, mixed with a watery fluid.

Q My discharge is creamy in color. Can this be normal?

A If the discharge is slight and nonoffensive and your doctor says it's normal, the creamy color is nothing to worry about. This is caused by cells from the lining. It is normal for these to be shed. However, if the discharge persists or if it has an unpleasant odor, tell your doctor, and he or she may carry out a Pap test.

Q I find that the discharge varies from time to time. Does this indicate some kind of abnormality?

A No, not necessarily. It is normal for there to be a cyclical variation in the amount of the normal discharge. It is usually heavier just before a menstrual period, and often the discharge contains an increased amount of mucus from the cervix at the time of ovulation.

Q My 11-year-old daughter is suffering from some vaginal discharge. Is this unusual, and how worried should I be?

A Vaginal discharge is not unknown in prepubescent girls. However, you must take your daughter to the doctor immediately. Your daughter's condition is most likely to be a bout of thrush, which is a yeast organism that thrives naturally in the vagina, and which can be cleared up quickly with some estrogen cream and by careful attention to hygiene. It may be possible that the discharge is due to retained material in the vagina: sometimes toilet paper can accumulate there, or your daughter may have introduced a foreign object herself.

There are many different causes of vaginal discharge, some trivial, some potentially serious, and an awareness of the significance of these can have great importance for health.

Most women are aware that a moderate degree of vaginal discharge is normal, and are not unduly worried by it. It is essential for the vagina to be kept slightly moist at all times (see Vagina), and it is kept in this condition by a watery fluid that passes through the vaginal wall from the blood vessels and tissue surrounding it. This movement of fluid is called transudation.

This normal, or physiologic, discharge is of moderate amount and, at worst, causes minor staining of the underwear. It is odorless, and is of a clear or slightly creamy color. It does not involve any itching or redness in the area surrounding the vaginal opening. Such a discharge may vary in amount at different times in the menstrual cycle (see Menstruation). It is also often more marked during pregnancy (see Pregnancy), and may be increased by the use of the contraceptive pill (see Contraception). The condition wrongly described as cervical erosion (see Cervix and cervical smears), in which some of the lining of the womb extends down over the cervix, can also cause an increase in the amount of normal discharge.

Abnormal vaginal discharge

Abnormal vaginal discharge is very common and causes considerable anxiety to many women. There is often reluctance to talk about it even to a doctor, but this is unwise since most causes of abnormal discharge can readily be cured and some may imply potential danger calling for immediate investigation. The most common, but not necessarily the most serious, causes of discharge are infective conditions causing inflammation of the vagina, or vaginitis. There are several common causes of vaginitis, but there are three specific organisms that cause about 90 percent of cases. These are the Candida organism that causes thrush, the Trichomonas organism that causes trichomonal vaginitis, and a germ called *Gardnerella vaginalis* that causes the condition of bacterial vaginosis. All three organisms are commonly transmitted by sexual intercourse (see Sex, and Sexually transmitted diseases).

Thrush

Several yeast organisms can cause thrush (see Thrush, and Yeast infections), but the most important are the Candida and Monilia species. Like all yeast organisms, these thrive in an environment with a

Using a Pap test, a sample of the vaginal discharge can be used to detect an infection. Here, a micrograph reveals the threadlike Leptothrix bacteria (iron bacteria), which are commonly associated with the protozoan Trichomonas vaginalis.

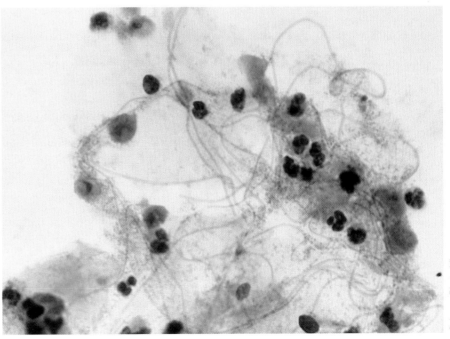

high sugar content (see Sugars). The importance of this knowledge is that untreated or poorly treated diabetes (see Diabetes), in which the urine is loaded with sugar, commonly causes genital and vaginal thrush in women. Apart from the treatment of the thrush infection, all such women must, as a minimum investigation, have their urine tested for sugar.

Thrush, or candidiasis, features strong itching around the vaginal area and a vaginal discharge that may be thick and white. This comes from colonies of the fungus that are partially adherent to the vaginal lining, and that may spread out onto the surrounding skin. Infected vagina and skin will often be inflamed, and the area is frequently very tender to the touch. The appearance is so characteristic that there is seldom much doubt as to the diagnosis. It is not, however, considered good medical practice to rely only on the appearance, and a swab should be taken for laboratory examination and positive identification. Candida organisms can readily be grown in culture, and the microscopic appearance of the typical branching strands of fungus is unmistakable to the expert.

A number of drugs are highly effective in the treatment of Candida infections, and these may be applied locally as creams or pessaries. Some of the drugs can be taken by mouth, and are highly effective.

Trichomonas vaginalis infections

The trichomonas is a single-celled microscopic organism of the type known as a protozoan. It is pear-shaped, and has an undulating membrane down one side and a number of delicate lashing tails at one end by which it moves about actively. A thicker, rapierlike process protrudes from the other end of the organism. Under the microscope the organism is easily identified by its appearance and by its active movements.

Infection with this organism may produce no detectable symptoms or only a minor discharge, but a heavy infection causes a profuse, greenish yellow, frothy discharge with an offensive smell. It is usually acquired by sexual contact with a male carrier, but can also be acquired from another woman if washcloths or other toilet articles are shared.

The discharge is associated with irritation in the vaginal area and soreness that may be severe. The organism causes numerous tiny spots of acute inflammation and damage to the lining of the vagina. The result is severe discomfort during sexual intercourse to the extent that the woman may prefer to avoid sexual contact. Vaginitis caused by sexually transmitted *Trichomonas vaginalis* is said to be as common as gonorrhea in sexually active women (see Gonorrhea).

As in all cases of abnormal vaginal discharge, it is essential for the doctor to make an accurate diagnosis so that the correct treatment can be given and the condition cleared up. The appearance of the discharge is not a sufficient indication of the cause. Trichomonas infection is diagnosed by placing a drop of the discharge on a microscope slide, covering it with a thin slip of glass, and examining it under the microscope. In 65 percent of cases of women with trichomonal infection, the organism can be seen on a Pap test.

Once the cause of the discharge is established, treatment with the drug metronidazole (Flagyl) can be started. This well-tried drug was first approved by the Federal Drug Administration in 1959 for the treatment of *Trichomonas vaginalis* infections. The drug acts by disrupting the helical structure of the DNA of the organism and preventing further DNA synthesis. It is taken orally.

Metronidazole reacts badly with alcohol, and this should be avoided during the course of treatment, which usually lasts for a week, otherwise there is likely

Keeping yourself informed about your body can be a lifesaver. If you are generally healthy, vaginal discharge can be quite normal. However, if you suspect you have an abnormal discharge, consult your doctor.

Patrick Bennett/Corbis

to be abdominal distress, nausea, vomiting, hot flashes, and headaches. If a woman has a trichomonas infection, her sexual partner must also be presumed to be infected. If the partner is not given the same course of treatment, reinfection after cure is likely. At least 30 percent of the sexual partners of a woman with trichomonal vaginitis are found to be carrying the organism in their genital tracts.

Gardnerella vaginalis infection

The organism *Gardnerella vaginalis*, usually in conjunction with other germs, can cause a condition known as bacterial vaginosis. This features vaginal and vulval itching and a vaginal discharge. The discharge is thin, grayish white, and often contains many small bubbles. Perhaps the most characteristic feature of Gardnerella infection is the occurrence of a typical musky or fishy odor, caused by the formation of amines—substances similar to those produced by the decomposition of organic matter. It is not claimed to be absolutely diagnostic of a Gardnerella infection since it is also found in Trichomonas infections. It is, however, absent in cases in which the discharge is caused exclusively by thrush. Doctors make use of this effect by adding a drop of 10 percent potassium hydroxide to a drop of the discharge on a microscope slide. The immediate appearance of the amine odor suggests Gardnerella or Trichomonas. This is called the whiff test.

Trichomonas can readily be seen on microscopy. A more precise indication of Gardnerella infection is the presence of what are called clue cells. These are cells from the lining of the vagina that, under the microscope, have a stippled appearance because they are covered with numerous bacteria. Treatment of Gardnerella infections is by metronidazole. Again, both partners must be treated.

There are many other sexually transmitted infections that can cause vaginal discharge. It is a common feature of gonorrhea and chlamydial infections. In both cases the discharge tends to be worse in the early stages of the infection. It must not be ignored since a reduction in the discharge commonly means that the infection is spreading to other organs of the pelvis to produce the persistent condition of pelvic inflammatory disease (see Pelvic inflammatory disease).

Discharge from retained material

Occasionally a tampon pushed high in the vagina will be forgotten and retained. The tampon will become infected and will cause a fairly profuse and unpleasantly odorous vaginal discharge. This is one of the easier causes of discharge to deal with, because removal of the offending tampon will soon clear up the prob-

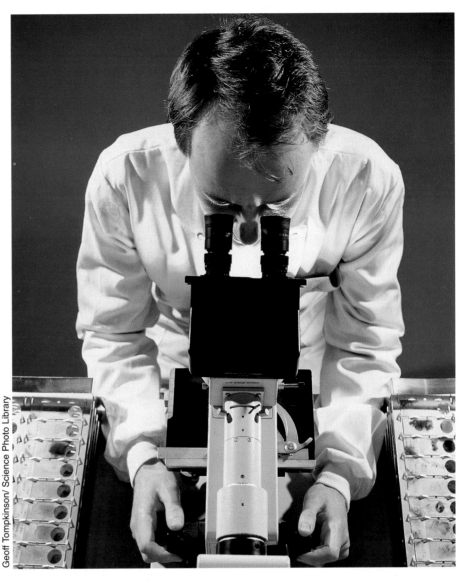

Geoff Tompkinson/ Science Photo Library

lem. Occasionally foreign bodies other than tampons are put in the vagina and forgotten about. Toilet paper has been known to accumulate in the vagina.

Removal of foreign vaginal material is usually easy. Not so simply cured is a discharge resulting from what are known as retained products of conception. These are the tissues of an embryo and its membranes and early placenta that are normally evacuated spontaneously from the womb, an indication of natural abortion of the pregnancy following death of the embryo (see Miscarriage). In roughly 10 percent of pregnancies the embryo dies early, usually because of severe malformation. In a small proportion of these cases, the material is retained. This also leads to infection and a vaginal discharge.

The treatment, in the case of an early abortion, calls for a minor surgical procedure known as evacuation of retained products of conception (ERPC). This is done by suction through a tube after

A laboratory technician examines preparations collected from a vaginal swab in order to detect infections. Abnormal discharges are sometimes malodorous and colored, and occasionally bloodstained.

gentle widening of the canal of the cervix with smooth dilators. In the case of a missed spontaneous abortion at a later stage, a drug called a prostaglandin, given in a vaginal pessary, and a drug called oxytocin, given in an intravenous drip, will cause the womb to contract and drive out the retained material.

Discharge after childbirth

Today, infection of the raw area inside the womb to which the placenta was attached is fortunately rare (see Childbirth). In earlier times it was one of the principal causes of maternal death following delivery of a baby. Puerperal sepsis killed millions of women before the cause was discovered and proper standards of obstetric hygiene

Kevin Fleming/Corbis

During infancy and childhood, it is not uncommon for girls to have some vaginal discharge. This is most often due to thrush (candidiasis), which is normally present in the vagina but which is kept in check by bacteria. Antibiotics, poor hygiene, and diabetes can cause the fungus to multiply. Good hygiene and estrogen cream will quickly clear up the condition.

instituted (see Obstetrics). Since the development of the sulfa drugs, and then antibiotics (see Antibiotics), deaths from this cause have become very rare in developed countries in the West.

Infection of the placental site may still occur, however, and early detection is important. Vaginal discharge is normal after childbirth and is called the lochia. It consists of cellular debris, mucus, and blood. The first indication that anything is going wrong is usually fever (see Fever), and this may occur within 24 hours of the birth. The temperature may rise suddenly or gradually. Such fever must always be assumed to be the result of infection until proved otherwise, and must always be reported to a doctor without delay. The diagnosis of puerperal sepsis becomes more likely if the vaginal discharge becomes more profuse, pus laden, and offensive. The absence of this, however,

need not affect the diagnosis. In this context, the vaginal discharge is of minor importance as a sign. Any suggestion of postpartum infection calls for urgent investigation and antibiotic treatment in the hospital. Delay could be disastrous.

Discharge caused by cancer
By far the most important cause of abnormal vaginal discharge is cancer (see Cancer) of the inner lining of the womb (endometrium). This form of cancer (endometrial cancer) is the second most common gynecologic cancer.

Over 30,000 cases and nearly 6000 deaths from this cause occur every year in the United States. It affects mainly women aged between 50 and 70, and especially those in the higher socioeconomic groups.

Other factors that slightly increase the risk of endometrial cancer include estrogen replacement therapy (see Estrogen, and Hormone replacement therapy), high blood pressure (see Blood pressure), obesity (see Obesity), and diabetes (see Diabetes). On the other hand, women who, before menopause (see Menopause), used contraceptive pills containing both estrogen and progesterone are at reduced risk of endometrial cancer compared with other women.

Vaginal bleeding or any bloodstained vaginal discharge after menopause at any time after six to seven months after the periods have stopped is the most common sign of endometrial cancer. When such cancer is present a bloodstained discharge occurs in 85 to 95 percent of women. Such a discharge must on no account be ignored, and no delay in reporting it to a doctor is justified. The worst reason of all for avoiding medical attention in this event is the fear of cancer. This is because the longer treatment is delayed, the more likely it is that the cancer will have spread outside the womb.

In Caucasian women, the cure rate (if the cancer is confined to the womb) is 95 percent. However, if cancer cells have spread to the lymph nodes in the pelvis the cure rate is 70 percent. If cancer has spread more widely to involve the ovaries (see Ovaries) and other pelvic organs the cure rate is only about 29 percent. All three rates are somewhat lower in black women.

It is uncommon for endometrial cancer to spread remotely to the lungs and the bones. Typically, spread occurs by local invasion and by way of the lymph drainage channels. Cancer can spread from the interior of the womb along the fallopian tubes to reach and involve the ovaries and other pelvic organs.

Cancer of the womb lining occasionally occurs in women before menopause. For this reason, any vaginal bleeding occurring outside the normal menstrual cycle or any new and unusual irregularity in the periods should be reported. Any bloodstained vaginal discharge that does not seem to be menstrual is an indication for immediate medical attention.

Medical investigation of a bloodstained vaginal discharge involves taking a careful history of the discharge, carrying out a pelvic and general examination and taking a small sample from the womb lining for pathological examination (see Dilatation and curettage).

Treating endometrial cancer
The treatment of endometrial cancer is surgical, supplemented with radiotherapy (see Radiotherapy) if the cancer has spread outside the womb. The results of treatment in early cancer are excellent, and a cure can usually be expected. If there has been wider spread of the cancer, progestational hormone therapy can substantially lengthen life but is unlikely to produce permanent remission of the disease. Eventual recurrence is, unfortunately, to be expected.

Because of the dangers of endometrial cancer, it is overwhelmingly important to report any bloodstained vaginal discharge that occurs after menopause.

Vagotomy

Q I had a vagotomy a few months ago. Since then I have had very severe diarrhea for which I have had to take medication. Does this mean I will have to be on medication for the rest of my life?

A Diarrhea after a truncal vagotomy is a well-recognized complication. It seems to be related to cutting the nerves that supply the majority of the intestine, and is more common in people who have had their gallbladder removed. In most cases it recovers on its own, but this may take several months. In persistent cases, further surgery may be needed.

Q I have heard that some patients who have a vagotomy have surgery on their stomach at the same time. Why is this?

A If the vagus nerves are cut at the level of the diaphragm, then as well as decreasing the acid secretion by the stomach, the surgery will lead to an inability to empty the stomach. Consequently a drainage operation has to be done as well. If the newer form of vagotomy is performed, the nerves are cut just as the tiny branches enter the stomach, and the nerves supplying the stomach-emptying mechanism are spared.

Q Does having a vagotomy affect the heart?

A No. The vagus nerve does supply the heart with nerves, and stimulation of these nerves causes the heart to slow down. But the vagus nerves are always divided much lower down, after the nerves to the heart have branched off.

Q After a vagotomy for a duodenal ulcer, am I likely to get the ulcer back again?

A Unfortunately there is no guarantee that any surgery for a duodenal ulcer will be 100 percent successful. However, a properly performed vagotomy should give a long-term success rate of well over 80 percent.

For those people suffering from duodenal ulcers, a vagotomy can be a lasting solution, effectively reducing the amount of acid produced by the stomach lining.

The word *vagotomy* means "cutting of the vagus nerve." The vagus are specialized nerves that emerge just below the brain (there are two, one on each side of the body) and pass down into the thorax, entering the abdomen through the diaphragm, just at the side of the esophagus (see Nervous system). The nerve then divides into various branches that supply the stomach, the liver, the gallbladder, and most of the intestines (see Stomach). Branches of the vagus nerve in the neck

Route of the vagus nerve

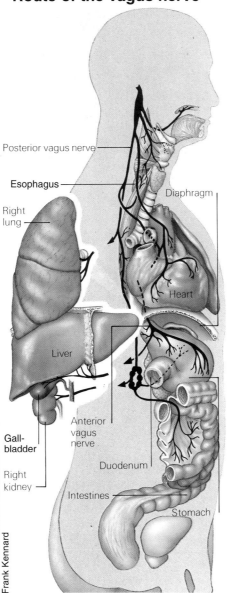

Posterior vagus nerve

Esophagus

Right lung

Diaphragm

Heart

Liver

Gall-bladder

Right kidney

Anterior vagus nerve

Duodenum

Intestines

Stomach

Frank Kennard

and chest also feed the heart. The function of the vagus nerve is to regulate the rhythm of the heart and the activity of the stomach and intestines. Stimulation of the vagus increases the output of acid by the stomach lining and relaxes the ring of muscle at the far end of the stomach, allowing food to pass into the duodenum (see Duodenum).

Why have a vagotomy?

The main reason for performing a vagotomy is to treat patients with duodenal or peptic ulcers, a condition in which an excess of acid is produced by the stomach lining (see Ulcers).

In the early 1950s it was found that cutting the vagus nerves at the point where they emerge into the abdomen, called a truncal vagotomy, led to a marked decrease in the amount of acid produced.

However, it was also soon realized that a large proportion of these patients developed problems with emptying the stomach. The stomach blew up with food and gas, and the ring of muscle that guards the outlet of the stomach stayed tightly shut (see Muscles). To overcome this problem, the combined operation of a vagotomy and a drainage procedure was devised. The drainage procedure consisted of either disrupting the muscular ring so that the stomach could always empty, or joining a loop of small intestine onto the main part of the stomach, thus bypassing the blockage.

The latest development is to divide only the tiny branches of the vagus nerve that supply the upper and middle parts of the stomach (the parts that produce the acid). This is called a highly selective vagotomy, and has the advantage that at no stage during the surgery is the stomach opened.

Side effects from a highly selective vagotomy are very rare and the technique is now widely used, with a success rate of over 80 percent.

The vagus nerve supplies a number of important organs; the liver and right lung have been lifted out of position to show its route clearly. Cutting or dividing the vagus nerve—performing a vagotomy—where it supplies the upper and middle sections of the stomach is a common operation used to treat duodenal ulcers caused by excessive acid production.

Valves

Q When my father had his aortic valve replaced, he had surgery for his coronary arteries. Is this usual?

A Yes. These days it is very common for people to have both types of surgery performed at the same time. Disease of the coronary arteries is very common in the general population, and most people who are investigated for heart valve abnormalities will also have their coronary arteries checked. If abnormalities are discovered, then grafts to bypass the blockages in the coronary arteries are made in addition to putting in a new valve; this results in a better recovery rate.

Q I have been told I have a prolapsing mitral valve. What is this and is it common?

A The mitral valve is located between the atrium and the ventricle on the left side of the heart. When this valve prolapses (becomes displaced), blood leaks back into the atrium while the ventricle is pumping. The condition is common, affecting 5 percent of women and 0.5 to 1 percent of men. It is not serious and is mainly detected by ultrasound.

Q I have aortic valve problems but I don't want to have surgery. However, the cardiologist seems anxious that I should. Why is this?

A No doctor is going to force surgery on a person who is unwilling, and doctors are even less likely to try and persuade you if they think there is any degree of risk to the procedure.

Nevertheless, replacement of the aortic valve is really a very safe procedure in all but the sickest of patients. The reason why your cardiologist is so anxious is probably because your aortic valve is obstructed—a disease called aortic stenosis. Not only will the symptoms of the disease be effectively relieved by surgery but, more importantly, your life may be saved by it since there is a high risk of sudden death in severe cases of the disease.

Though no longer the most common kind of heart disease, heart valve problems still happen to many people. Advances in investigation and surgery have meant that much more can be done for those who are affected.

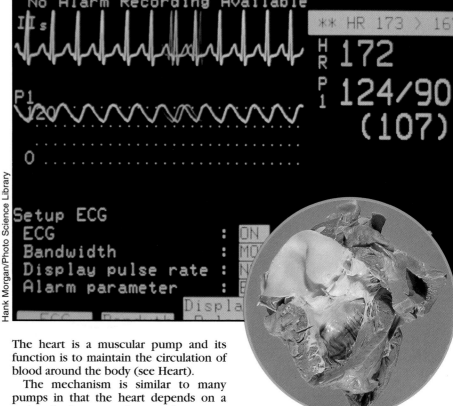

Hank Morgan/Photo Science Library

The display from an EKG machine used to monitor patients in an intensive care unit (above). The EKG provides information on the degree of valve disease. One cause of this problem is the buildup of chalk in a malformed valve (inset).

The heart is a muscular pump and its function is to maintain the circulation of blood around the body (see Heart).

The mechanism is similar to many pumps in that the heart depends on a series of valves to work properly.

On the right-hand side are the pulmonary and tricuspid valves; on the left-hand side are the aortic and mitral valves. The four valves open and close automatically to receive and discharge blood from and to the chambers so that it can flow in only one direction.

The pulmonary and aortic valves are similar in structure. They have three leaf-like cusps, or leaflets, and are made of tough but thin fibrous tissue. The mitral and tricuspid valves are more complicated, though they are similar in structure. The mitral valve has two leaflets, while the tricuspid valve has three.

Each of these valves sits in a ring between the atrium and the ventricle. The bases of the leaflets are attached to the ring, and the free edges touch each other and close the passage between the ventricle and atrium when the valve is closed. These free edges are also attached to a series of fine strings called the chordae tendineae that pass into the ventricle and stop the valve from springing back into the atrium when under pressure.

Problems

Only two things can go wrong with a valve. It can either become blocked so that blood can't pass through (stenosis), or it can allow blood to leak backward in the opposite direction to the normal circulation (incompetence or regurgitation).

In the past, rheumatic fever was found to be the most common cause of valve disease, with other causes being rather rare (see Rheumatic fever). In the case of rheumatic fever, the inflammation almost exclusively affected the valves on the left side (aortic and mitral), and could subsequently lead to stenosis or incompetence.

Today congenital abnormalities are probably the most common forms of valve disease. Stenosis or incompetence can

Valves—viewed from above

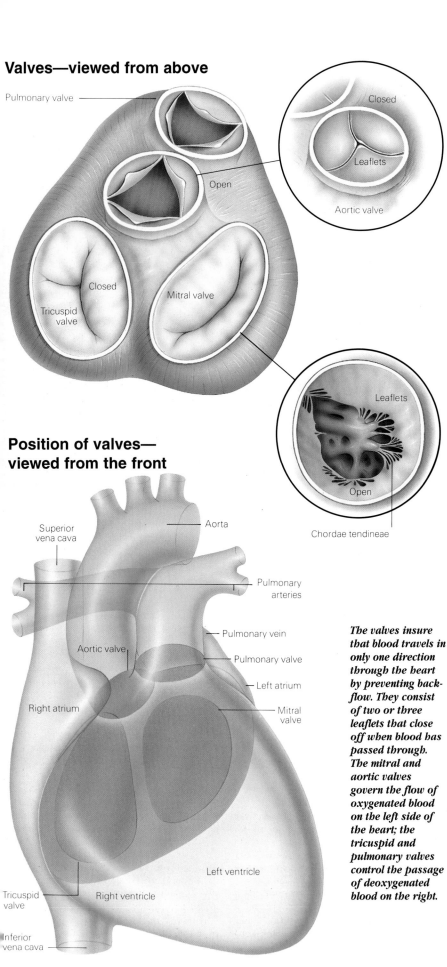

Pulmonary valve

Open

Closed

Leaflets

Aortic valve

Closed

Tricuspid valve

Mitral valve

Leaflets

Open

Chordae tendineae

Position of valves— viewed from the front

Superior vena cava

Aorta

Pulmonary arteries

Pulmonary vein

Aortic valve

Pulmonary valve

Left atrium

Mitral valve

Right atrium

Left ventricle

Tricuspid valve

Right ventricle

Inferior vena cava

The valves insure that blood travels in only one direction through the heart by preventing backflow. They consist of two or three leaflets that close off when blood has passed through. The mitral and aortic valves govern the flow of oxygenated blood on the left side of the heart; the tricuspid and pulmonary valves control the passage of deoxygenated blood on the right.

occur as a result of minor abnormalities of structure of any of the valves; however, the aortic and pulmonary valves are most likely to be affected. Problems may not come to light until late in life when the wear and tear starts to put strain on the valve. An abnormal valve may thicken and get deposits of calcium (chalk) in it over the years, causing a reduction in efficiency. Abnormal valves also appear to be at risk of picking up germs from the bloodstream, which grow on the valve and start to destroy its substance. This gives rise to a disease called infective endocarditis, which can be very serious.

As well as isolated involvement of a single valve, there may be congenital problems that can affect many parts of the heart and give rise to problems, sometimes as early as immediately after birth. One of the most common is called Fallot's tetralogy: this involves an obstruction to the pulmonary valve, together with a hole between the two ventricles (ventricular septal defect).

Another abnormality that can cause minor problems is mitral valve prolapse. This happens because there is some slack in the valve and its chordae tendineae, which allows it to balloon back into the atrium, resulting in a leakage of blood.

Symptoms of valve disease

There are relatively few ways in which valve problems come to light. Murmurs are usually picked up by a doctor using a stethoscope (see Murmurs of the heart). Aortic and mitral problems may cause a buildup of fluid in the lungs due to increased pressure, which results from an obstruction or leaking. This leads to breathlessness.

Excessive thickening of the muscular wall of the heart, as a result of the extra strain that a blocked or leaky valve puts on it, may lead to heart pain (angina). Finally, the heart's rhythm may be disturbed as the orderly contraction of muscle breaks down.

Investigation and treatment

Often the symptoms of minor valve problems can be controlled by pills, but in some cases surgery may be needed.

To decide if this is necessary, a cardiologist will make a number of tests, including an ordinary chest X ray and an electrocardiogram (EKG); these give a good idea of the level of strain the heart is under. An echocardiogram, which uses ultrasound to look at the heart (see Ultrasound), may be performed to picture the valves.

Finally, a cardiac catheterization procedure may be performed; this will measure the pressure in the various chambers of the heart and appropriate surgery can then be carried out.

Varicose veins

Q Do varicose veins run in families? Both my mother and my father have had trouble with them, and I am wondering whether I will be affected?

A Yes, they do run in families, but no definite inherited link has been identified. All that can be said is that you are more likely to develop varicose veins than you would be if neither of your parents had them. There is not much you can do to stop them from developing, apart from avoiding standing still for long periods.

Q I have a few varicose veins and I would like to have them treated, but my husband and I would like to have more children. Is it better to wait until after I have had all my children before having them treated?

A In general it would be better unless, of course, they are causing a lot of trouble at the moment. There is no doubt that pregnancy makes varicose veins worse, and it would be more sensible to have them treated after having all your children.

Q I have a friend who has a very bad ulcer on her ankle, and also has varicose veins. Are the two connected?

A They may be. Sometimes particular sorts of varicose veins can lead to breakdown of the skin in the lower leg with the formation of an ulcer. However, most patients with varicose veins do not have an ulcer, and so the two do not invariably go together.

Q I have heard that varicose veins can be treated with injections, thus making surgery unnecessary. Is this true and, if so, does having injections make it difficult to have an operation later on?

A Some varicose veins can be treated by injections. The ones that are suitable are small ones, confined to the area below the knee. Having injections does not affect subsequent surgery, should it prove necessary.

Our upright stance, with all its many advantages, has not come without a price. For many, this price may include varicose veins—those twisted knots of vein that snake embarrassingly, and often painfully, across the lower legs.

Ron Sutherland

One might think that a doorman's job is a cushy one, straining only his capacity for politeness. In fact, standing immobile for long periods puts him at increased risk of getting varicose veins.

Veins are said to be varicose when they become tortuous, thin walled, widened, and visible below the skin (see Veins). The veins in the superficial tissues of the legs are most often affected.

There is no known cause for varicose veins of the legs, but there are many factors that may lead to a worsening of varicose veins if they are already present. Varicose veins run in families, but there is no clear-cut reason for this (see Heredity). They are also much more common in women than they are in men.

The veins

The blood that supplies the tissues of the lower limb normally flows down the arteries to the feet, then back up the veins, and so to the heart. In the lower limb, there are two systems of veins: the deep system and the superficial system. It is the

Removing varicose veins

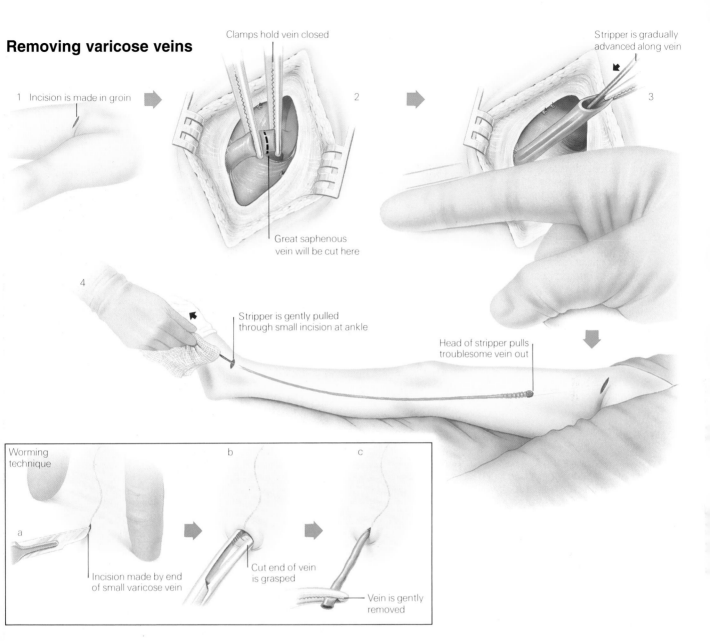

1   Incision is made in groin

Clamps hold vein closed

2

Great saphenous
vein will be cut here

Stripper is gradually
advanced along vein

3

4

Stripper is gently pulled
through small incision at ankle

Head of stripper pulls
troublesome vein out

Worming
technique

a

b

c

Incision made by end
of small varicose vein

Cut end of vein
is grasped

Vein is gently
removed

superficial system that is affected because it consists of veins in the tissues between the muscle and the skin, veins that can easily be seen and are called varicose when they become enlarged.

Both the superficial and deep veins contain valves every inch or so. These valves consist of tiny folds of the lining of the vein, and they allow blood to flow up the limb, but not the other way.

In patients with varicose veins, these valves are found to be defective. It is not clear whether the defective valves cause the varicose veins, or whether it is the other way around. However, the final effect of having defective valves is that the blood in the vein can flow down the vein, leading to stretching of its wall.

The superficial veins of the lower limb are divided into two main veins, the long saphenous and the short saphenous veins. The long saphenous vein carries

blood from the front of the foot up the inner side of the leg and goes deep into the thigh just below the groin. The short saphenous vein carries blood from the outer side of the foot up to the back of the knee, where it also goes deep to join the deep system of veins. The long saphenous vein and its many branches are the most common sites of varicose veins.

Aggravating factors
Although there are no obvious causes of varicose veins there are a number of factors that increase their possibility.
Pregnancy: Many women notice varicose veins after pregnancy. It is probable that the veins were abnormal before pregnancy, but that pregnancy made them worse. There are two theoretical reasons why this should happen. First, the presence of an enlarged uterus leads to considerable pressure on the veins in the

(1) The patient lies on a tilt table with the feet raised. The troublesome veins have already been marked on the skin. An incision is made in the groin area and the fascias are divided until the great saphenous vein is revealed. (2) The vein is lifted, clamped, and divided; all the branches are tied off. (3) The stripper, a thin tube, is then introduced into the groin end; it is advanced down the vein, with the surgeon's finger tracing the vein's path to insure that the stripper's way is clear. (4) A small transverse incision is made on the inside of the ankle and the stripper is withdrawn through it. Again, the surgeon traces the path of the vein. The leg is raised to reduce bleeding. (Inset) The worming technique is used to remove tortuous tributaries. Small incisions are made at sites of uncomfortable veins. Sections are removed using artery forceps. All incisions are stitched, and, finally, bandages are applied to the leg.

Q Is there anything that can be done to treat the patches of tiny purple veins that I seem to have developed on my legs? They do not bother me, apart from their unsightliness.

A Unfortunately these groups of tiny veins, or venular flares, as they are called, are impossible to treat. They are associated with varicose veins, however, and it may be that if you have treatment for the varicose veins they will cease to get any worse. Don't forget that minor blemishes on the legs may be a lot less unsightly than scars from operations, or brown skin stains from injection treatment.

Q Is it true that certain jobs can cause varicose veins?

A Probably. Standing still for long periods of time increases the amount of blood in the veins of the legs and may worsen varicose veins. However, it is probably a combination of the tendency to develop varicose veins and the prolonged standing that leads to the final outcome. There are many people who have varicose veins who do not stand for long periods, and conversely there are many people whose job entails standing who do not have varicose veins. For those people who do have to spend long periods of time standing, some form of exercise during a break is advisable. Also, as you stand working, make a point of squeezing and relaxing your leg muscles; this helps pump blood up the veins.

Q There seems to be a lot of argument about whether or not varicose veins cause pain in the legs. Can they cause pain, and if so, what sort of pain?

A Varicose veins can cause pain in the legs, but usually only if the veins are severely affected. The pain is usually worse at the end of the day, and may be felt at night as a sort of night cramp. It is very important that pain in the legs is not automatically attributed to varicose veins, since there may be another abnormality in the leg, such as arthritis or arterial disease, causing the pain.

One type of treatment involves injecting different parts of the vein with a special substance, causing inflammation (right). The leg will then be bandaged very tightly, so that the varicose vein is compressed.

pelvis, causing increased pressure in the veins of the leg. This pressure may cause the veins to become swollen. Second, hormones that are produced during pregnancy lead to a general softening up of the supporting tissues to allow the baby's head to pass through the birth canal, and the supporting tissues of the veins may also be similarly affected (see Pregnancy).

Obesity: Varicose veins can be brought on through obesity because of increased pressure inside the abdomen, together with general weakening of fibrous tissue in the wall of the vein (see Obesity).

Prolonged standing: Jobs that involve prolonged standing may put an undue strain on the veins of the legs, especially if they have to be kept still.

Injury: Sometimes a large varicose vein develops at the site of an injury, such as where a baseball has hit a player's leg. This may be the only varicose vein in an otherwise normal leg (see Bruises).

Deep vein thrombosis: Occasionally patients who have had a deep vein thrombosis may develop varicose veins in the lower leg, but these are usually of a different pattern compared with the more common varicose veins, which start in the superficial veins (see Thrombosis).

Effects of varicose veins

Varicose veins do not look pleasant, and by far the most common reason for people to seek medical help is because the veins are unsightly. But varicose veins can also cause complications and these may necessitate surgical or other treatment.

Because they are thin-walled and near the surface, varicose veins are susceptible to injury. This, coupled with the fact that the blood flow is much more sluggish in varicose veins, can lead to a thrombosis in the vein. The resulting inflammation around the thrombosis, known as phlebitis, causes pain and redness in the affected area.

For unknown reasons, some patients who have varicose veins develop very bad eczema on the lower leg (see Eczema). This condition can be treated with skin preparations, but if the varicose veins are removed, then the eczema usually disappears of its own accord.

Varicose veins in all their unsightliness ... They are more common in women than men, but it's comforting to realize that there are many types of treatment available (including surgery, injections, and bandages), and that they can be controlled.

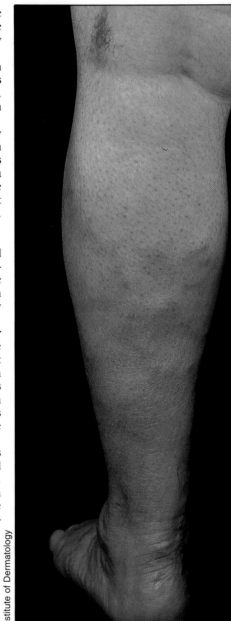

Institute of Dermatology

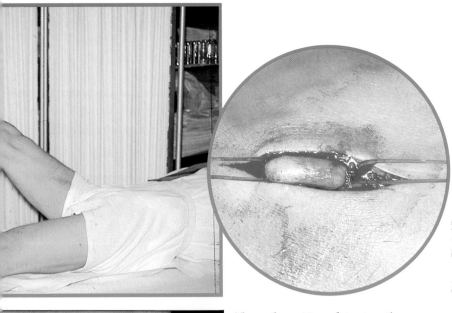

The modern approach to operating on varicose veins involves making an incision in the groin area and pushing a tube down the vein (above and below). As the tube works its way down, any obstructions in the vein are cleared. The tube is then removed and the incision stitched up.

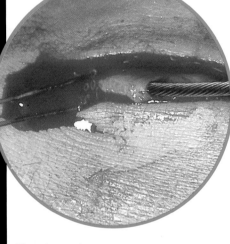

and it is here that careful examination of the pattern of the individual patient's veins is of vital importance. By examining the patient, first when he or she is lying down and then standing up, the surgeon determines whether the long or the short saphenous vein is at fault, and at which point along the vein the trouble arises.

It is usually found that the valves in the upper part of the long saphenous vein (in the groin) are causing the problem, allowing blood to leak back down the vein (see Valves). Therefore, if the long saphenous vein is tied off in the groin, the pressure is taken off this vein at points lower down. The blood that would normally flow through the long saphenous vein finds its way back to the heart via a different vein, of which there are dozens in the leg.

This sort of surgery, although it may seem quite elaborate, is relatively minor for the patient. Usually he or she is in the hospital for one or two days and can get up and walk the day after surgery.

Injections: In this form of treatment a special substance is injected into different parts of the vein, causing the lining of the vein to become inflamed. The leg is then tightly bandaged, and remains so for about a month, so that the vein is compressed. The object of the treatment is to get the opposite walls of the vein to stick together permanently, thus effectively closing it (see Bandages, and Injections).

The main disadvantage of this form of treatment is that it is only effective on small varicose veins, and only if they are situated below the knee (it is virtually impossible to get a bandage to stay on the thigh for more than a few hours).

Bandages: There are no other forms of treatment that are capable of actually removing varicose veins once they are present, but the wearing of support hose can help to prevent varicose veins from getting any worse. This hose is specially designed to give firm, even pressure all the way up the leg, and it is usually quite comfortable to wear.

Taking care

If you have varicose veins, the chances are that you will always have a few prominent veins for the rest of your life. Even if you have the existing ones treated, there is no guarantee that they will not appear elsewhere after treatment. However, there are some things you can do to try and prevent them from reappearing!

Try not to do too much standing, if at all possible. Walking is fine, but do not stand still for long periods.

When you sit down, always try to put your feet up on a stool or chair, so that the blood in the legs can flow more easily back up the body to the heart.

Treatment

Various forms of treatment have been tried for varicose veins, but modern treatments include surgery, injections, and other remedies, such as the wearing of bandages and support hose.

Surgery: The aim of surgery for varicose veins is twofold. First, an attempt is made to remove the unsightly veins. Second, an operation is done to prevent the veins from coming back again (see Surgery).

The first part of the treatment involves making several tiny little cuts in the skin over the veins and removing them a segment at a time. The distance between the cuts will vary, but may be 2 in (5 cm).

The second part of the operation—treating the root cause of these particular varicose veins—may be more difficult,

Vasectomy

Q I am thinking of having a vasectomy but am worried that it will affect my virility. Does this ever happen?

A Generally there is no medical reason why a vasectomy should have any effect on virility, or any aspect of your sex life except fertility. A few men do find a temporary slackening of sexual desire after surgery but this is usually caused by psychological factors. For example, it may be due to anxiety about the surgery having some effect on sexual performance or sexual desire.

Q How soon after having a vasectomy is it safe to have intercourse without using some kind of birth control?

A Sperm capable of fertilization have been known to survive in the seminal vesicles for as long as six months after vasectomy, but it is usually more like four to six weeks. However, it is important not to rely on these figures; and specimens of semen should be examined under a microscope to make certain that there are no sperm remaining in the seminal fluid before you have intercourse without using some method of birth control.

Q My wife died soon after I had a vasectomy. I am now planning to remarry and both my future wife and I want to have children. Is this impossible, or is there any way in which the vasectomy can be reversed?

A Vasectomies can sometimes be successfully reversed, but this is a difficult procedure with no guarantee of success in the end. Surgery involves finding the cut ends of the vas deferens and meticulously sewing the various layers together again.

Even if this is done there is no guarantee that the internal tube will remain open; and if it is open, sperm antibodies can prevent the development of satisfactory sperm. At present, the pregnancy rate in the partners of men who have had vasectomies reversed is no more than 40 percent.

Male sterilization is one of the most reliable forms of birth control. It requires only minor surgery, but should never be undertaken lightly because there is no guarantee that the effect can ever be reversed.

The decision to have a vasectomy has to be a rational one: it should only be made after a great deal of thought and discussion with both your partner and your doctor.

Vasectomy is a permanent form of sterilization for males, and is an increasingly common form of birth control in the United States for men whose families are complete or for those who do not wish to have children. It is equivalent to the operation in a woman in which the fallopian tubes, along which the eggs pass from the ovary to the womb, are either cut, tied, clipped, or sealed off, so that she cannot become pregnant.

Both operations are intended to result in a permanent inability to have children. Therefore no couple should consider sterilization (see Sterilization) unless they are certain that there is no possibility of their wanting children in the future. Before deciding to have a vasectomy it is always advisable for a man to discuss the matter thoroughly with both his partner and doctor since there is no guarantee that the procedure can be reversed in the future.

How it works

Sterilization in males consists of removing a section of the vas deferens, which is the duct that sperm (see Sperm) pass along when released from the testes (see Penis,

and Testes). Sperm are manufactured from cells that make up the walls of small tubes (seminiferous tubules) that form each testis. When sperm have matured they collect in larger tubes, the vasa efferentia. These join together and pass out of the testis at the epididymis, a long coiled tube almost wrapped around the outside of the testis. When the epididymis leaves the area of the testis it becomes a long thin channel, called the vas deferens. This is grouped together with the arteries, veins, and lymphatics that supply the testis. Together they form a thick cord called the spermatic cord.

From the scrotum, or bag in which the testes lie, the two spermatic cords pass up into the lower part of the abdomen and loop over the lower end of each ureter (the tube carrying urine from the kidney to the bladder) before joining the urethra (the tube that takes urine away from the bladder) where it runs through the prostate gland. At this junction, the newly made sperm are stored in pouchlike structures, called seminal vesicles, until they are required.

During ejaculation (see Orgasm) the sperm, now in a fluid called semen, are pushed forcefully down the urethra and out at the tip of the penis. If this happens during sexual intercourse (see Intercourse, and Sex), the sperm are propelled deep into the woman's vagina.

There are many ways in which birth control (see Contraception) can be achieved. Some, such as using the condom and the diaphragm, depend on creating a physical barrier. Others, such as the IUD, or coil, interfere with the fertilized ovum establishing itself in the womb; and another, the Pill, interferes with the production of the monthly egg. Sterilization in a male consists of removing a section of the vas deferens, which gives this method the name vasectomy. This works on the basis that if a piece of the vas deferens is missing it will be impossible for sperm to pass along it from the testes to be released and thus bring about fertilization.

Advantages and disadvantages

All methods of birth control have their own particular advantages and disadvantages, and it is very important that individuals choose the one that is best suited to their personal needs and circumstances. Vasectomy, because it is generally irreversible, is not something to be undertaken lightly.

Men who consider having a vasectomy are usually in their late 40s or 50s, already have children, feel that their families are complete, and prefer this method of birth control to any other.

Vasectomy has the great advantage of being absolutely reliable and permanent. However, its permanency can be a disadvantage since a reversal of the surgical procedure is difficult and expensive, and, in many cases, impossible.

The decision about whether or not to have a vasectomy should not be made without consultation, although ultimately the responsibility must lie with the man alone. Doctors insist that patients fully understand what is involved, and may want to have a signed statement to this effect before they will undertake surgery.

Nevertheless, it is also important that a decision to have a vasectomy is taken

Vasectomy surgery is simple. Local anesthesia is given; an incision is made in the skin of the scrotum (1). Part of the vas deferens is pulled out (2). It is cut in two places about 1 in (2.5 cm) apart and the section is removed (3). The ends are folded back (4). The site is closed and the procedure is repeated on the other side (5).

jointly by both partners. Although it is the man who will have the vasectomy, it will inevitably have some effect on his relationship with his partner. Before planning a vasectomy a man should discuss the advantages and disadvantages with his partner and family physician.

Surgery

Because the surgery required for a vasectomy is relatively straightforward, it does not require hospitalization, and can be done in the doctor's office or family planning clinic. The vasectomy is carried out under local anesthesia (see Anesthetics).

Two or three small shots are given into the site of the operation to deaden the area. The section of the vas deferens chosen for removal is that part which is most easily accessible and lies at the neck of the scrotum, just below where it joins the rest of the body.

A small vertical cut is made through the anesthetized skin and the vas deferens is identified. It is then cut in two places 1 in (2.5 cm) apart, and the intervening

How a vasectomy is performed

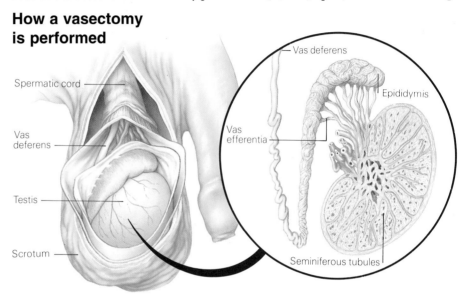

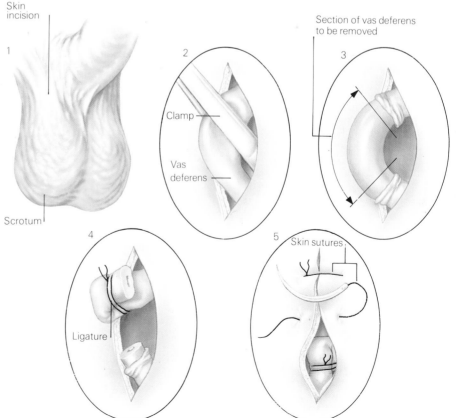

Q Is there a noticeable scar after a vasectomy?

A Usually the skin heals so well that you would have to look very carefully to find the scar.

Q A friend of mine had a vasectomy and he told me that the whole area became swollen and turned blue. Is this usual?

A Fortunately not. It would appear that your friend developed a scrotal hematoma. This occurs when a severed blood vessel oozes into the scrotum, and this happens only rarely.

Q What should a man thinking about having a vasectomy bear in mind before going ahead with surgery?

A The most important thing for him to understand fully is that although reversal may sometimes be possible, the operation should be regarded as a permanent measure. It is vital that he doesn't enter into it with the expectation that he may be able to change his mind at a later date and have it all reversed. Apart from that, he and his partner need to be sure that they will not want more children in the future. They also need to be sure that their relationship is stable, and likely to last so that there is no question of the man wanting to reserve the possibility of having children with another partner in the future. For these reasons, vasectomy is usually the chosen method of contraception for older men.

Q Have the major Western religions made any pronouncements on vasectomy?

A The Protestant Church feels that vasectomy is a voluntary business, but stresses that young and unmarried men should not consider having surgery. The Catholic Church is opposed to any form of birth control apart from the rhythm method. The Orthodox Jewish view is as firmly against the procedure as the Catholic one; and to date there has been no statement of opinion from the Muslim religious authorities.

In India vasectomy has become a controversial issue, not least because of suggestions of coercion. Good health education should allay fears (right).

The evergreen entertainer and bon vivant Dean Martin was one celebrity known to have had a vasectomy, and he talked freely about his surgery (above).

section is then removed. The ends are usually folded back on themselves before being securely tied with a material, such as silk, which will not dissolve or disintegrate. The wound (see Wounds) is closed with a few stitches (see Stitch) and the procedure is repeated on the other side. The whole operation only takes half an hour or less.

After surgery

The wound usually heals in a few days (see Healing), after which the stitches are removed. There may be some soreness when the anesthesia wears off, but this is entirely normal. In a few patients there may be some bleeding into the wound, and this can cause discomfort, pain, swelling, and some discoloration for a few days. Intercourse is likely to be painful for a day or two, and most men avoid having sex until the stitches are removed.

It is important to realize that there is a substantial time lag between surgery and the time when the patient is in fact infertile. This is because a certain number of sperm are stored in two little pouches called the seminal vesicles. They have

already passed up the vas deferens and escaped before the vasectomy has been performed. These sperm can remain capable of fertilization for several months after surgery. Usually it is reckoned that by the time three months have elapsed they should all have been used up, but there are cases where pregnancy has occurred up to six months after the vasectomy operation.

The exact time cannot be predicted, but it is related to the number of times that the man ejaculates after surgery. If he has frequent sexual intercourse, then he will use up the remaining sperm more quickly. To guard against unwanted pregnancy during this time other forms of contraception, such as a condom, should be used. It is customary to examine two specimens of semen at eight and 12 weeks after surgery, and, if these contain no sperm, then it is considered safe to carry on with unprotected intercourse.

If seminal analysis after six months still shows the presence of sperm, then the patient should be investigated for the possibility of having two vasa deferentia on one side, one of which has been missed.

In the later stages of surgery to remove a section of the vas deferens (below), the cut ends are folded back on themselves and ligatures are made. They are securely tied with material that will not dissolve or disintegrate. A reversal of the process, called reanastomosis, aims at the reconstruction of a tube between the epididymis and the seminal vesicle, and is commonly performed on only one side. The ease with which surgery can be done depends on how much of the vas deferens was removed.

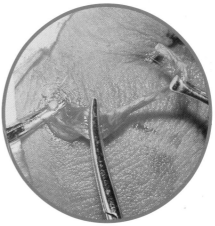

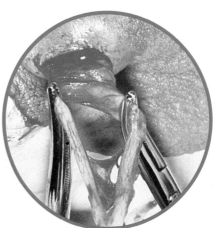

Effects of vasectomy

It is important to realize that the vasectomy procedure is simply an interruption to the flow of sperm into the part where the semen is collected. Even though millions of sperm are released during normal intercourse, they are so small that their total volume will not make any appreciable difference to the volume of semen.

The other function of the testes, that of producing male hormones (see Hormones), which are released directly into the bloodstream, is not affected in any way by a vasectomy; nor is a man's sexual drive or ability. A very few men experience psychological problems that do affect their sexual performance, but psychotherapy (see Psychotherapy) or counseling (see Counseling) should clear these problems up. In extreme cases, the man may choose to reverse the vasectomy surgically.

There is some evidence that tying off the vas deferens on each side can lead to the formation of antibodies against the patient's own sperm. This occurs in very few patients and is of no relevance unless the patient wishes to have a reversal of his vasectomy. However, in this case the main obstacle to a successful reversal is the difficulty of the mechanics of successfully joining up two tiny tubes in the midst of a large amount of scar tissue. The success rate of reversal is around 30–40 percent.

Apart from the occasional case of the development of antibodies to sperm, there are no other known effects. The possibility that vasectomy might cause an increase in the incidence of atheroma (see Arteries) has not yet been proven by any scientific research or evidence.

Outlook

Vasectomy is virtually always completely and permanently successful. In approximately one in 2000 cases the two ends of the severed vas deferens do manage to join up again, resulting in an unexpected and apparently miraculous pregnancy of the man's partner. If this occurs the man can safely undergo another vasectomy.

Attempts have been made to develop a surgical procedure that would be less permanent, and thus more acceptable to a larger number of men. However, no such surgical procedure is contemplated or is generally available at the present time.

Vegetarianism

Q Is it true that a vegetarian diet is healthier than one that involves eating meat?

A As far as diet goes, eating meat is not harmful in itself. However, eating anything to excess can be dangerous, and a heavily meat-centered diet can, for example, produce too high an intake of fats. Remember, though, that meat is an excellent source of protein and iron, which the body needs. If these substances are not eaten in meat, they must be found elsewhere. The body also needs a certain proportion of fat, so avoiding meat without careful supplements can be bad for you. However, a well-balanced vegetarian diet can be very healthy, and is even pre-scribed for certain conditions that are caused or aggravated by a high intake of saturated fats or a low intake of fiber. A vegetarian diet tends to be high in fiber and low in saturated fats.

Q I have just become a vegetarian. What should I do when I eat at friends' homes?

A Presumably you became a vegetarian either out of conviction or because a change of diet was called for. The best approach is to have the courage of your convictions and tell your host in good time that you are vegetarian. No friend would feel inconvenienced, provided that you tell him or her early. After all, you wouldn't think twice about stating dietary preferences if you were, say, a diabetic. Your vegetarianism is nothing to be ashamed of.

Q Will my children get all the vitamins they need from eating a purely vegetarian diet?

A A vegetarian diet that is properly balanced will contain all the vitamins that you are ever likely to need, provided it is carefully planned. The kind of vegetarianism you choose is also relevant. If, for example, you are actually vegan and do not eat meat or animal products of any kind you *must* give your children vitamin B$_{12}$ supplements if you want them to follow the same diet as you.

Not so long ago vegetarians were afflicted with a reputation for being eccentrics. But as public awareness of the dietary advantages of vegetables has grown, so too has respect for those people who prefer not to eat meat.

Vegetarianism is a way of life in which plant foods are eaten in preference to, or to the exclusion of, animal products. Historically vegetables have only recently come into their own. Knowledge of nutrition has increased greatly in this century (see Nutrition), and during the 1920s fashion, led by such knowledge and by economic necessity, moved away from the heavy, meat-centered Edwardian meals of 10 to 12 courses to a lighter, healthier, more balanced diet (see Diet). Between the two World Wars consumption of fruit and vegetables rose dramatically in the Western world. By the end of World War II, for example, there were 70,000 vegetarians registered in Britain. Registration enabled a vegetarian to exchange the meat ration for up to 2 lb (900 g) of nuts a week.

A way of life
For many people vegetarianism is a complete way of life that involves more than just diet. Naturism, homeopathy

In the West, vegetarianism is a practice based on personal preference. In the poorer parts of the world, however, the economics of necessity are paramount: vegetables may be all that's available, or affordable.

(natural medicine), spiritualism, and yoga all have links with vegetarianism (see Homeopathy, and Yoga).

There are many forms of vegetarianism, but most vegetarians fall into one of five main groups. At the least rigorous end of the scale are those who will eat white meat, such as chicken or fish, and animal products, such as cheese and eggs, but will avoid red meat. Next are the lacto-ovo (milk-egg) vegetarians, who avoid all forms of flesh, including fish and fowl, but will eat eggs and dairy products. Following this group are the lacto vegetarians, who avoid all flesh and also eggs, on the ground that eggs are embryos and therefore flesh. Then there are those who follow a macrobiotic diet, part of a whole lifestyle based on hatha yoga, which con-

Growing soybeans in Zaire (left). Their value as a source of protein is readily apparent: 3.5 oz (100 g) of soybeans contain nearly twice as much protein as the same weight of chicken. Soy "meat"—textured vegetable proteins based on soy—is being used more and more as a substitute for the real thing.

centrates on whole grains, cereals, and some vegetables, but also includes fish (see Macrobiotics). Finally there are the vegans, who eat no flesh or animal products of any kind.

Why become a vegetarian?

There are probably almost as many reasons for becoming a vegetarian as there are vegetarians. The motive may be ethical, economic, ecological, social, emotional, spiritual, or medical. One obvious and widespread reason is a simple dislike of meat, its taste or appearance, or both. Other reasons based on personal dislike include that of one person who became a vegetarian after seeing a particularly bloody automobile crash: the mutilated bodies reminded her of a butcher's shop, and she has been unable to eat meat ever since.

In early cultures there were often social reasons for people eating a vegetarian diet. Some Indian and African communities have no tradition of hunting, and so no source of fresh meat. Instead they live on cereals and plants. Economic pressures may also be relevant: with the

That steak on your plate was once part of an animal that was dismembered in a slaughterhouse. Is it so surprising that the thought of this butchery makes some people stop eating meat?

rising cost of fish and meat, many people cannot afford this type of food.

Perhaps more commonly, there are intellectual reasons for becoming a vegetarian. The Vegan Society was begun by vegetarians who felt that the methods used in dairy farming, especially the early separation of cow and calf, were in some ways more cruel than those of meat production. In protest, they refused to eat animal products of any kind.

Most vegetarians avoid meat and meat products because they are distressed by the idea of animals being slaughtered to provide it, by the methods of slaughter, or by the treatment of the animals on the way to the slaughterhouse.

There is also the ecological and economic argument that the starving people of the world could be better provided for if our diet were not so meat centered. Fifty percent of the world cereal crop is fed to animals, and it takes 10 tons of vegetable protein fed to an animal to produce one ton of animal protein (see Protein). The theory is that if less grain were used to raise fewer animals for slaughter, more would be available for humans.

These diagrams represent how, in terms of land use, it is more economical to grow crops rather than graze animals destined for slaughter and the dinner table.

The economics of vegetarianism

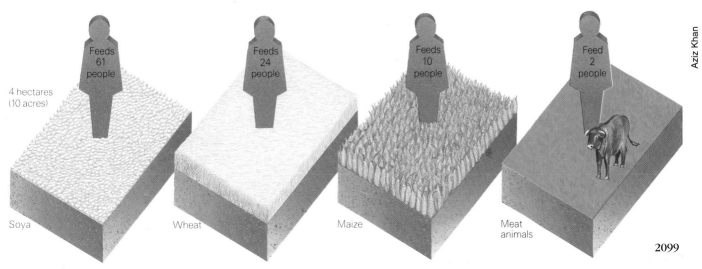

4 hectares (10 acres)

Feeds 61 people — Soya

Feeds 24 people — Wheat

Feeds 10 people — Maize

Feed 2 people — Meat animals

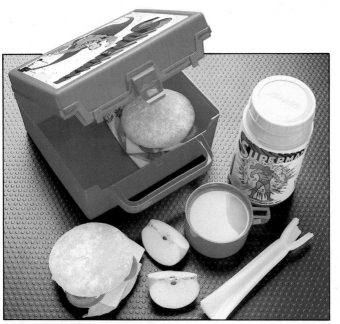

A tempting lunch box for kids to take to school. What's special about this one is that the food in it is vegetarian and contains all the nutrients necessary for a well-balanced meal. The crux of adopting a vegetarian diet is that it must be balanced, containing the vitamins your children are likely to need; vitamin supplements (inset) can provide reassurance.

Several religious and spiritual sects advocate vegetarianism as part of a pure, simple life. The macrobiotic lifestyle, for example, centers on the belief that pain and disease are the results of spiritual imbalance, and that concern for the origin of food is one way to restore the balance. A pure natural diet is thought to rid the body of harmful toxins and, in conjunction with yoga and prayer, promotes spiritual well-being.

Finally, some people become vegetarians for health reasons. Although a meat-free diet is not necessarily better for everyone, certain conditions—especially heart and digestive diseases—can be improved by the low saturated fat and high-fiber intake of a vegetarian diet.

A balanced vegetarian diet

Planning a vegetarian diet requires much thought and care. Vegans, especially, must be aware that the quality of protein obtained from individual plant sources is low when compared with animal protein. However, by combining certain plant proteins a high-quality protein can be obtained. For example, cereals and legumes complement each other.

To insure that protein requirements are met, the vegan who is not obtaining the benefits of high-quality protein from eggs and cheese should eat a diet of mixed protein sources. Such a combination might include cereals, nuts, legumes, potatoes, and oil seeds.

A properly balanced vegetarian diet can have health advantages. Vegans tend to weigh less than omnivores (those who eat many kinds of food, flesh and vegetable), which can be an advantage. Also, vegetarians eat a greater amount of fiber, which guards against constipation (see Constipation) and intestinal diseases.

Other conditions that a vegetarian diet has improved or even cured in some cases include infantile eczema, childhood asthma, acne, and, in adults, diabetes, hypertension, circulatory problems, blood clots, angina, and migraine.

The most widely discussed argument for vegetarianism on health grounds, however, is the avoidance or alleviation

of heart disease (see Heart attack, and Heart disease). One of the most common causes of heart attacks is the accumulation of fatty deposits along the walls of the coronary arteries. Diets rich in fats and particularly saturated fats (fats with a high concentration of hydrogen atoms), which are found predominantly in animal products, appear to contribute to the disease (see Fats).

Heart disease is almost unknown in nonindustrial vegetarian communities. However, the Scandinavians, who eat a higher proportion of animal fat than any other European nation, also have the highest incidence of heart disease. The Italians, who eat the lowest proportion of animal fat but consume large quantities of vegetable fat, have the lowest incidence.

Be careful with your diet

A commitment to vegetarianism, and especially veganism, can, however, lay the incautious follower open to danger. Overly eager acceptance of the intellectual tenets of vegetarianism could lead a person into a neglect of the many other factors that contribute to good health.

Weight loss, often accompanied by a loss of energy, is a common effect of changing over to a vegetarian diet. This can be serious in someone who is already underweight. More serious illnesses that are connected with veganism in particular are spinal ataxia, a condition causing unsteady gait, stooped posture, and loss of balance and sensation in the legs; and megaloblastic anemia, a deficiency in the blood (see Anemia). Both of these conditions, caused by vitamin B_{12} deficiency, are quite rare (see Vitamin B), but deficiency of this vitamin is the major health risk for vegans. Cobalt is a vital constituent of this vitamin; because vitamin B_{12} is found only in animal foods or microorganisms, in a vegan diet it can be gained naturally only by eating vegetables old enough to have a growth of mold on them. One way to avoid such a deficiency is to include a vitamin B_{12} supplement in the diet. There is vitamin B_{12} in eggs and cheese, so it is really only vegans who are at risk.

Vitamin D is also absent from plant foods. However, individuals can make this vitamin by the action of sunlight on the skin. Vitamin D deficiency can occur in children reared on a vegan diet if they are not sufficiently exposed to sunlight. It would be wise, especially in winter, to give children extra vitamin D in the form of drops (see Vitamin D).

The choice is yours

Ultimately the choice of diet is a personal one, based on belief, preference, or circumstances. But whatever rules you apply should result in a properly balanced diet, with the right proportions of fats, carbohydrates, proteins, vitamins, and minerals, and containing an appropriate number of calories.

Changing one's diet should always be a slow and careful process, as any sudden change can be a shock to the system. Always consult a dietitian before making any radical change in the amount or type of food you eat. A well-balanced diet and plenty of sensibly planned exercise are vital for health. Whether that diet is vegetarian depends on individual needs and preferences.

Bury Peerless

The Jains, members of a religious sect in India that expresses reverence for all forms of life, are the strictest of vegetarians, and wear masks to avoid inhaling insects. A cornucopia of delights for a vegetarian (below); with such variety, vegetarianism need never be dull.

Graham Strong

Veins

Q My father had to have open heart surgery recently for his angina and they removed a vein from his leg. How was this vein used in the surgery?

A The vein from the leg is in fact used to form a bypass for the blocked coronary arteries that were the cause of your father's angina. Although veins are designed to carry blood at much lower pressure than arteries, they can cope with the extra strain usually imposed on the arteries very well.

Q I have heard that you may get clots in the legs if you go on an air flight. Is this true, and is this particularly dangerous?

A Yes, there is some truth in this. If you are sitting still for a long time, then the rate of blood flow in the deep veins of your legs slows down. This is largely because the muscles in your legs, which are active when you are moving about, also help to pump the blood back toward the heart; this pumping is lost when you sit down. There is also pressure from the seat on your thighs as you sit, which will tend to reduce the rate of blood flow. Once the rate of flow falls the blood clots more easily. The danger of blood clots in the deep veins of the legs is that they can break off and float around the circulation to get stuck in the lungs, so the thing to do is to try and keep your feet moving when you are on a long flight, and to make sure that you get out of your seat every hour or so if this is possible.

Q How long can a needle be left in the arm of a patient who is being drip fed?

A Nowadays the needles are nearly all thin plastic tubes called cannulas. A simple cannula in the arm usually lasts only a few days. In intensive care units, where drips may be required for very long periods, longer fine tubes called catheters are used, and these can be put into the big veins in the chest. These central lines are designed to last longer than the small cannulas in the arm.

After giving up oxygen and nourishment to the tissues, blood is carried back to the heart by the veins. These specially designed channels play as important a part as the arteries in the efficient working of the circulation.

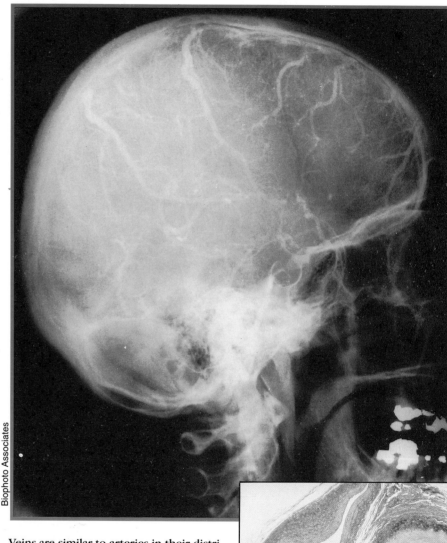

Biophoto Associates

Science Photo Library

Veins are similar to arteries in their distribution; the arteries and veins associated with a particular organ or tissue often run together, but there are major differences. For example, many veins have valves, which the arteries do not, and the walls of an artery are always thicker than those of a vein of the same size, while the central channel, or lumen, will be much bigger in the vein than the artery (see Arteries and artery disease).

Structure and function

Veins are tubes of muscular and fibrous tissue. Their walls have an outer layer, the *tunica adventitia*; a middle layer of muscle fiber, the *tunica intermedia*; and an inner lining, the *tunica intima*. They

The carotid angiogram (top)—a type of X ray of blood vessels—graphically illustrates the network of veins carrying blood away from the head. The micrograph (above) shows transverse sections of a vein and an artery; the vein is on the left.

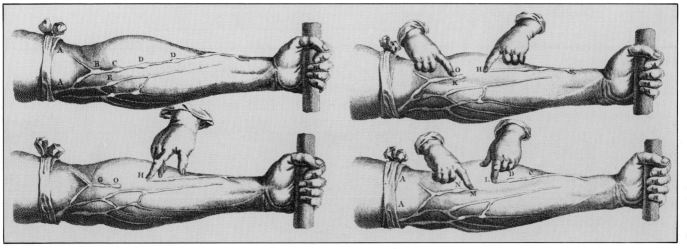

contain only a thin layer of muscle. After passing through the capillaries from the arteries, blood enters the venous system. It first passes into very small vessels called venules, which are the venous equivalent of arterioles. It then makes its way into small veins and back toward the heart along the veins that are large enough to be seen under the skin. Veins of this size contain valves that prevent blood from flowing back toward the tissues. The valves have little half-moon-shaped cups that project into the lumen of the vein, and these make the blood flow in only one direction.

Eventually, blood flowing back to the heart enters one of two large veins; the inferior vena cava receives blood from the lower half of the body, and the superior vena cava receives blood from the head and arms. These vessels are about 1 in (2–3 cm) wide, and they enter the right atrium of the heart. Blood passes from here into the right ventricle, and then into the lungs via the pulmonary arteries. It leaves the lungs by means of the pulmonary veins, which enter the left atrium of the heart (see Heart).

Special types of vein
There is one area where the veins are arranged in a very different way from the arteries, and this is in the intestines. Here, instead of draining into a vein that passes straight into the heart, blood from the intestines is drained into what is called the hepatic portal system of veins. This allows the blood, which may be rich in digested food, to be carried directly to the liver (see Circulatory system).

Once blood from the intestines reaches the liver, it passes in among the liver cells, in special capillaries that are called sinusoids, and then enters the system of veins called the hepatic veins. These eventually lead on to the inferior vena cava, and thus into the heart. This system insures that food passed into the venous

Vein networks

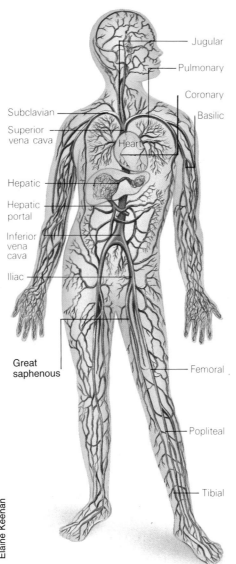

The body's complex system of veins returns blood in the direction of the heart (as opposed to arteries, which carry it away) through the conduits called the venae cavae.

Elaine Keenan

William Harvey, who proved that the blood circulates (1628), illustrated how blood in the arm flows continuously in one direction, controlled by valves in the veins.

system from the intestines is brought to the liver for chemical processing in the most efficient way (see Digestive system, and Liver and liver diseases).

Other areas where there are special kinds of venous structure are in the extremities—the hands, feet, ears, and nose. Here it is possible to find direct communications between the small arteries and veins, where blood may flow through from one to the other without having to go through a system of capillaries in the tissues. The main function of these arteriovenous connections is related to the control of body temperature. When they are open, heat loss increases and the body cools down (see Temperature).

There are similar connections between the arteries and veins in the genital areas. These allow for the engorgement of blood that occurs in the genitals as a result of sexual excitement (see Genitals).

What can go wrong?
One serious problem that affects veins is the tendency of blood clots to form in them. This is likely to happen because of the slowness with which blood flows along the veins, in contrast with the rapid flow maintained in the arteries. Smoking and the Pill increase the risk of clotting, although the low dose of estrogen in modern contraceptive pills has much reduced this danger (see Blood).

Another major trouble is caused by the upright stance of human beings—this leads to considerable pressure in the veins of the legs since they are supporting quite a high column of blood. This can result in twisted, engorged veins in the legs (see Varicose veins). However, problems affecting the veins are minor compared with those arising from arterial disease.

Ventricular fibrillation

Q Is ventricular fibrillation always fatal?

A An attack of ventricular fibrillation is likely to be fatal unless treatment is given immediately. This consists of administering an electric shock to the heart to convert its activity back to normal. Alternatively if you thump someone hard on the breastbone within half a minute of their losing consciousness, you can convert their heart rhythm back to normal without the aid of electricity, but the chances of success diminish as the ventricular fibrillation becomes established. A few patients can have an attack of ventricular fibrillation and survive without being given treatment because the electrical activity of their heart reverts on its own. As a general rule, however, ventricular fibrillation is fatal without treatment.

Q My doctor told me that I have atrial fibrillation. Does this mean that I am at risk of ventricular fibrillation?

A No. In atrial fibrillation the atria of the heart are beating in an uncoordinated way. This has little impact on the overall function of the heart since the two ventricles are still able to pump. In ventricular fibrillation no blood is pumped through the heart, and death will follow unless the heart's electrical activity is restored to normal. Atrial fibrillation—a common and relatively minor heart problem—does not lead to ventricular fibrillation, so you shouldn't worry.

Q Is it true that heart surgeons may deliberately put the heart into ventricular fibrillation? Isn't this dangerous?

A It is done. But in the carefully controlled circumstances of heart surgery, where the work of the heart is taken over by the bypass machine, there is very little risk involved. The reason for putting the heart into ventricular fibrillation is that it moves less and so is therefore easier to operate on. It can be easily reversed by using a defibrillator, which restarts the heart.

Thousands of people who are walking around today have been treated for attacks of ventricular fibrillation. All would have died but for the treatment they were given—treatment that only became available in the 1960s.

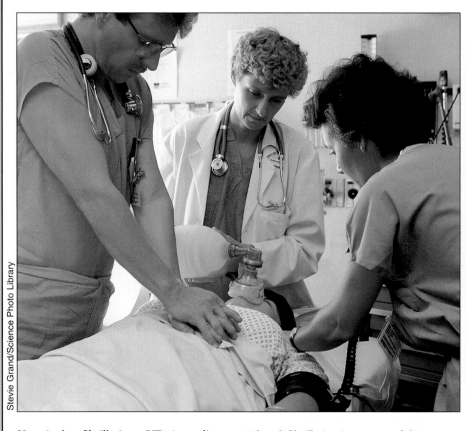

Stevie Grand/Science Photo Library

Ventricular fibrillation (VF) is a disturbance of the orderly electrical activity of the heart. Because the fibers that make the heart's pumping chambers start to relax and contract in a totally uncoordinated way, the heart is unable to pump blood. This means that, within seconds of an attack, a person will become unconscious and death will follow in a minute or two. Urgent treatment is needed, whether it be from a paramedic team that can get to the patient quickly, or in a coronary care unit.

Causes of VF
The main cause of VF is a heart attack, which is responsible for many of the deaths from the condition. A heart attack usually arises from coronary artery disease, where the heart's own blood supply becomes obstructed (see Heart attack, and Heart disease).

Other heart problems can also cause VF, particularly those where there is an electrical disturbance of the heart. This disturbance may eventually lead to vari-

When defibrillation is unsuccessful in restoring normal heart rhythm after a heart attack, chest compression and artificial respiration are necessary.

ous disorders where the heart beats too fast. In some cases the heart rate is so fast that the heart can only cope for short periods of time before VF becomes a serious possibility. Sometimes the heart is affected by a disease that involves its own muscles—called cardiomyopathy—and in a few cases this may lead to a rise in the heart rate, and so bring on VF.

Mechanism of VF
The regular and automatic beating of the heart results from a very sophisticated timing system that conducts electrical impulses to the various parts of the heart. These impulses lead to the heart muscle contracting, and they are ordered so that the ventricles contract after the atria and both sets of chambers have an adequate time to relax and recover for the next heartbeat.

In the various diseases that raise the rate of heartbeat, the mechanism becomes disrupted so that the chambers beat at a very fast and inefficient rate. In VF, the whole system breaks down so that individual muscle fibers contract and relax quite independently, with no overall contraction of the heart, and no pumping of blood.

Treatment

The revolution in treatment of VF has been the introduction of defibrillators. These work by delivering a shock across the heart when two electrical pads are placed on the chest, one on the breastbone (sternum) and one at the apex of the heart, just below the left nipple. During heart surgery, two much smaller pads are placed on the actual surface of the exposed heart, and a much lower current is used (see Electrocardiogram).

The basic principle of defibrillation is that an electric shock will cause the simultaneous electrical discharge of all the cells in the heart. This gives the normal conducting system what might be described as a clean slate on which to work, and enables it to reinstate normal, orderly electrical activity.

Like any other effective form of treatment, defibrillation is not without its dangers. A shock can actually put a heart into VF, although this is only a risk when this form of treatment is being used for less serious disturbances of the heart rate; once the patient is in VF, there is obviously nothing to lose. Further, when defibrillation is performed, neither the patient nor his or her bed must be touched. The electrical pads, or paddles, have insulated handles to protect the operator.

Prevention

Great efforts are made to identify patients who are at risk of VF, so that drugs can be prescribed to lessen that risk. One of the main indications that someone may be likely to suffer from VF is when they have already suffered an attack. Such patients

The heart's normal pumping action

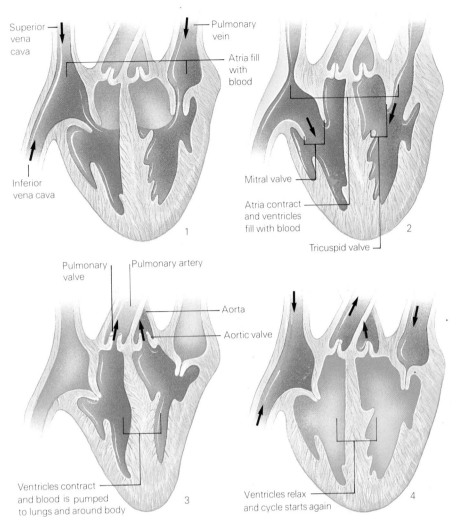

A number of electrical impulses insure the efficient working of the heart. They govern the rhythmic and coordinated action of the atria, ventricles, and valves (above). Ventricular fibrillation is most likely to occur after a heart attack, so a patient may need treatment by defibrillation while at home (below).

will usually be given an intravenous infusion of the local anesthetic lignocaine, which reduces the likelihood of extra electrical activity of the heart.

Much can also be done in coronary care units to reduce the risk of VF after a heart attack. Since the risk is greatest during the initial 24 to 48 hours after a heart attack, patients usually stay in a coronary care unit until the critical period has passed. Even so, a number of patients still suffer attacks of VF after this time.

VF outside the hospital

Unfortunately most heart attacks are unexpected, so patients are most likely to suffer from VF before they can reach the safety of a coronary care unit. The critical period is within the first two hours, and hence it is imperative to get effective treatment to them immediately. Ideally there should be teams of paramedics available to rush to the spot when someone collapses with VF. Such teams exist in most US cities, and people trained in resuscitation techniques can often help.

Verruca

Q I am a frequent swimmer at my local swimming pool. Does this make me more vulnerable to verrucae?

A Yes. This is the most likely place to catch the infection because after swimming the soles of the feet are softened and the skin's defenses are consequently weaker. If you have verrucae, always wear protective footwear such as flip-flops at the pool; otherwise you will spread the infection to others.

Q My 13-year-old daughter has a verruca. Is her younger brother likely to catch it?

A Yes. At his age he probably has no immunity to the virus, and so is at risk of being infected. There are two ways of preventing this. First, if you treat your daughter's verruca every day with one of the proprietary wart paints and then cover it with a waterproof adhesive bandage, she will not shed the virus around the house. Second, if both she and her brother use their own towels and footwear, and dry their feet immediately after bathing, he will also be less likely to pick up the infection.

Q Do preparations bought over the counter really help in treating verrucae?

A Yes, they certainly do, and in two ways. First, daily application of a wart paint and rubbing down the horny cap with a pumice stone or emery board will rapidly relieve the pain of walking on a verruca. Second, treatment kills the surface virus, thereby reducing the danger of spreading it to others. About 50 percent of verrucae respond to such simple measures. The problem is that the treatment must be continued until the verruca has completely gone, which usually takes about three months. Too often the sufferer gets discouraged, and so doesn't persist with the treatment for long enough. It is easy to tell if a verruca is cured, because it ceases to hurt. Tiny black spots can be seen in it, and the skin then returns entirely to normal.

Many of us know how painful a verruca can be, and how persistent. Fortunately, however, even the most stubborn ones can usually be cured, and very often simply by the sufferer's sheer perseverance with a simple treatment.

Kelly-Mooney Photography/Corbis

The verruca virus is easily spread if the conditions are right. It is particularly prevalent among children, especially when their feet are wet. Keep a verruca covered and dry, and make sure that children's feet are thoroughly dried after bathing. A public pool is often a source of infection, so anyone with a verruca should wear plastic or rubber beach shoes.

The word *verruca* is simply the Latin for a wart, and has been adopted into the English language to refer to a wart on the sole of the foot (see also Feet, and Skin and skin diseases). Doctors are consulted more often about verrucae than other warts because they are more painful and annoying than warts elsewhere on the body (see Warts). Sometimes doctors also refer to verrucae as plantar warts.

Cause

Warts are caused by a virus that enters the skin through tiny injuries, especially if the skin is wet and soggy. Most verrucae arise on the weight-bearing parts of the sole of the foot, that is the heel and ball, not the instep.

A virus is a particle of living matter that can only reproduce itself inside a living cell, borrowing some of the cell's contents for this purpose. After the virus enters the epidermal cell there is an incubation period of several months, while the virus is multiplying and spreading, before enough skin cells are infected and deformed to produce a visible wart.

The epidermal cells deformed by the virus cause a hard, horny swelling (the wart), which on the sole of the foot is pressed inward by standing and walking, thereby irritating the sensitive nerve endings under the skin.

There are several strains of human wart virus. Verrucae are due to one strain, although the patient often has warts elsewhere. Another strain that affects only the soles of the feet causes a mosaic wart. This looks like a honeycomb, and is actually a mass of closely packed polygonal warts, often at least 1 in (2.5 cm) across. Mosaic warts are extremely resistant to treatment and often last for several years but, fortunately, are not nearly as painful as verrucae.

Verrucae, like other common virus diseases, are unusual in infancy but begin to occur during the school years, reaching a peak at about age nine. They then decline in frequency, becoming rarer after the middle twenties. Curiously, the sex incidence is equal up to the age of six but then they become more common in girls.

Appearance

Like verrucae, corns (see Corns) are also painful and callous, and it may be difficult to tell them apart. However, if the horny cap of a verruca is pared away, four distinguishing features will be clearly seen.

First, the verruca becomes wider the more skin is pared away. It is shaped like a pyramid with the point at the surface and there is more hidden in the skin than is visible above it. It also has a calloused collar, which pushes aside the tiny lines on the skin of the sole. These never run

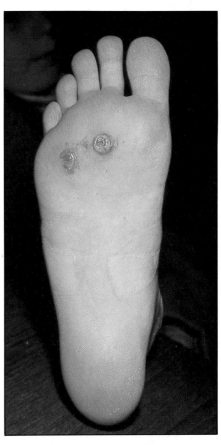

John Watney

Verrucae are particularly painful because they are pressed into the sole of the foot by standing and walking. The calloused skin of each verruca should be rubbed down daily, and a proprietary wart paint applied.

across the verruca but encircle it and its collar. Finally, when the skin can no longer be pared without causing pain, pinpoint bleeding spots appear. If the verruca has already been killed, however, the tiny blood vessels are clotted, showing as a few speckled black spots on the surface. This is therefore a sign that the verruca is healing.

In contrast, a corn is widest at the top and narrows to a point within the skin. On paring, it shows a white, smooth appearance like ground glass, and it has no collar. A callus is simply thick skin with a greatly increased epidermal layer. The fine skin lines run through it and are often more obvious in the thick skin of a callus.

Verrucae occur where the sole touches the ground but rarely at an exact point of pressure as is the case with corns and calluses. Therefore, if the bit of hard painful skin has been present less than two years in a child or young adult, and is not exactly over a bony knot, it is probably a verruca. If it has been present more than two years over a bony knob in an older person, it is probably a corn or a callus. Occasionally a verruca may arise in a callus, and will be revealed by careful paring.

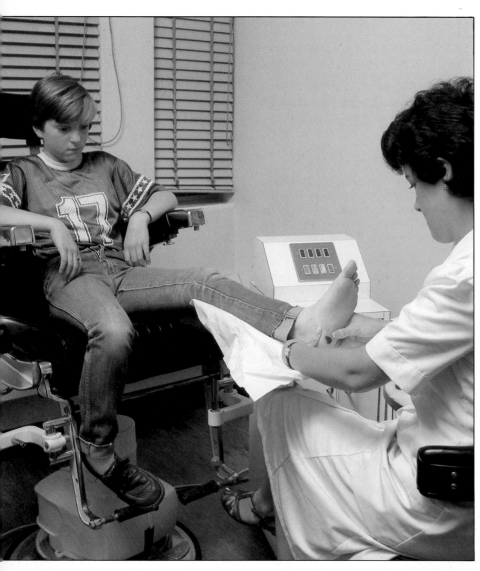

The key to curing a verruca is persistence, since some can take months to disappear. The progress of the verruca should be checked every month by your doctor, a nurse, or podiatrist: they will be able to tell when it has healed completely.

Progress

The verruca wart virus, which is relatively harmless and only affects a tiny area of the outer layer of skin, is often overlooked by the body's defenses for many months (see Immune system). This is why warts last so long. Other viruses, like the chicken pox virus (see Chicken pox), spread throughout the body and rapidly stimulate its chemicals and cellular defenses, so that the illness clears in a week or two. Warts, on the other hand, can last for months or even years.

When the body finally notices the verrucae and mounts an offensive, they shrivel up and disappear leaving no scar. This accounts for the success rate of many wart charms. About 20 percent clear in

six months and the majority within two years. Once this immunity is learned it is readily available to prevent reinfection. Sometimes, as a result of illness or the use of immunosuppressive drugs (see Immunosuppressive drugs), this immunity fades and warts recur, so that further treatment will be needed.

Treatment

There are no medicines or injections to kill the verruca virus in the way that antibiotics (see Antibiotics) kill bacteria. The aims of local treatment are to destroy the skin cells containing the virus, and to stimulate the body's own defense mechanisms. It is thought that by killing the cells and the virus inside them, the body's defense mechanisms are more readily stimulated. Moreover, local treatment that kills the surface virus makes the verruca less infectious to others.

Local treatments that can be safely used in the home include paints, gels, and soaks that contain salicylic acid (a drug

that loosens and removes the tough outer layer of skin), formaldehyde, or related drugs. Rubbing down the calloused cap of a verruca relieves the pain of walking on it, and, if this is not done, a layer of dead, hard tissue builds up over the verruca, shielding it from the paint you have to put on.

If there are many small verrucae, an alternative treatment is to soak the affected sole in a saucer of formalin in solution every night and morning for 10 minutes. Since formalin dries out the skin, causing it to crack, the skin between the toes and around the verrucae should be protected with petroleum jelly.

Salicylic acid can be used in the form of plasters, although preparations such as Chlorsal and Posalfilin, which are much stronger, can cause inflammation in normal skin and should only be used under medical supervision.

Any treatment may take up to three months. If the verruca persists, treatment by freezing is the next step, and this has to be given by a doctor or at a hospital. If this treatment is unavailable, the core of the verruca will have to be scooped out under local anesthesia, and the base and sides cauterized. The resulting hole is covered with a sterile dressing, and kept dry until it heals. Verrucae are never cut out since this would leave a scar that might be persistently painful.

Prevention

Most verrucae are caught at swimming pools. This is because the skin barrier is weaker when it is wet. People with verrucae should therefore wear thin rubber or plastic beach shoes.

In the home, a child can be prevented from spreading the virus by using his or her own towel and bath mat, and by covering the verruca with a waterproof adhesive bandage.

Treating a verruca

- Wash the foot in warm water, soaking it for at least five minutes
- Dry with a towel (make sure that no one else uses the towel)
- Rub the hard skin away with an emery board or pumice stone
- Apply a drop of paint to the verruca and let it dry
- Cover with an adhesive bandage
- Have your nurse or doctor check the verruca each month
- Continue treatment daily until the nurse or doctor thinks it is cured
- See your doctor if the verruca becomes more painful

Vertigo

Q I often feel dizzy when I stand up suddenly, especially after having a hot bath. Is this vertigo, and if so, does it mean that something could be seriously wrong?

A No, this is not vertigo. It is called postural hypotension. It means that your blood pressure is dropping slightly but suddenly so that the blood supply to your brain is reduced a little. It happens to everyone occasionally and does not usually signify anything serious, unless it happens often, in which case you should see your doctor.

Q Some years ago my father had a serious heart infection and he has suffered from vertigo ever since. Could this be due to his treatment?

A There are some antibiotics that can cause vertigo as a side effect, though this is an uncommon reaction, and your father may have needed these drugs when he was ill. These antibiotics can damage the inner ear's balance receptors and for this reason their use is reserved purely for life-threatening situations.

Q How do trapeze artists avoid getting vertigo, which would be dangerous when they work so high in the air?

A Such people avoid vertigo by practicing. They are trained to ignore the violent stimulation of their balance sensors, which would otherwise be bound to cause vertigo. The artists perform regular, progressive exercises that gradually enable them to prevent vertigo. Similar exercises can help some people who suffer from vertigo for medical reasons.

Q Why do some people get vertigo when looking down from great heights?

A People who are afraid of heights usually feel faintness rather than true vertigo. Vertigo refers to a feeling that the world is spinning around you, or that you are moving or swaying when you are really standing still.

People often confuse vertigo with a fear of heights. In fact, it can be a symptom of a variety of conditions, from the normal effects of spinning on a merry-go-round to the distressing results of some sort of brain damage.

Vertigo is a common and often distressing symptom that occurs when the delicate balance mechanisms in the inner part of the ear or brain stem are damaged or disturbed. Many of the causes of vertigo are not at all serious, but occasionally vertigo may indicate some very worrying disease.

The balance mechanism
The position of the head is continuously monitored by sensitive mechanisms in the inner ear, which act like levels. When the head is moved the fluid inside the inner ear's balance center is set in motion. As this fluid moves it stimulates tiny hairs that are connected to nerve fibers. These nerve fibers inform the brain of the head's rotary motion. If the movement stops suddenly, the fluid continues to move and the brain continues to get messages that the head is still turning (see Brain).

Information from the inner ear is sent to the brain stem, the area of the brain responsible for interpreting information from the balance centers. But the brain stem also receives information about the body's position from the eyes and other position sensors. These other sensors tell the brain that the movement has stopped.

Children discover at an early age that spinning around and around makes them delightfully dizzy. They obviously relish such a deliberate episode of vertigo.

This contradictory information confuses the brain, which is receiving false and incoherent messages. A picture of an unstable and chaotic world is formed in the brain stem and this results in vertigo.

This common type of vertigo can be cured very simply by spinning a little in the opposite direction. This sets the fluid sensors in contrary motion to counteract the first spin. Ballet dancers and circus performers, who have to spin violently during their routines, can train themselves not to suffer from vertigo.

Medically, vertigo can be caused in two ways: there can be something wrong with the inner ear mechanism so that the messages get confused, or the brain stem itself can be damaged so that messages are not properly analyzed.

Problems in the inner ear

The part of the inner ear that contains the balance sensors is called the labyrinth, because it curls into a spiral. The labyrinth can sometimes be the site of a viral infection, which can cause sudden and severe vertigo, called labyrinthitis. Sometimes the sensation of spinning is so strong that it causes vomiting, and even slight head movements can cause dizziness.

This condition is called positional vertigo and the symptoms may continue during convalescence. Fortunately drugs that sedate the balance centers in the brain stem can be a very effective treatment for the unpleasant spinning sensation.

Persistent positional vertigo is caused by tiny specks of hard material that are a by-product of the infection in the labyrinth.

These tiny specks of material or stones lie near the tiny hairs within the inner ear, rolling onto these sensory hairs whenever the head moves. As they do so they stimulate the nerve endings and tell the brain that the head is spinning when information received from all the other sensors says that the body is still.

Peering up into the Manhattan skyline can bring on dizziness: the confused brain wants to believe that the buildings are moving rather than the clouds (top). Flamenco dancers avoid spinning themselves dizzy by spotting, when they focus their eyes on one spot for as long as possible and come back to the same spot each time around.

Image Bank

2110

Labyrinthitis can be caused as a result of other types of ear infection, such as otitis media. This type of ear infection is common among children, but fortunately vertigo is a rare complication (see Otitis).

Ménière's disease can cause vertigo. It happens when there is swelling in the fluid cavities of the inner ear, including the balance mechanisms (see Ménière's disease). It is not known why this happens, but it is usually characterized by severe vertigo with partial loss of hearing and a continuous buzzing in the affected ear. The buzzing is called tinnitus (see Tinnitus).

The symptoms of vertigo can be treated with special drugs. Unfortunately, however, the partial deafness is sometimes permanent, and Ménière's disease is one of the causes of vertigo that requires the sufferer to seek prompt medical advice.

Damage to the brain stem

Nerve messages from the inner ear are analyzed by a collection of cells in the brain stem called the vestibular nucleus. Damage to this interpretative part of the system can also cause vertigo.

In older people the blood vessels that supply the brain stem can become furred or even blocked. Starved of sufficient oxygen, cells in the brain stem stop working and messages from the inner ear are no longer properly analyzed.

Sometimes the blood vessels get kinked in the neck as a result of arthritic neck joints. This may mean that the blood

How vertigo occurs

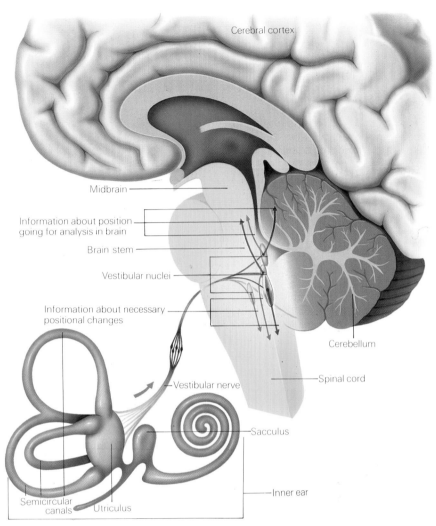

Cerebral cortex

Midbrain

Information about position going for analysis in brain

Brain stem

Vestibular nuclei

Information about necessary positional changes

Cerebellum

Vestibular nerve

Spinal cord

Sacculus

Inner ear

Semicircular canals

Utriculus

Mike Courteney

Vertigo can be brought on by two different sets of conditions: either confused messages are sent to the brain from the semicircular canals in the ears, or some damage to the vestibular nucleus causes the messages that are received to be incorrectly analyzed.

supply is momentarily blocked when the head is turned suddenly. This can produce vertigo. Occasionally tumors or patches of inflammation may affect the vestibular nucleus, producing vertigo.

All these types of vertigo can be eased by drugs, but the root cause also has to be found and treated by your doctor.

Vertigo caused by drugs

There are many drugs that cause vertigo, perhaps the most common being alcohol. Large quantities of alcohol can make the world appear very unsteady indeed, especially when lying down with closed eyes. Closing the eyes is likely to bring on sudden, mild vertigo since the eyes provide information that can contradict the confused messages coming from the balance centers in the inner ear.

Vertigo caused by drugs is usually a sign of slight overdose, which can be relieved by simply reducing the prescribed dose. However, one or two of the more powerful antibiotics can cause vertigo by raising the blood pressure, which can then damage the delicate balance mechanisms. Fortunately these drugs are rarely used.

Outlook

Persistent or regular vertigo should always prompt a visit to your doctor so that it can be investigated. Provided this is done, the outlook is generally very good.

The brain's ability to unscramble confused messages is remarkable. Most forms of vertigo will actually disappear in time, because the brain eventually learns to interpret the conflicting messages and to ignore those that are false.

Virginity

Q I am 20 years old and a virgin. My partner wants to sleep with me, but I am afraid that losing my virginity will hurt. Are my fears well-founded?

A The first time can be painful for some people, both for men and women. But the terrifying stories whispered about losing one's virginity have no basis in fact. All they do is make people tense and nervous. If the hymen is intact, there may be some pain when it is ruptured. In the majority of women, however, tampons and such normal activities as sport will have stretched the hymen to the point where the bleeding and pain are slight. It is more likely that any pain that you might feel will be caused by the fear and nervousness, making you tense and likely to have insufficient lubrication in your vagina. The anxiety will pass in a few days. Take it slowly, make sure that both you and your partner are aroused and comfortable; you will find that the pleasure will soon outweigh any pain you felt the first time.

Q My boyfriend says that I don't love him because I don't want to go beyond heavy petting. What can I say to him?

A You could equally claim that he doesn't love you because he wants to force or persuade you to do something you don't wish to do. Sex never proved anything, certainly not love. People have sex for many reasons, and too often out of the misguided conviction that it is expected of them. Don't fall into this trap: if you do not want to make love then that is your right, and your boyfriend should respect your decision. Wait until you feel it is the right time.

Q I'm about to go to college and I'm still a virgin. Is this at all unusual?

A It is true that by the age of 19 virgins are in the minority, and about 75 percent of your colleagues will have lost their virginity. However, it's nothing to be ashamed of. The choice of how you run your sex life is your own.

All aspects of sexual behavior can provoke the deepest of emotional reactions. And nowhere is this more true than over the issue of virginity—or, more precisely, its loss.

Bokelberg/Image bank

A virgin is simply someone who has never had sexual intercourse (see Intercourse, and Sex). We usually think of women when we talk of virgins, but in fact the word actually applies to both sexes equally. Rather unfairly, however, the stigma attached to women losing their virginity outside marriage has generally been greater than for the male sex. Medically speaking, virginity is a physical state and you cannot be "almost" a virgin. You either have or haven't had sexual intercourse. Since there is one physical change that can occur to a woman on her first experience of sex, this is seen by many people and cultures as proof of virginity.

The hymen
The majority of virgin women have a thin membrane that partially closes off the vagina (see Vagina). This is called the hymen (see Hymen). It can be very thin or fairly tough; it can close off the vagina almost completely, leaving only a small opening for the monthly period, or be so flimsy as to be no barrier at all.

Hymens can be stretched or broken over the years by virgins who have used tampons for their periods, masturbated, or even engaged energetically in some sports. Hymens can also be stretched or

Adolescence is a time of rapid change, especially in attitudes toward the opposite sex. It is important that young people take on their adult roles at their own pace and do not allow themselves to be pressured into premature sexual activity.

broken during heavy petting. However, none of these conditions will cause a girl to lose her virginity.

Conversely, hymens can be tough enough to resist complete penetration by the man and, in some cases, will stretch but not break. There have been cases of virgin births, with women giving birth although their hymens were still intact!

In most cases the thin membrane will be in place and will break the first time the woman has intercourse. This may cause bleeding and pain in some women. On subsequent occasions the ring of tissue will wear away until it becomes virtually nonexistent. But the lack of a hymen, or lack of pain and bleeding, is absolutely no proof that the woman was not a virgin.

Advantages and disadvantages
Are there benefits to being a virgin? Virgin women, of course, do not have unwanted pregnancies or catch sexually transmitted

diseases (see Sexually transmitted diseases), which certainly are advantages. There is some evidence that nuns are less likely to suffer from cancer of the cervix (see Cervix and cervical smears), but are more likely to have breast cancer (see Breasts) than women who are sexually active. Cancer of the cervix may be linked to early sexual activity and a greater number of sexual partners, while breast cancer seems to occur more frequently in women who have not been pregnant (see Cancer). But are there emotional rather than physical benefits? If you have been brought up to believe that it is important to remain a virgin, either until a specific time, like marriage, or for

Catholicism places a high value on a woman's virginity on her wedding day. A bride (left) disembarks in Venice dressed in white as a symbol of her virginity. Catholic women are taught to emulate the Virgin Mary who epitomizes purity and grace and the sanctity of the closed body.

life, then there is a strong chance that you will suffer emotionally if you give in to the persuasion of other people.

Many societies place great emphasis on women being virgins on their wedding day. This is probably because in a patriarchal, or male-ruled, society the only way a man could be certain his property and name were being handed on to his son was to make sure his woman did not get pregnant by another man—especially before the wedding! In such societies visible proof may even be demanded, and bloodstained bedsheets have to be displayed after the wedding night. Indeed, some Italian gynecologists do a flourishing trade in surgically restoring hymens for such an occasion.

Defloration

Losing your virginity is something that should happen happily, leaving no feelings of fear, guilt, or self-disgust. In fact, it is hardly something you should lose, but something you give and share with

someone you love. The first time you make love is very important, less for the mere tearing of a membrane than for the psychological impact invested in the occasion. Virginity is also a state of mind, and a 30-year-old mother can be virginal in her approach to life, while a 14-year-old may be tough, cynical, and far from innocent even though he or she has never had sex. The most important thing about giving up your virginity is being sure that you are doing so at the time that is right for you. Nobody should lose his or her virginity (or, indeed, ever have sex at any time in life) simply because "Everybody's doing it," or "Good heavens, you're not still a virgin at your age."

There are no firm rules about when men or women should lose their virginity. Like all good things, waiting, anticipating, and planning can enhance the event, so leaping into bed with your first partner, or as soon after your 16th birthday as possible, is hardly a good idea. The right time is when it feels right.

Alan Hutchison Library

John Topham Picture Library

Viruses

Q Why is it that viruses cannot be treated with antibiotics?

A Bacteria that respond to antibiotics are complicated organisms, although each consists of only one cell. Viruses, on the other hand, are very simple, consisting of a core of nucleic acid (genetic material) surrounded by a protein capsule. Antibiotics work by impeding the activity of the bacterial cell without harming human cells. Since the virus has no metabolic activity to disrupt, the principle of antibiotics is of no value whatsoever.

Q Is it likely that treatment will be able to affect the course of minor viral diseases like the common cold?

A It doesn't seem likely that any form of direct treatment will be discovered in the next few years, although there is always the chance of a breakthrough in research. However, the answer to these minor viral infections may well be prevention rather than cure, although so far it is very difficult to make a vaccine against the common cold since there are so many different viruses that cause it. But the use of the antiviral substance interferon may prove to be a possible means of prevention. Interferon is made by human cells following invasion by a virus, and it has recently been shown that a nasal spray of interferon can reduce the risk of catching a cold. At the moment interferon is very expensive to produce, but genetic engineering might make it a practical proposition in the future.

Q Why do so many different kinds of viruses produce similar symptoms, like colds?

A This is a very effective way for the virus to multiply and infect someone else. The virus multiplies in the tissues of the nose and throat to cause a streaming cold, and when the sufferer sneezes he or she liberates clouds of droplets containing viruses into the air. These then settle on the mucous membranes of other people, and continue the life cycle of the virus.

Influenza, measles, and rabies are disparate diseases that have the common link of being caused by viruses. As yet no adequate treatment exists for viral diseases, but the most dangerous can be effectively prevented.

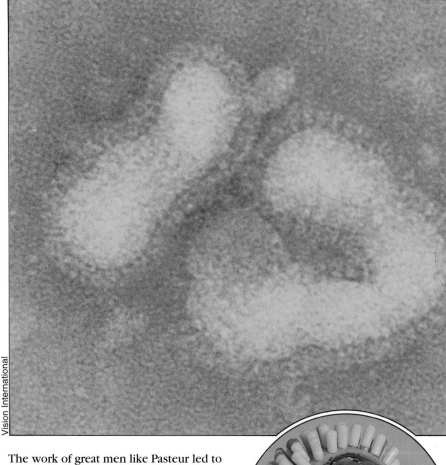

Vision International

The work of great men like Pasteur led to the discovery of bacteria—the cause of many of our most serious illnesses. However, by the end of the last century there were still many diseases for which a bacterial cause was suspected but not found. Pasteur himself had demonstrated that rabies was an infection and had produced a vaccine against it, although he had not been able to find a bacterium that caused it. He rightly deduced that this was because the organism was too small to be seen under a microscope.

The first virus was found in 1892 and was identified as tobacco mosaic virus. This virus causes disease in plants rather than in man. Following this discovery it was shown that foot and mouth disease, which occurs in cattle, was caused by a similar minute organism.

It was demonstrated that these viruses were able to travel from plant to plant or animal to animal after passing through a filter too fine to let a bacterium through.

Viruses are extremely simple structures that usually consist of a thin protein membrane containing one of the nucleic acids, DNA or RNA. The influenza virus (above) is a typical example. It is also wrapped in an outer envelope, as shown in the model (inset). It can change its protein structure with each new infection in order to fool the body's immune system.

Research was carried out in the light of knowledge at the time but was impeded by the fact that it was still not possible to see viruses. It was the electron microscope that first revealed what viruses actually look like.

What are viruses?

Viruses are very tiny organisms. For example, a polio virus is 20 nanometers across (a nanometer is one-thousandth of a micrometer, which in turn is one-thousandth of a millimeter).

The basic structure of viruses is so simple that it is questionable whether they should be regarded as living matter at all. Essentially they consist of no more than a capsule of protein that contains their genetic material in the form of one of the nucleic acids, DNA or RNA. These are the substances that carry the genetic message from generation to generation in all living things. It is the DNA that is passed on in the process of reproduction and is contained in the nucleus of living cells. The DNA then sends messages to the chemical factories inside the cells, instructing them to make various types of protein. These messages are carried by the RNA.

Viruses work by invading the cells of the organism they are infecting. Once a virus is inside a cell, it liberates its DNA or RNA content. These substances interfere with the cell's own function and the protein-producing apparatus of the

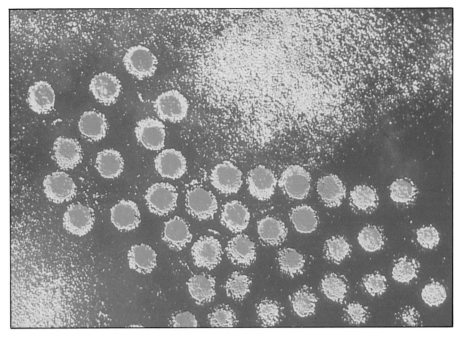

Science Photo Library

cell starts to work for the virus instead of for the cell itself. Having taken control of a cell, the virus manufactures more viruses, so that more cells and finally other individuals can be infected.

Thus viruses are very lifelike in their ability to pass on their own characteristics from generation to generation by the use of genetic material. The two nucleic acids, DNA and RNA, are the basic stuff of life, and even if they are only contained in

The hepatitis A virus is often found in bad food and water. The infection thus occurs in areas with poor sanitation.

a thin capsule, they make up what is virtually a living organism.

Structure

Viruses are extremely small, the smallest being 20–30 nanometers across and the largest 10 times that size. Most viruses are

How a virus multiplies

Viruses are totally parasitic since they only multiply in the cells of other organisms. When a virus invades a host cell (1) its genetic material mingles with that of the host cell (2), which then starts to produce more viral genetic material (3). Finally, the new viral particles (4) become enveloped again in a protein membrane and emerge from the cell (5) to invade other cells.

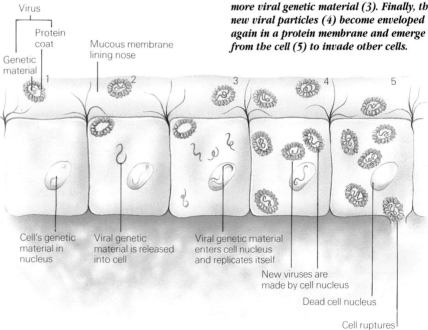

Virus
Protein coat
Genetic material
Mucous membrane lining nose
1 2 3 4 5

Cell's genetic material in nucleus

Viral genetic material is released into cell

Viral genetic material enters cell nucleus and replicates itself

New viruses are made by cell nucleus

Dead cell nucleus

Cell ruptures releasing viruses

Elaine Keenan

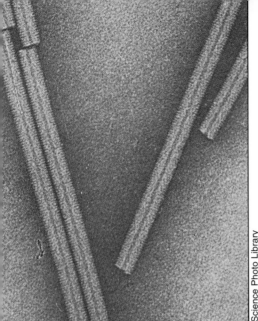

The first virus to be discovered was the tobacco mosaic virus. It is viewed here under the electron microscope, which enabled research to progress.

more or less round in shape. Exceptions are the rabies virus and its related viruses, which are bullet-shaped, and the smallpox virus and its related viruses, which are brick-shaped.

Viruses are basically classified according to whether they carry the nucleic acid DNA or RNA. The nucleic acid core of a virus is called the genome and the protein capsule the capsid. The capsid is made up from many identical protein blocks called capsomeres. The way in which the capsomeres line up around the genome dictates the overall shape of the individual virus particle.

Different groups of viruses have different shapes, one of the most common being the icosahedron, a structure with 20 flat sides of equal size, effectively forming a sphere. The capsid of other viruses forms a hollow cylinder. These differences in structure can only be determined by pictures taken with an electron microscope (electron micrographs). Some viruses have another structure on top of their capsid, aptly called an envelope.

All these variations place a virus in a particular group. The viruses that cause human disease are now all classified with one important exception—the hepatitis viruses (see Hepatitis).

Viruses and bacteria

There is an enormous difference in size between viruses and bacteria. For example, a streptococcus is 50 times greater in diameter than a polio virus.

An individual bacterium is able to reproduce itself by splitting in two, and it can live independently, having the apparatus to carry out many metabolic pro-

cesses within its cell wall. All bacteria contain DNA and RNA (see Bacteria). In contrast, although viruses can survive outside the cells of other organisms, they need these cells for any kind of metabolic activity. Individual viral particles (virons) also need the apparatus of host cells to multiply. They do this by making exact copies of themselves according to instructions from their DNA or RNA, a process known as replication. They only contain one kind of nucleic acid.

How are viruses spread?

Viral diseases can be very infectious. A disease like measles is so infectious that until vaccination was introduced, it was certain that virtually every child in the US would get it. A new epidemic used to occur about every two years.

The measles virus, like many others, is spread by droplet infection. A cough or sneeze from an infected person will carry the virus into the air to be inhaled by someone else (see Measles).

The polio virus and enteroviruses (primarily infecting the intestines) enter the body via the digestive tract. Another group, the togaviruses, which are carried by insects, make their way into the body through the skin as the result of an insect bite. And that most horrific of infections, rabies, also enters via a bite from an animal that has been driven to distraction by the disease (see Rabies).

Once inside the body, viruses invade the cells at the site of entry.

The rhinoviruses that are responsible for the common cold enter the cells of the mucous membrane joining the nose to create symptoms in the nose and upper airways (see Common cold).

Viruses in the laboratory

Viruses are not only difficult to see but are very difficult to grow in the laboratory since they depend on living cells for replication. In the early days of virology it was not possible to grow viruses at all, but only to pass them from one laboratory animal to another.

The first advances in this field came with the realization that bacteria could be grown inside fertilized chickens' eggs. The influenza, mumps, and herpes viruses can all be grown in this way by injecting infected tissue into the inside of the egg. This will produce a collection of tiny colonies just like those on a bacterial culture plate.

The next step was the development of tissue cultures, which are collections of mammalian cells grown in a test tube. Preparing a culture is not a routine technique of investigation, but it is vitally

Vaccination is essential for preventing the deadliest viral infections, especially in Third World countries where so many other serious health problems are rife.

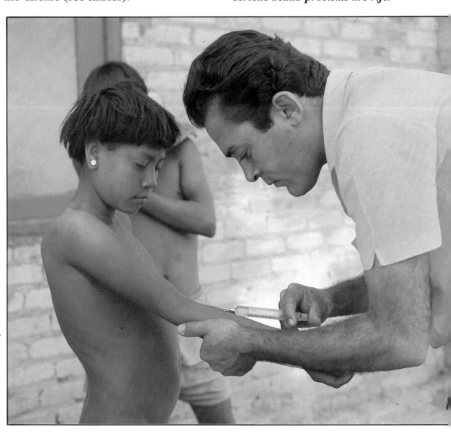

The work pioneered by Louis Pasteur continues under sophisticated modern conditions at this French research center. Here scientists have developed vaccines against polio, rabies, and other viruses.

important in the making of vaccines that protect us against the most dangerous and widespread viral infections.

A particular viral infection is usually diagnosed by monitoring the levels of antibodies in a patient's blood over a period of two weeks.

Treatment of viral infections

If there were any really effective method of treating a specific virus, then doctors would need a diagnosis earlier than two weeks after the onset of infection. However, there are very few specific treatments for viral diseases.

Recently, however, there has been one important breakthrough in the search for such a treatment. This is the development of the drug acyclovir, which has the property of killing cells infected with the herpes group of viruses while leaving the normal cells untouched. The virus can therefore no longer replicate itself. This drug may prove useful against all kinds of herpes infections and is already very valuable in treating the overwhelming kind of infection that people with deficient immune systems inevitably suffer from (see AIDS, and Immune system).

Prevention

Although viral infections cannot yet be satisfactorily treated, many of the serious ones can be successfully prevented. Smallpox has been totally eradicated worldwide through a combination of vaccination and isolation of cases. It is also possible to vaccinate against measles, German measles, yellow fever, polio, and rabies (see Vaccination).

There are some infections, however, against which it seems impossible to produce an effective vaccine. One of these is influenza. The influenza viruses have a remarkable ability to change their protein structure as they pass from person to person (see Influenza). These minor changes enable them to fool the body's immune system with each new infection. This explains why we get so many attacks of the same disease in a lifetime.

A vaccine will be effective if it is made from the current strain of a virus, but for this to be possible, a manufacturer would have to predict accurately the strain, which would be a very difficult proposition. The problem is multiplied in the case of the common cold, since there are many viral strains, so it is unlikely that prevention or treatments for the cold will be available in the near future.

Institut Mérieux

Vitamin A

Q I know a daily dose of halibut-liver oil is good for children. Is a double dose twice as good?

A Halibut-liver oil is a valuable source of vitamin A, but it is dangerous to exceed the recommended dose. Because vitamin A is stored in the body, excessive amounts can be toxic.

Q I've heard that vitamin A helps prevent colds. Is there any truth to this?

A Vitamin A aids the body in producing mucus-secreting cells, and this is one of the ways the body protects itself from germs. It works by removing them from the body—by the nose in the case of a cold. So a lack of vitamin A makes you more likely to catch colds.

Q Will eating carrots help me see in the dark, or is this just an old wives' tale?

A There is some truth in this old wives' tale. The carotene contained in carrots provides vitamin A, which helps your eyes to adjust to dim light quickly.

Q Is a poor diet the only cause of vitamin A deficiency?

A No, poor diet is in fact rarely the cause of vitamin A deficiency in developed countries. The usual cause is the failure of the intestine to absorb enough vitamin A, which may be due to cystic fibrosis or some other damage to the intestine. Deficiency can also occur as a side effect of long-term treatment with anticholesterol drugs. Diets that combine low levels of fat (essential for the absorption of vitamin A) with low levels of retinol can also cause a deficiency.

Q What are the symptoms of vitamin deficiency?

A Initially, a deficiency in vitamin A results in night blindness (the inability to see in dim light). If the deficiency persists, the eyes become dry and inflamed, eventually causing damage to the cornea and finally blindness.

Deficiency in vitamin A is relatively rare in the West, but where it does occur, generally due to malabsorption, serious problems can arise, including eventual blindness.

Vitamin A is one of the vital groups of vitamins that the body needs to function properly. It enables us to see in a dim light, keeps our skin healthy, insures normal growth, and renews the body tissue. With only a few exceptions, we obtain all the vitamins we need from our food, and the minute amounts the body requires mostly exist in their natural state in food. Vitamin A, however, is largely manufactured by the body from a food substance called carotene.

Sources of vitamin A

The vitamin A in our food comes in two different forms from two different sources. The pure form, called retinol, is found in foods such as fish liver oils, liver, kidney, cheese, eggs, and butter, having already been manufactured by the animal concerned. The second form we make ourselves from carotene, which is found in such vegetables as carrots, spinach, cabbage, and tomatoes.

In fact, when a vegetable is orange, yellow, or dark green in color, what you are seeing is its carotene content, and the darker the green of the vegetable, the greater the carotene content. Spinach and watercress therefore contain more in each pound than cabbage, and dark green cabbage provides more than lighter colored vegetables.

Carotene is converted into retinol in the liver and in the small intestine, and then some of the vitamin A (whether it be converted carotene or retinol itself) is absorbed into the bloodstream and circulated around the body to be used in its everyday functions, while the rest is stored in the liver.

Although vitamin A is not present in many foods, those that contain it are fortunately readily available. A fifth of our average intake comes from vegetables, mainly carrots. Turnips and potatoes are no substitute, however, since they contain no carotene. Milk and butter are other common sources; margarine, to which vitamin A is added artificially, contains almost as much as butter and is therefore just as good.

Foods rich in vitamin A tend not to lose their vitamin content easily, though prolonged exposure to light and air can reduce the amount. Cooking at normal temperatures has no serious effect, but frying at a high temperature in butter or margarine will result in loss of vitamin content.

Vitamin A deficiency

Itching, burning, and reddened eyelids are among the problems caused by lack of vitamin A, and a drastic deficiency can lead to blindness. The children of poorer nations are often vulnerable and a cause is early weaning onto an unsuitable food like skimmed milk, which can contain little or no vitamin A. However, prepared baby foods almost always have essential vitamins added to them.

In more affluent societies the diet tends to be better balanced, and most people get as much vitamin A as is needed, about two-thirds of it coming from retinol and one-third from carotene.

Nevertheless, a deficiency of vitamin A can cause night blindness (see Night blindness). Doctors have long recognized night blindness as a medical condition. Normally it takes about seven to 10 minutes for the eyes to become used to a dim light; so if you are dazzled for some time after seeing another car's headlights at night, or if you find it difficult to distinguish objects in the twilight, see your doctor to find out if you have vitamin A deficiency. Taking halibut-liver oil capsules is the quickest cure, since it is one of the best sources of vitamin A.

If you are on a high protein diet, you could risk a deficiency simply because the body uses up the vitamin much faster when converting protein into body tissue and energy. However, there are other times when the body uses up its store of vitamin A too quickly, such as when it is in high fever (see Fevers).

Taking certain drugs also causes a loss. Your doctor will advise you as to how much vitamin A is needed should any of these situations arise.

Excessive vitamin A

The 40 or so vitamins can be divided into two types: those that can be stored by the body and those that cannot. Because vitamin A is stored in the liver, daily intake is not essential, although regular supplies are needed. There is some danger, however, in taking too much vitamin A. This is very unlikely to result from intake through food but can occur if large amounts are taken in such concentrated forms as halibut oil capsules. Symptoms may include insomnia, weight loss, dryness of the lips, and aching limbs. In general, however, taking slightly more than is needed is unlikely to harm you.

Vitamin A: Are you getting enough?

The daily requirement for different age groups and the vitamin A content in the foods listed are given in micrograms (1000 micrograms = one milligram, or one-thousandth of a gram).

There is no need to worry if you are unable to take the correct amount every day as long as the amount you take over a week gives the correct daily average.

Age group	Daily requirement
Babies under 12 months	450
Children: 1–6 years	300
7–8 years	400
9–11 years	575
Adolescents (12+)	750
Adult men and women	750
Expectant mothers:	
first 4 months	750
until the birth	900
during breast-feeding	1200

Food	Vitamin A content
Apricots, dried, 2 oz (57 g)	340
Butter, 1 oz (28 g)	282
Cabbage, 4 oz (114 g)	56
Carrots, 4 oz (114 g)	2267
Cheese, 2 oz (57 g)	238
Cod-liver oil capsule, 1	180
Cream, heavy, 2 tablespoons (30 ml)	130
Egg, 1	80
Halibut-oil capsule, 1	1200

Food	Vitamin A content
Kidney, 4 oz (114 g)	340
Fish, oily, 4 oz (114 g)	52
Liver, ox, 4 oz (114 g)	6800
Margarine, 1 oz (28 g)	255
Milk, whole, 7 fl oz (0.2 L)	80
Peas, frozen, 4 oz (114 g)	56
Prunes, dried, 2 oz (57 g)	90
Spinach, 4 oz (114 g)	1136
Tomato, 1.5 oz (42 g)	49
Watercress, 1 oz (28 g)	142

Di Lewis

Vitamin B

Vitamin B is essential for the regulation of the body's processes. Unlike most other vitamins, it is not stored in the body and needs to be consumed daily. Fortunately it is present in a wide variety of foods.

Q I'm on the Pill and suffering from headaches and depression. Would I benefit from a general vitamin supplement, or would I be better taking one of the B vitamins?

A Since the Pill often results in pyridoxine deficiency, you can offset this by taking more of this vitamin, and adding brown rice, liver, chicken, mackerel, peanuts, brewer's yeast, and wheat germ to your diet. Start with 2–5 mg and increase the daily allowance if symptoms do not disappear. For a general supplement, take B complex capsules.

Q Will heavy drinking cause a vitamin B deficiency?

A Yes. Heavy drinking impairs the body's ability to use thiamine, one of the B vitamins. The poor concentration, fatigue, and weight loss alcoholics suffer from may be due as much to thiamine deficiency as excess drinking. Drink less, or if you find it difficult to cut down, make sure your diet contains more milk, whole meal bread, beef, fortified cornflakes, and peanuts.

Q My children will only eat white rice and white bread. Could they get beriberi?

A It's extremely unlikely. The association of beriberi with white cereals is not due to eating the cereals, it is due to eating virtually nothing else. White rice and bread provide carbohydrate intake and are not a source of thiamine. Wheat flour (and hence bread) is by law supplemented with thamine, and most diets contain many other sources of thiamine.

Q I have been prescribed a vitamin B supplement. Is it possible to take too much?

A Theoretically no, since the vitamin is not stored in the body and any excess is excreted. Very large doses, however, might constitute a major challenge to your system, and it is possible that some sort of toxic effect could follow.

Vitamin B is a complex of at least eight separate water-soluble vitamins: B_1 (thiamin), B_2 (riboflavin), B_3 (niacin), folic acid (folacin), B_6 (pyridoxine), B_{12} (cyanocobalamin), biotin, and pantothenic acid. They can be obtained in adequate supplies by eating a well-balanced diet (see Diet), since B vitamins are present in a wide variety of foods.

However, B vitamins can be easily destroyed, and their absorption and use by the body is affected by drugs (see Side effects) or excessive alcohol. If a deficiency occurs, disease can result.

Uses

The B vitamins have a number of uses in the body. They act with enzymes to maintain chemical actions (see Enzymes), particularly to do with breaking down foods. They are involved in the process of providing the body with energy, basically by converting carbohydrates into glucose. They are vital in the digestion (see Digestive system) and use of fats and protein. The B vitamins are also necessary for the normal functioning of the nervous system (see Nervous system), and for the maintenance of muscle tone in the gastrointestinal tract (see Stomach).

Pyridoxine (B_6) assists in hormone production (see Hormones), and it must be present for the production of antibodies and red blood cells. Folic acid and B_{12} are also involved with red cell formation. Riboflavin maintains the skin, liver, and eyes. Other vitamins in the group also perform functions necessary to good health.

Sources

Almost all the B vitamins occur in brewer's yeast (the richest natural source), liver and other organs, and whole grain cereals. Cow's milk, eggs, nuts, legumes, and green leafy vegetables are also rich in many of the B vitamins.

B vitamins, particularly biotin, are also produced by bacteria in the human intestine. These bacteria grow best on milk, sugar, and small amounts of fat in the diet.

How vitamin B is lost

The body does not store vitamin B, making regular daily replenishment vital. Because the B vitamins dissolve in water, much of their nutrient value can be lost in cooking. Premature harvesting and long and improper storage also cause vitamin B loss. Thiamin is most affected, and nicotinic acid the least.

Food processing also affects the B vitamins in foods. Milling wheat to produce white flour results in a lowering of the thiamin and nicotinic acid content. Milling and the extraction of bran and germ from rice means that polished rice contains less thiamin. Cereals that have been processed contain fewer vitamins.

Canned meats contain fewer vitamins than home-cooked meats. Light affects riboflavin in bottled milk.

Ideally all vegetables and fruits should be ripened on the plant and eaten raw, with the skin still on, immediately after being harvested. Since such ideal circumstances are impractical for most people, attempts should be made to buy fresh produce only in quantities that can be used promptly, and to cook them (preferably by steaming, not boiling in water) as little as possible. Often frozen vegetables and fruits contain more vitamin B than those improperly shipped and stored.

Deficiency

Deficiency of vitamin B can occur both from low intake and from its destruction, for example, by excessive alcohol or sugar intake. A lack of vitamin B can lead to various conditions, including beriberi, although this is rarely found in developed countries in the West.

Wet beriberi arises from a thiamin-free diet, and is characterized by edema (waterlogging and swelling of the body; see Edema). Dry beriberi occurs through a thiamin deficiency, but the deterioration in health is slower and edema may not appear. Both forms of beriberi affect the functioning of the nervous system, but the brain is usually unimpaired.

Infantile beriberi is a disease that affects children breast-fed by thiamin-deficient mothers. Here, brain malfunction takes place, together with convulsions, uneasiness, and loss of voice. In rare cases beriberi might arise following fever, pregnancy, or hard physical labor.

In the United States, thiamin deficiency occurs almost exclusively in alcoholics, primarily due to a poor dietary intake (see Alcoholism). However, it has also been demonstrated that severe alcoholism affects intestinal absorption of thiamin.

A varied diet is the best guarantee of adequate vitamin B, which is present in many foods and drinks.

Pellagra is another vitamin B–related condition present in areas where there is poverty and famine, but it also occurs in people whose diets consist mainly of fats and carbohydrates, or alcohol. It is a result of inadequate supply of nicotinic acid, and symptoms include burning and itching, skin blotches, weakness, diarrhea, and depression.

Pernicious anemia (see Anemia) is a disease that occurs in people who lack the ability to absorb and utilize vitamin B_{12}, and in vegans, who shun milk, eggs, meat, and fish. B_{12} can be taken in pill form or by injection, while eating raw liver is also a cure (see Vegetarianism).

Sores on the skin, often at the corner of the mouth, are usually caused by a deficiency of riboflavin (see Sores). Riboflavin deficiency also causes lesions of the cornea (see Cornea). A deficiency of folacin is indicated by a very red tongue, diarrhea (see Diarrhea), and sometimes anemia, poor growth (see Growth), and graying hair. Pyridoxine (vitamin B_6) deficiency can cause anemia, irritability, kidney stones (see Kidneys and kidney diseases), and muscle twitching (see Muscles, and Twitches and tics).

Lack of biotin can lead to tiredness (see Tiredness), depression (see Depression), nausea (see Nausea), skin problems (see Skin and skin diseases), and aches and pains. A deficiency of pantothenic acid is rare because it is found in most foods.

When a supplement is necessary

The need for vitamin B increases during infection or stress (see Stress), as well as during pregnancy (see Pregnancy) and in the presence of certain drugs. The contraceptive pill creates a greater need for pyridoxine. Women on the Pill who experience headaches or depression may need to add it to their diet (see Contraception).

Pregnant women can benefit from taking two B vitamins. If there are early signs of toxemia, such as swelling feet, ankles, and fingers, an increased dose of pyridoxine can be taken, and should be continued during breast-feeding. Vitamin B is also used as an antisickness treatment. Pregnant women should also take folic acid, which is often given in a combined pill with iron supplements. Folic acid deficiency is the most common vitamin deficiency in the United States, but is easily corrected with supplements.

Folic acid is involved in the making of red blood cells. The body has to produce more of these cells in pregnancy to help with the nourishment and development of the fetus (see Fetus). Without folic acid, a pregnant woman will risk such complications as toxemia, premature

Vitamin B

How much vitamin B complex do you need in a day?

Age group	Thiamin (mg)	Riboflavin (mg)	Nicotinic (mg)
Babies under 1 year	0.3 to 0.5	0.4 to 0.6	5 to 8
Children aged 1 to 6	0.7 to 0.9	0.8 to 1.1	9 to 12
Children aged 7 to 10	1.2	1.2	16
Male adolescents	1.4 to 1.5	1.5 to 1.8	18 to 20
Female adolescents	1.1 to 1.2	1.3 to 1.4	14 to 16
Men	1.4	1.6	18
Women	1.0	1.2	13
Pregnant women	1.3	1.5	15
Lactating women	1.3	1.7	17

Vitamin B in the diet

You only need to eat a normal, balanced diet in order to satisfy your daily requirement of vitamin B. As can be seen from the chart below, a variety of foods contain vitamin B components. Vitamin amounts are given in micrograms (1000 microgram = one milligram). Quantities of pyridoxine, B_{12}, folic acid, pantothenic acid, and biotin required are miniscule and are present in an everyday diet.

Thiamin

1 large slice of whole wheat bread	150
4 oz (114 g) cured, cooked ham	600
4 oz (114 g) wheat flakes cereal	600
1/2 cup (70 g) blackberries	200

Riboflavin

4 oz (114 g) cabbage	1000
1 whole wheat bread roll	100
4 oz (114 g) liver	3500
1 egg	250

Nicotinic acid

small glass of milk	1800
4oz (114 g) hard cheese	7000
4oz (114 g) beef	8000
1/2 cup roasted peanuts	1200

Sources of vitamin B

	Milk	Tea/coffee	Whole wheat bread	Cheese	Liver	Potatoes	Eggs	Peanuts	Whole grain cereals	Chicken	Green vegetables	Kidney	Beef	Brewer's yeast	Beer
Thiamin (B_1)	x		x			x		x	x		x		x	x	
Riboflavin (B_2)	x			x	x	x	x		x	x	x	x			
Nicotinic acid (B_3)	x	x		x		x	x	x	x		x		x		x
Folic acid			x		x			x	x		x	x		x	
Pyridoxine (B_6)			x		x	x		x	x		x	x	x		
B_{12}	x				x							x	x	x	
Biotin	x				x		x	x				x		x	
Pantothenic acid	x		x		x		x	x	x	x	x	x	x	x	

birth, and hemorrhaging, all the result of a condition called megaloblastic anemia, which causes tiredness and weakness. Breast-feeding mothers are advised to increase their niacin intake.

Doctors recommend additional pyridoxine to alleviate the symptoms of premenstrual syndrome (see Premenstrual syndrome), such as headaches, depression, and painful breasts.

Finally, the use of steroids (see Steroids), the hormone estrogen (see Estrogen), and dieting (see Slimming), create a need for pyridoxine. This can also be helpful for acne (see Acne and pimples), and in in helping to alleviate the side effects of menopause (see Menopause).

Toxicity

Overconsumption is rare with B vitamins, since they are not stored in the body. However, excessive amounts of nicotinic acid (a form of niacin) may cause flushing, headache, cramps (see Cramp), and nausea. Too much folacin may mask the presence of pernicious anemia. Large supplements of vitamin B_6 have been shown to cause sensory nerve damage.

Other B vitamins

There are several other substances that are considered by some to be B vitamins. B_{13} (orotic acid), for example, has been synthesized in Europe and is found in organically grown root vegetables, while B_{17} (laetrile) is the one B vitamin that does not occur naturally in brewer's yeast. Some of these substances have been promoted by faddists as cures for various ailments. Scientific evidence is lacking, however, and a physician's advice should be sought before taking large doses of either these or other vitamins.

Vitamin C

Q My grandmother says that freezing and canning take all the goodness out of foods. Is she right about vitamin C?

A Not entirely, although there may be a slight loss when vegetables are blanched for freezing, and a further slight loss if frozen vegetables are stored for a long time. But fresh vegetables that have also been stored may yield less vitamin C than frozen ones since it is readily destroyed by contact with air. The heat processing that takes place during canning also affects vitamin C, although sometimes the manufacturer will add extra and this will be stated on the can's printed label.

Q How can I best preserve vitamin C when cooking fresh vegetables?

A Vegetables should be prepared immediately before they are used. Cook in the minimum amount of boiling salted water, or, even better, steam them, for as little time as necessary. Do not leave vegetables soaking in the cooking water, and serve immediately. Prolonged cooking and keeping them hot can destroy almost all the vitamin C content. The best way of preparing potatoes is to bake them in their skins. Never add sodium bicarbonate to the water to improve the color of vegetables—this reduces the vitamin C value, too. Even cutting and slicing them does this, as does cooking in copper or iron pans. Undoubtedly, the best way to eat vegetables is raw.

Q I have heard that smokers and heavy drinkers should take extra vitamin C. Is this true?

A It has been found that levels of vitamin C are lower in heavy smokers or drinkers whose diet is otherwise quite adequate. If you are a heavy smoker or drinker, it would seem a reasonable precaution to take more than the basic recommended daily allowance of vitamin C. Better still, cut down your consumption of tobacco and alcohol.

Vitamin C is considered to be one of the most vital vitamins. However, it is not enough just to eat the right foods—they must be properly prepared too, otherwise the vitamin content may be sharply reduced or lost altogether.

Fruit is rich in vitamin C, especially citrus fruits like oranges, lemons, and limes.

Vitamin C is probably the most controversial of all the vitamins. Great claims have been made for its healing and protective powers, not only in connection with the common cold (see Common cold), but in aging (see Aging), heart disease (see Heart disease), and many other conditions. The official view remains skeptical, however, although no one denies that even in affluent societies we are more likely to be deficient in vitamin C than in any other nutrient.

Unfortunately for us, vitamin C does not occur in many foods, and in those that do contain it, the amount will vary according to season, freshness, and cooking method. Nor can the body store vitamin C, so it needs regular replenishment.

Vitamin C is vital for maintenance of the body's connective tissue, that is, the skin, fibers, membranes, and so on that literally hold it together. Collagen, a protein that is important for the formation of healthy skin, tendons, and bones, depends partly on vitamin C for its manufacture, and the vitamin is also needed for the release of hormones (see Hormones) and the production of other chemical substances that play a part in our survival and resistance to infection.

Even so, this vitamin remains something of a mystery. Its complete function is unknown, but some research scientists consider it to be the most essential of all the vitamins.

Vitamin C deficiency
The extreme form of deficiency in vitamin C is a condition called scurvy (see Scurvy). When this occurs, the connective tissue disintegrates so that blood vessels break down and there is bleeding

People at risk from vitamin C deficiency

Older people—perhaps living alone, existing on canned and packaged foods

Young people—perhaps in college dormitories, living on junk foods

Food faddists—advocates of macro-cereal-based diets who do not understand the body's nutritional needs

Bottle-fed babies—given cow's milk formulas without vitamin supplements or orange juice

How much vitamin C do you need?

Food	Approximate vitamin C content (micrograms)
4 oz (14 g) fresh blackberries	220
4 oz (14 g) fresh strawberries	70
4 oz (14 g) lemon juice	60
1 fresh orange	60
4 oz (14 g) canned orange juice	40
Half grapefruit	20
4 oz (14 g) canned pineapple	12
4 oz (14 g) boiled brussel sprouts	40
4 oz (14 g) boiled cabbage	24
4 oz (14 g) frozen peas	12
4 oz (114 g) raw green peppers	112
4 oz (114 g) boiled potatoes (according to season, new potatoes contain most)	4–20
1 fresh tomato	10

Daily vitamin C requirements

The requirements for different age groups is given in micrograms (1000 micrograms = one milligram, or one-thousandth of a gram).

Babies under 12 months	15
Children 1–8 years	20
Adolescents 12–14 years	25
Adults	30
Expectant mothers and during breast-feeding	60

Vitamin C was not actually identified as the curative agent until 1932. The name ascorbic acid (used to describe vitamin C when it is manufactured) is derived from the term antiscorbutic, meaning the ability to prevent and cure scurvy. Today, this deficiency can be cured very quickly with high doses of vitamin C, but if the condition is neglected there could be permanent damage.

Sources of vitamin C

If we were prepared to live on rose hips, we would be very well provided with vitamin C, as this is the richest natural source available. Paprika is good, too, but since neither this nor rose hips are on everyone's daily menu, we have to rely on other sources (see Diet).

Fortunately vegetables such as potatoes, which do feature in most people's diets in the Western world, contain some vitamin C, as do brussels sprouts, cauliflower, and cabbage. Among fruits, black currants are best, followed by strawberries. Further down on the list, but available all year round, are citrus fruits (oranges, lemons, limes, and grapefruit). Rose hip syrup is obviously brimming with vitamin C, and is available from most health food stores.

There is not much vitamin C in apples or pears, virtually none in milk (though sometimes vitamin C is added), none in cereal grains, dried peas and beans, nuts or dried fruit (the drying process effectively rids fruit of any vitamin value). Although all green and root vegetables and fruit contain a certain amount, this varies from season to season. For example, new potatoes contain three times as much vitamin C as old ones.

When extra is needed

Some distinguished experts maintain that we need far more than the normally recommended daily allowances. It is generally acknowledged that the body requires additional vitamin C after a severe illness or injury, and there have been experiments showing that burns (see Burns) heal faster when a vitamin C solution has been applied to the skin in conjunction with injections or doses taken by mouth.

High doses of vitamin C have also been used successfully in experiments carried out to reduce levels of cholesterol (see Cholesterol, and Heart disease) in the arteries, and it is thought that the vitamin might offer protection against gastric bleeding in those who have to take large regular amounts of aspirin for such conditions as arthritis (see Arthritis, and Aspirin and analgesics).

This of course brings us to the vexed question of vitamin C and the common cold, over which many claims have been made and much research carried out. The current verdict is "not proven," with no conclusive evidence that points to vitamin C being an effective protection against, or treatment for, colds. However, if you have one cold after another every winter, there is no harm in trying this.

Too much vitamin C

The body excretes any surplus of this vitamin and any massive dose of vitamin C that is not utilized by the body is simply flushed away in urine. This means that there is no possibility of an overdose according to our present knowledge. On the other hand, people seem to be able to function healthily and normally on small amounts.

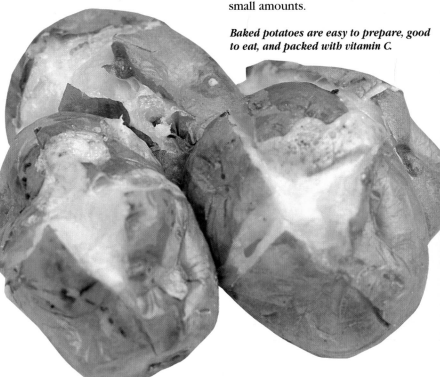

Baked potatoes are easy to prepare, good to eat, and packed with vitamin C.

into the skin, joints, and from the gums. Teeth are loosened, bruises appear, and resistance to infection is lowered.

Scurvy was one of the earliest deficiency diseases to be discovered. In 1497 Portuguese navigator Vasco da Gama lost more than half his men through its effects, owing to the inevitable shortage of fresh fruit and vegetables on long voyages. In 1753 British naval surgeon James Lind showed that scurvy could be prevented and cured by giving victims orange and lemon juice, although he was unaware of the reason for this.

Vitamin D

The sunshine vitamin is essential for the normal growth and development of a child's bones, and for the maintenance of healthy bones in an adult.

Q Will sitting under a sunlamp give me enough vitamin D?

A No. You will get a certain amount of vitamin D but not as much as you need. Diet is much more important, and you must make sure that yours contains a sufficient amount of vitamin D. Sufferers with seasonal affective disorder (SAD) sometimes claim that using a sunlamp is an effective treatment for the condition, and it is possible that SAD is related to a deficiency in vitamin D.

Q I sunbathe in the yard when the weather permits. Do I need to worry about having enough vitamin D in my diet?

A If you lived, say, in Hong Kong, you could afford not to worry about vitamin D in your diet. There, the average Chinese diet is low on vitamin D, but signs of deficiency are rare because of the higher than average annual amounts of sunshine. Those who live in temperate climates get less sunshine. So diet is very important. Try to eat a helping of canned fish once a week at least. If, as a nation, we ate more oily fish such as herring, which is a particularly rich source, we would have all the vitamin D we need.

Q My son is going on a trip to southern Europe in August. For how long will he benefit from the vitamin D he absorbs there?

A The body can store vitamin D for several months. It is estimated that one square centimeter (0.155 square inches) of skin can absorb 0.45 micrograms in three hours. In the Northern Hemisphere, the highest rates are found in the blood in September. A survey of children who had spent some weeks at the coast in summer showed that they had much higher reserves of vitamin D as compared to children who had not, and these reserves were still present the following February. While sunshine is undoubtedly good for you, you also need to be aware of the damage that can ensue from staying out too long in hot sun without taking precautions.

Vitamin D is sometimes called the sunshine vitamin for the very good reason that we derive part of our essential supplies from exposure to the sun. We also obtain it from what we eat (see Diet), but there is some danger of deficiency since it does not occur in many foods. We need vitamin D so that it can work with calcium (see Calcium) to make healthy bones (see Bones). Vitamin D helps the absorption of calcium and phosphorus from the intestinal wall and maintains correct levels in the bloodstream.

Sources of vitamin D

There are two main types of vitamin D. When we derive it from sunshine, it is through ultraviolet rays hitting the skin and converting cholesterol in the skin into cholecalciferol, or vitamin D_3 (see Cholesterol). The other main kind of vitamin D is called ergocalciferol, or D_2, and is manufactured from plant materials such as yeasts.

Comparatively few foods contain vitamin D. Besides cod-liver oil, it is most richly available in herrings, kippers, canned salmon, and sardines. If you think you are not taking a sufficient amount you could increase your supplies with a daily spoonful of cod-liver oil or a helping of canned fish once or twice a week. Margarine is required to have vitamin D added to it during production, and evaporated milk usually has extra, too. Butter and fresh milk have much smaller amounts, but because of their daily use, they are a good source. Eggs contain some vitamin D as well.

We need to be aware that the ultraviolet rays in sunlight can be both beneficial and harmful to our health. Vitamin D is crucial to the body's production of vitamin D; at the same time, it can cause serious long-term damage to the skin, including cancer. Make sure that you regulate your exposure to the sun sensibly.

Spectrum

Vitamin D—How much do you need?

It is not necessary to maintain the intake on a daily basis, but over a period of a week the intake should average out. The figures here are in micrograms (1000 micrograms = 1 milligram or one-thousandth of a gram).

Age range	Vitamin D intake
Babies under 1 year	10
Children age 1 to 4	10
From age 5 upward	2.5
Adults	2.5
Pregnant and breast-feeding women	10

Vitamin D content in foods
(figures in micrograms)

Food	Vitamin D content
Glass of milk	0.16
Canned sardines in oil 4 oz (125 g)	14.16
Hard cheese 2 oz (50 g)	0.14
Cod-liver oil 1 tbls (15 ml)	60.00
1 egg	1.00
Fortified evaporated milk 4 fl oz (125 ml)	0.44
Fried liver 4 oz (125 g)	0.44
Herring 4 oz (125 g)	25.60
Kipper 4 oz (125 g)	25.52
Margarine 2 oz (50 g)	4.50

Vitamin D deficiency

The main result of vitamin D deficiency is rickets in children (see Rickets). Rickets is a condition of defective bone growth, causing bowlegs, knock-knees, distorted appearance of the ribs, and narrowed chest and pelvis (see Growth).

Early symptoms include restlessness, sweating, lack of muscle tone, and softening of the bones of the skull. The baby's teeth may be slow in appearing or may be soft and susceptible to decay (see Teeth and teething). The bones are fragile and easily broken, and there may be muscle spasms and twitching (see Twitches and tics). Extra vitamin D can reverse the effects if it is given early enough, but damage can be permanent. Fortunately rickets has now been virtually wiped out in the Western world.

An adult form of vitamin D deficiency is known as osteomalacia, and this causes bone softening and breakage, muscular weakness, pain, and tenderness. This can affect older people if they live on a diet that is low in calcium and vitamin D. Osteomalacia is often associated with osteoporosis, which also increases risk of breakage (see Osteoporosis).

Excessive vitamin D

Since vitamin D is stored in fat (see Fats), any extra is not easily expelled from the body. Instead, it is stored in the liver and can lead to certain poisonous effects if the intake is too high. Early signs of vitamin D poisoning include loss of appetite, nausea, and vomiting (see Liver and liver diseases). Since vitamin D helps absorption of calcium, there may be unhealthily high concentrations of this in the blood, leading to brittle bones, hardening of the arteries, and growth failure in children.

Today vitamin D, mainly in the form of D_2, is recommended for pregnant and breast-feeding women, and children under age five. As long as you follow the instructions and take no further D_2 supplements beyond those suggested by the doctor, the dosage will be safe.

Vitamin E

Q Should I give my family muesli for breakfast? I have heard that it contains a lot of vitamin E.

A It depends on the muesli. Look at the label on the packet to see if the contents include whole or rolled oats, nuts, and sesame seeds; all these contain vitamin E.

Q Does vitamin E improve sexual performance?

A Vitamin E does have this reputation, but there has yet to be definite proof. Possibly the greatest benefit is psychological.

Q Could my iron tonic interfere with my body's ability to absorb vitamin E?

A Medications containing iron work against the absorption of vitamin E, which is why iron should be taken at a different time of day—in the morning if vitamin E is taken in any extra form in the evening. Mineral oils such as castor oil, sometimes taken as a laxative, also impair absorption of vitamin E and other nutrients. And the female hormone estrogen, which is contained in the contraceptive pill and in hormone replacement therapy for menopause, may impair absorption. Some people taking iron or estrogen have a daily teaspoon of wheatgerm oil, though this is probably not necessary.

Q Should I use vegetable oils in my cooking as a good source of vitamin E?

A In theory, yes, since these oils contain vitamin E. At the same time, however, a high consumption of polyunsaturated vegetable oils actually creates an increased need for the vitamin. This is because vitamin E has a biochemical effect on polyunsaturated fats that uses up supplies. Polyunsaturated fats are often recommended by doctors for patients with high cholesterol levels, since the fats help reduce these levels, but remember that more vitamin E is needed to maintain a balance.

Research into the benefits of vitamin E is still in progress, but some people claim that it has remarkable curative and rejuvenating powers. Is there any truth in this?

For years vitamin E has had a very poor reputation. This is because, in the past, doctors' interest in vitamins (see Vitamins) has been concentrated largely on the effects of deficiency, even though vitamin E deficiency is very rare. Recently, however, a new and exciting role for this neglected vitamin has appeared.

Vitamin E has long been the Cinderella of the vitamins. Until recently, pharmacology textbooks have dismissed the fat-soluble vitamin E as unimportant. Some have even said that it is of no medical relevance in humans. These views have recently undergone a radical change.

History

In 1922 it was discovered that female rats required an unknown substance in their diets to sustain normal pregnancies. Without this substance, they could ovulate and conceive normally, but within about 10 days the fetus died and was absorbed. Male rats deficient in this substance were also found to have abnormalities in their testes.

The unknown substance turned out to be a new vitamin, and was given the designation vitamin E. Fourteen years later it was chemically isolated from wheatgerm oil, and was found to be any one of a range of eight very complicated but similar molecules known as tocopherols.

The news of the availability of the new vitamin was greeted with interest, and, for a time, vitamin E enjoyed a reputation as the antisterility vitamin. Doctors prescribed it freely and illogically as a treatment for infertility (see Infertility), although there was no reason to suppose that the people concerned were deficient in the vitamin.

Like all the other vitamins, this one was used on the fallacious basis that it could benefit, in people who were not deficient in it, those conditions caused by its deficiency. By association, vitamin E was also used, quite pointlessly it turned out, to try to treat various menstrual disorders, inflammation of the vagina, and menopausal symptoms. Soon the interest died down, and for many years the vitamin was largely forgotten.

Vitamin E deficiency

Human vitamin E deficiency is very rare because the vitamin occurs widely in many foods, especially in vegetable oils. Deficiency occurs only after many months on a severely restricted diet (see Diet) or in people being artificially fed. A daily intake of 10 to 30 mg of the vitamin is said to be sufficient to keep the blood levels within normal limits, and this will always be provided by any reasonable diet. Human milk contains plenty to meet the baby's needs. When deficiency does occur, however, the effects can be devastating.

Severe deficiency can cause degenerative changes in the brain (see Brain damage and disease) and nervous system (see Nervous system), impairment of vision (see Eyes and eyesight), double vision, walking disturbances, anemia (see Anemia), an increased rate of destruction of red blood cells, fluid retention (see Edema), and skin disorders (see Skin and skin diseases). It must be emphasized that these deficiency effects are extremely uncommon. In the last few years the reason for them has become apparent.

Free radicals

Chemists have known about free radicals for about 100 years. It is only recently, however, that it has become apparent that they are implicated in disease. Free radicals are highly active, short-lived chemical groups that contain an atom with an unpaired outer orbital electron. The stable state is a pair of electrons, and if only one is present the atom will quickly capture an electron from a nearby atom, causing a form of molecular damage known as oxidation. When this happens the deprived atom itself forms a free radical. In this way a chain reaction can be set up that can quickly damage tissues.

For many years, chemists have known that free radical oxidation action can be controlled, or even prevented, by a range of antioxidant substances. Antioxidants are used to prevent lubricating oils from drying up, and to protect plastics from free radical damage.

Foodstuffs have long been protected from free radical damage by antioxidants. When fat goes rancid it does so by a free radical oxidation reaction. This can be prevented by antioxidant additives such as BHA (butylated hydroxyanisole), BHT (butylated hydroxytoluene), and tocopherol (vitamin E).

Natural body antioxidants

Medical interest in the possibility that free radicals were involved in disease processes was aroused when it was dis-

Vitamin E—How much do you need?

United States recommended daily allowances are as follows. The amounts are given in micrograms (1000 micrograms = 1 milligram, or one-thousandth of a gram).

Age range

Babies under 1 year	5000
Children under four years of age	1000
Children over four and adults	3000

The main vitamin E foods

Figures are given as the number of micrograms in 100 grams (3.527 oz)

Bran	2000
Almonds, shelled	2000
Butter	2000
Cornflakes	400
Potato chips	6100
Eggs	1600
Hazelnuts, shelled	2100
Peanuts, fresh or roasted	8100
Muesli	3200
Sunflower oil	1800
Whole wheat bread	200

Vitamin E can help keep your skin young and healthy looking. Eating a good balanced diet should provide enough vitamin E, but supplements, either in the form of capsules or lotions, can also be taken.

covered that the body has its own natural antioxidants. One of the most effective of these is vitamin E. This vitamin is especially important because it is fat soluble and much of the most significant free radical damage in the body is damage to the membranes of cells and to low density lipoproteins. Both vitamins contain fat molecules. Vitamin C (see Vitamin C) is also a powerful antioxidant, but it is soluble in water, not in fat. This means that it gets distributed to all parts of the body. The two vitamins are both highly efficient at mopping up free radicals, and cooperate in doing this.

The tocopherols
Among the richest natural sources of the tocopherols are seed germ oils, alfalfa, and lettuce. They are widely distributed in plant materials. Tocopherols are almost insoluble in water but dissolve in oils, fats, alcohol, acetone, ether, and other fat solvents. Unlike vitamin C they are stable to heat and alkalis in the absence of oxygen, and are unaffected by acids at temperatures up to 212°F (100°C).

Because vitamin E consists of so many slightly different tocopherols, worldwide standardization is difficult and a little arbitrary. The international unit of vitamin E is taken to be equal to 1 mg of alpha-tocopherol acetate. For all practical purposes of dosage, however, you can consider 1 international unit to be equivalent to 1 mg.

Antioxidant properties
All the tocopherols are antioxidants and this appears to be the basis for all the biological effects of the vitamin. The effects of vitamin E deficiency are, it seems, the effects of inadequate antioxidant protection. Vitamin E is involved in many body processes, and, in conjunction with vitamin C, operates as a natural antioxidant, helping to protect important cell structures, especially the cell membranes, from the damaging effects of free radicals. In animals, vitamin E supplements can protect against the effects of various drugs, chemicals, and metals that can promote free radical formation.

In carrying out its function as an antioxidant in the body, vitamin E is, itself, converted to a radical. It is, however, soon regenerated to the active vitamin by a biochemical process that probably involves both vitamin C and another natural body antioxidant, glutathione.

Dangers of overdosage
Publicity about the antioxidant value of vitamins E and C has led many people to take these vitamins on a regular daily basis, sometimes as part of an organized therapy. Like vitamin C, vitamin E is generally regarded as being a fairly innocuous substance and few if any warnings are heard of the dangers of overdosage (see Overdoses). For adults, this is probably reasonable, but there are limits to the amounts that can be safely taken. Recommended dosages for vitamin E should not be exceeded.

There is, however, a special caveat in the case of babies. Although free radicals are generally destructive, the body also uses them for beneficial purposes. They are, for instance, the mechanism by which phagocyte cells destroy bacteria (see Bacteria). This action is unlikely to be interfered with in adults, but it is known that dangers have arisen from overdosage of vitamin E in premature babies (see Premature babies).

Large doses of vitamin E have been shown to interfere sufficiently with the action of these cells of the immune system to cause a dangerous form of intestinal infection (see Digestive system). So supplementary vitamin E should never be given to babies except under strict medical supervision.

Vitamin K

Q My young nephew is a hemophiliac. Would giving him vitamin K prevent him from bleeding if he is injured?

A Unfortunately not. The abnormal bleeding tendency in hemophilia is due to an inherited deficiency of one of the clotting factors, Factor 8. Factor 8 is not one of the three clotting factors that depends on vitamin K for its production. Your nephew must rely on conventional treatment when an injury causes bleeding.

Q I've heard that if you take antibiotics you will kill the bacteria in the gut that produce vitamin K. Is this true?

A Only powerful antibiotics that are taken over long periods will kill all the intestinal bacteria. A vitamin K deficiency would then take about two weeks to appear. However, antibiotics in everyday use have little or no effect on the bacteria that produce vitamin K, so extra vitamin K is not required.

Q I am two months' pregnant. Will I need extra vitamin K?

A No. Vitamin K is not one of those vitamins that you need to take in increased amounts during pregnancy.

Q I had gallstones, and had to have my gallbladder removed. Do I need to take extra vitamin K?

A Bile, which is stored in the gallbladder, is necessary for the absorption of vitamin K from the intestines. Extra vitamin K would only be needed if the bile ducts were blocked and the bile failed to reach the intestines from the liver. Patients with gallstones or who have had gallbladder surgery hardly ever need extra vitamin K.

Q How can I be sure that I am getting enough vitamin K?

A Even if you do not eat foods containing vitamin K, you need not worry because your intestinal bacteria will provide you with an adequate supply.

By helping the blood to clot, vitamin K performs a vital function in the body. Deficiencies are rare and usually easily treated.

Vitamin K consists of vitamin K_1, a yellow oil found in a variety of vegetables, and vitamin K_2, a yellow waxy substance produced by bacteria. Although we get a supply of vitamin K_1 from such leafy vegetables as spinach and green cabbage, a normal diet will only provide us with a proportion of our needs. We get the remainder of vitamin K_2 from the bacteria that live in our intestines, and this insures that we always have a steady supply. In healthy people a deficiency resulting from an inadequate diet is rare.

Vitamin K deficiency

Vitamin K is used by the liver to produce 13 blood components known as the clotting factors (see Liver and liver diseases). A deficiency results in the decreased production of three of these 13 factors, the most important of them being prothrombin. When an injury occurs, the ability of the blood to coagulate will be impaired. Small cuts will bleed vigorously, and large bruises will form under the skin in response to even minor injuries. In severe cases of vitamin K deficiency, serious and even fatal hemorrhaging may occur (see Hemorrhage).

Because vitamins K_1 and K_2 are fat soluble (they are dissolved and stored in fat), a deficiency may occur in diseases that cause decreased digestion and absorption of fats and oils (see Fats). These include a bile duct obstruction and celiac disease (See Bile, and Celiac disease). This deficiency can easily be treated with vitamin K injections or with tablets of synthetic vitamin K.

Some liver diseases, such as cirrhosis and hepatitis (see Cirrhosis, and Hepatitis), interfere with the utilization of vitamin K, and vitamin supplements in large doses may then be required. This deficiency is sometimes difficult to treat and can be very dangerous in patients with liver failure, who may develop uncontrollable internal bleeding.

Finally, vitamin K deficiency is often found in the newborn, and may cause serious damage both from blood loss and from bleeding into the brain and other vital organs (see Birth). Intestinal bacteria are not present at birth; milk contains very little vitamin K; and the supply from the mother's bloodstream does not last long. To make up this deficiency, some newborn babies are given a small shot (1000 micrograms) of vitamin K.

Camilla Jessel

Babies are sometimes given vitamin K at birth because they have no intestinal bacteria to produce it and the supply from the mother's bloodstream is quickly depleted.

Excess vitamin K

Vitamin K is nontoxic (that is, not poisonous) if taken in excessive amounts because the liver controls the rate of production of the clotting factors.

Some patients have an increased tendency to thrombosis, or blood clot formation (see Thrombosis). These blood clots obstruct the healthy blood vessels in which they are first formed, and may also be carried around the body in the bloodstream to obstruct blood vessels elsewhere. The limbs, lungs, brain, and heart may suffer serious damage. Thrombosis is not caused by excess vitamin K, but in such patients further blood clot formation can be prevented by taking drugs such as warfarin that stop the liver from using vitamin K to produce clotting factors.

Vitamin K—How much do you need?

The figures below are only rough estimates. Daily requirement cannot be calculated accurately because so much of our intake is supplied by intestinal bacteria. The figures given below are in micrograms (1000 micrograms = 1 milligram, or one-thousandth of a gram).

Age group	Daily requirement		
Babies under one year	500–1000		
Children under ten years	1000–2000		
Adults	4000		

Pigs' liver			400–800
Eggs (each)			20
Cows' milk			2
Human breast milk			20
Potatoes			80

Vitamin K content of food

Figures given are micrograms per 100 gm (3.53 oz) of food

		Spinach	4200
		Green cabbage	3200
		Carrots	100
Lean meat	100–200	Peas	100–300
Ox liver	100–200	Tomatoes	400

Vitamins

Q What are vitamins and how important are they?

A Vitamins are organic substances present in minute amounts in food. Put simply, they help make our bodies work. Because they cannot be made in the body, vitamins must be obtained from the diet or from sunshine. We require only small amounts of them, but they are nevertheless absolutely essential to normal metabolism, and a serious deficiency will lead to disease.

Q I am feeling very low in energy. Is this because I have a vitamin deficiency.

A It is most unlikely that a person on a normal Western diet would be suffering from a vitamin deficiency. On the other hand, it does sound as though you are depressed, and vitamins are unlikely to help with depression. In fact, the only times extra vitamins should be taken is when you have an abnormal diet or are on a restricted diet.

Q My hair has started to fall out in great clumps, and I have bald patches on my scalp. Could this be a vitamin problem?

A This doesn't sound very likely. Hair has circles of growth and then rest, and it is normal to notice more hair loss at some times than others. Furthermore, any number of conditions or factors can be responsible for hair loss and baldness—from overperming to alopecia. It would be worthwhile obtaining medical advice.

Q Can taking too many vitamins be harmful?

A Taking too much vitamin A and D can be harmful. Too much vitamin A can result in fragile bones, liver and spleen enlargement, and appetite loss. Overdoses of vitamin D can cause vomiting, headaches, weight loss, and calcium deposits in the kidneys and arteries. When taking vitamin supplements, always strictly follow the dosage recommendations given by your doctor.

Everyone knows that vitamins are important and that a deficiency can cause illness. But there is more to the vitamin story than that. There have been some interesting and important developments in recent years.

Vitamins are chemical compounds necessary for normal body function. Nearly everything that happens in the body is mediated by chemical activators called enzymes (see Enzymes), and vitamins are essential components in many of the enzyme systems of the body. They operate within the cells, assisting in the synthesis of tissue-building material, hormones (see Hormones), and chemical regulators; they participate in energy production; and they assist in the breakdown of waste products and toxic substances. The B group of vitamins (see Vitamin B), for example, function as coenzymes, substances without which the vital enzyme-accelerated chemical processes of the body cannot occur or do so abnormally.

A well-balanced diet

In general, we get all the vitamins we need from a normal, well-balanced diet (see Diet). The quantities needed for health are very small. With the exception of vitamins C (see Vitamin C) and E (see Vitamin E), vitamins taken in excess of the minimum requirement are simply wasted. In the case of vitamins A (see Vitamin A) and D (see Vitamin D), excessive intake can actually be dangerous and even fatal (see Overdoses).

Vitamin deficiency is uncommon in well-nourished populations but can occur in people on fad diets or those practicing extreme forms of vegetarianism (see Vegetarianism); in people with malabsorption disorders; in alcoholics who get enough calories from alcohol to meet their energy requirements and who feel no need to eat (see Alcoholism); and in people taking certain drugs, such as hydralazine, penicillamine, and estrogens (see Side effects).

Vitamins are conventionally divided into the fat-soluble group A, D, E, and K, and the water-soluble group, vitamin C (ascorbic acid) and the B vitamins. Because of their metabolic function, they are found in highest concentration in the most metabolically active parts of animal and plant tissues, the liver and seed germs.

Recent developments

The most recent development in the vitamin field is the recognition that two vitamins, C and E, have properties that are distinct from their previously known functions. Both of these vitamins are powerful antidioxidants, and there is increasing evidence that large daily doses of them have substantial health benefits.

The new knowledge is that the immediate cause of much tissue damage in disease and environmental injury is the action of powerfully destructive chemical groups known as oxygen free radicals. Much research has shown that doses of the order of 1000 milligrams of C and 400 milligrams of E can have a substantial effect in mopping up free radicals and preventing them from causing molecular damage.

Antidioxant vitamins

In particular, it is now becoming widely accepted that the mechanisms of arterial damage leading to the deposition of cholesterol (see Cholesterol) and other material in the lining of arteries (see Arteries and artery diseases) involves free radical action. Major research projects are increasingly supporting the probability that the resulting disease, atherosclerosis, which leads to heart attacks (see Heart and heart disease) and strokes (see Stroke), can be countered by regular large supplements of antioxidant vitamins.

Atherosclerosis is the cause of more premature deaths and severe morbidity in developed countries than all other major diseases put together.

Mothers and babies, in particular, benefit from a well-balanced, vitamin-rich diet.

Image Bank

Vitiligo

This condition causes pale patches to appear on the skin, usually on the face and hands. Though these can be unsightly, vitiligo is not a serious disease.

Q I have found white spots developing on my hands. Could this be vitiligo?

A Yes, quite possibly. Vitiligo usually starts as small white spots on parts of the skin exposed to the sun, like the backs of the hands. If this is going to develop into vitiligo, the spots will enlarge and run into each other, perhaps over a few months. Vitiligo is not serious in itself, but it would be wise to consult your doctor about it.

Q Can you inherit a tendency to vitiligo?

A Yes. Though there is no definite pattern of inheritance, about 30 percent of sufferers have a family history of the condition.

Q Vitiligo appeared on my face and hands some years ago, and now I have been told my thyroid gland is failing. Could there be a connection?

A Yes, vitiligo seems to be associated with all the autoimmune diseases of hormone glands. An autoimmune disease is where the body's immune system turns against its own tissue for some reason. Vitiligo can be associated with failure of the thyroid and of the adrenal glands, and it can also be associated with pernicious anemia. More than one of these diseases can occur in the same patient, and the fact that all these problems tend to occur together has led to the suggestion that vitiligo, too, is an autoimmune disease. Most doctors believe this to be the case, though there is no definite proof.

Q Does vitiligo get better of its own accord?

A No. Unfortunately this condition is unlikely to improve much, and, once the pigment has been lost from the skin, there is little chance of it returning. On the positive side, though, the disease is no more than a slight cosmetic embarrassment, and the only problem is the increased risk of sunburn. Makeup can conceal any unsightly patches.

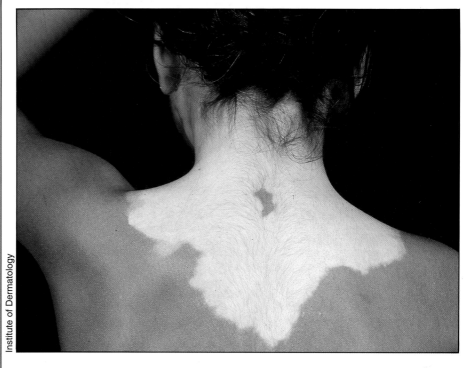

Institute of Dermatology

Vitiligo is a condition where areas of skin lose their pigment and show up as very pale patches. Fortunately the disease has no serious consequences to health, although it can represent a very important cosmetic problem to the sufferer.

Vitiligo is not uncommon: it may occur in as many as one percent of the world's population. Although many people are affected, the extent of the problem is often very slight. It seems that women are more likely than men to seek advice, mainly for cosmetic reasons, but in fact the overall incidence may actually be the same in both sexes.

Causes and symptoms

Most doctors now favor the theory that vitiligo is an autoimmune disease. An autoimmune disease is one where the body's own immune system has turned against some part of the body (see Immune system). Often the hormone-secreting glands are involved. Since vitiligo is often associated with autoimmune failure of hormone glands, it is thought to be an autoimmune disease, with antibodies being produced to pigment-producing cells. However, there is no proof that such antibodies really occur.

The disease has only one symptom, the disorder of pigmentation that can be seen

Although not a serious threat to health, the patchy loss of pigment that is the characteristic symptom of vitiligo can cause a considerable amount of distress.

on the skin. Usually this is found in areas that are exposed to the sun, such as the backs of the hands, although eventually it may become more widespread.

The depigmented areas of skin start as small spots, which then run together to produce enlarging areas of pale skin. Often the areas bordering the depigmented skin are more heavily pigmented than usual.

About half of the sufferers start losing pigment before they reach age 20. The pale areas may develop quite quickly over the course of a few months, and then remain unchanged for years.

Hair growing in pale areas may also lose its color in the course of time.

Treatment

There is no really satisfactory treatment. Drugs called psoralens have been tried, often combined with ultraviolet light, but although there may be some improvement, there is also a risk of toxicity. Steroid creams may be used on the affected patches, and this can produce limited improvement (see Steroids).

Vocal cords

Vocal cords, two strong bands of tissue inside the larynx, vibrate as air exhaled from the lungs passes over them, producing the sound that is a basis for speech.

Q Why do boys' voices change so drastically during puberty?

A The voice changes most dramatically in boys because of the sudden growth that occurs in the larynx. The voice breaks, dropping in pitch as the larynx grows and the vocal cords slacken off. This is triggered by the production of male hormones such as testosterone. The actual tone of the voice is probably inherited.

Q I have been told that I must have a laryngectomy. What does this mean, and will I be able to speak afterward?

A A laryngectomy entails the removal of the larynx, including the vocal cords, and is usually performed as a result of cancer. A small round hole is made in the neck and windpipe so that the patient can breathe. The hole is known as a tracheostomy, and the larynx and the surrounding malignant tissue are removed. Unfortunately the removal of the vocal cords means that any voice produced after the operation must be artificial. There are a number of ways by which an artificial voice may be achieved. Esophageal speech can be learned by swallowing air into the stomach and belching in a controlled manner. Alternatively, artificial vocal cords can be used in the form of a small vibrator that is placed on the neck at the site of the removed Adam's apple. When the patient exhales and mouths the words, artificial vibration of the air coming through the throat produces a functional if rather monotonous metallic voice. Recently attempts have been made to implant an artificial larynx, using synthetic reeds for the vocal cords.

Q I lost my voice a few days ago and now have a rasping cough. What should I do?

A If you smoke, stop. It worsens the condition. Rest the voice and try not to speak for a few days. Steam or linctus inhalations may help but if it does not improve in two weeks, see the doctor.

The vocal cords serve a function similar to that of the reed in a wind instrument such as a clarinet. When a musician blows air over the reed, the thin wood or plastic vibrates, producing the basic sound that is then modified by the pipes and holes of the instrument. Similarly, the vocal cords vibrate when someone vocalizes, and the sounds produced are modified by the throat, nose, and mouth.

Structure
The vocal cords are housed in the larynx. They consist of two delicate ligaments, shaped like lips, which open and close as air passes through them. One end is attached to a pair of movable cartilages called the arytenoids, while the other is firmly anchored to the thyroid cartilage, which is part of the Adam's apple. The arytenoid cartilages alter position so that the space between the cords (the rima) varies in shape from a wide V during speech to a closed slit during swallowing.

How sound is produced
The vibration of the vocal cords during speech (see Speech) occurs when the rima narrows and air from the lungs is expelled over the cords and through the larynx. The loudness of the voice is controlled by the force with which the air is expelled, and the pitch by the length and tension of the cords. The natural depth and timbre of the voice is due to the shape and size of the throat, nose, and mouth. This is why men, who generally have large larynxes and long, slack vocal cords, tend to have deeper voices than women who have smaller larynxes.

Disorders
Most disorders of the vocal cords are characterized by hoarseness of the voice due to inflammation of the larynx. This is called laryngitis (see Larynx and laryngitis), and it could occur merely as a result of cheering the local football team or because of a viral infection such as a cold. Laryngeal tumors may also cause laryngitis: these are usually nonmalignant and take the form of polyps, cysts, or growths sometimes known as singers' nodes—an occupational hazard for those people who sing for a living. They develop through constant rubbing of the vocal cords through overuse, and will usually have to be removed by surgery.

Position and structure of the vocal cords

Heavy or rapid breathing

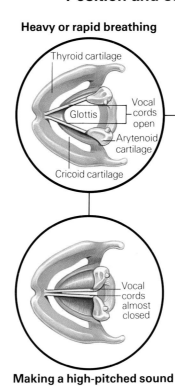

- Thyroid cartilage
- Glottis
- Cricoid cartilage
- Vocal cords open
- Arytenoid cartilage
- Vocal cords almost closed

Making a high-pitched sound

Mike Courteney

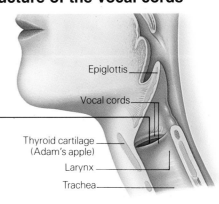

- Epiglottis
- Vocal cords
- Thyroid cartilage (Adam's apple)
- Larynx
- Trachea

The vocal cords (below) are housed in the larynx, which is situated in the throat. The details show their relative positions when they are open and closed.

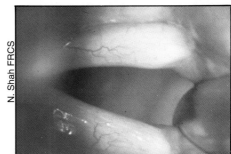

N. Shah FRCS

Vomiting

Q What is the best first-aid treatment for vomiting?

A Avoid solid foods that are likely to make you vomit more. Drink plenty of bland fluids—water or sips of soda—and avoid alcohol. If you find it impossible to keep the fluids down, suck ice cubes. A teaspoonful of baking soda diluted in a teacup of water or milk can also help. As you feel better, eat dry bread, soups, and custards. Work back to your normal diet over three or four days.

Q I have often heard people say that they had almost vomited up their insides. Can this really happen?

A No. This is just a figure of speech and rather colorfully describes a severe bout. If the vomiting is caused by food poisoning or severe gastroenteritis it can be extremely unpleasant and distressing. But no matter how violently or persistently you vomit, there is no possibility at all that you will damage your internal organs.

Q Is it necessary always to see your doctor about vomiting?

A No. In the majority of cases vomiting only lasts for a day or two and usually has a fairly obvious cause. But if you get regular bouts of vomiting, or if it is accompanied by abdominal pain, or if you have recently had a knock on the head, or if there is a possibility you may be pregnant, then you should see your doctor. Also go to your doctor immediately if the vomit contains blood.

Q I have had repeated vomiting bouts for some time, and have been persuaded to go and have tests. But I am rather worried. What is involved?

A After initial examination by your doctor, you may be sent for an X ray of your stomach. A visit to a gastroenterologist may be required, and he or she may take a direct look in your stomach with an endoscope. The tests are simple and should cause you no pain.

Vomiting may be accompanied by nausea, dizziness, and faintness—it is an exhausting and unpleasant experience. But it is a mechanism of survival that warns us of danger.

Vomiting refers to the forceful ejection of the contents of the stomach through the mouth. Commonly known as throwing up, it is an unpleasant and often exhausting experience. It can be caused by a number of conditions and is usually triggered by the middle ear, gastrointestinal tract, or the brain. The condition may be brought on by motion sickness, food poisoning, or unpleasant odors or sights, in which case it usually lasts no longer than two days. Or it may be a symptom of a more serious complaint, such as a heart attack or cancer.

Mechanism

The actual mechanism behind the ejection of food is straightforward. At the onset of vomiting, the pylorus (a muscular valve through which food normally passes from the stomach into the intestines) closes (see Digestive system). The waves of stomach contractions that normally push food downward into the intestines go into reverse, causing pressure inside the stomach to build up, the larynx (windpipe) to close, and the contents of the stomach to burst up through the esophagus and out of the mouth.

There are three main areas of the body which, when stimulated, can bring about vomiting; although the mechanism is the same in each case, the causes are different.

Stomach irritation

Irritation of the stomach lining is the most common cause of vomiting. This can be brought on by a surprising variety of conditions, including gastritis, gastroenteritis (see Gastroenteritis), peritonitis (see Peritoneum), appendicitis (see Appendicitis), and ulcers (see Ulcers); tonsillitis can also cause vomiting in young children (see Tonsils). These types of complaint are associated with viral infections and inflammation, and should be treated as soon as possible by your doctor.

The most common cause of stomach irritation is eating or drinking to excess, or eating contaminated or impure food (see Food poisoning). The body protects itself against potentially harmful substances and tries to expel what it has recognized as dangerous. The bout of vomiting is usually short-lived, lasting only a day or two, and is rarely a serious condition.

For some people, sea travel has always been a challenge! This detail from a 19th-century caricature shows some wretched passengers on a transport ship and illustrates a hazard still true today.

Mary Evans Picture Library

VOMITING

The mechanism of vomiting

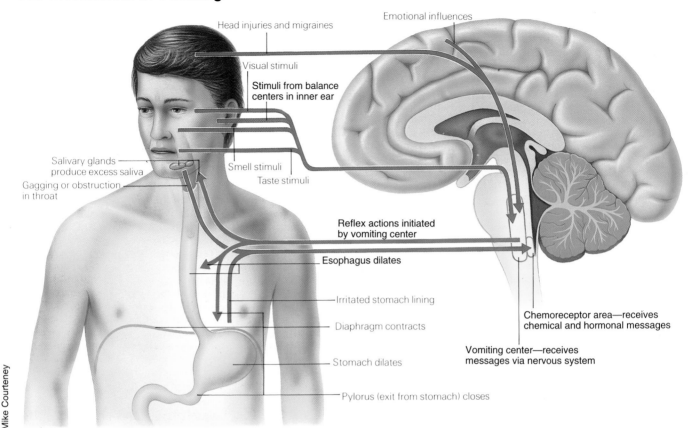

Head injuries and migraines

Emotional influences

Visual stimuli

Stimuli from balance centers in inner ear

Salivary glands produce excess saliva

Smell stimuli

Gagging or obstruction in throat

Taste stimuli

Reflex actions initiated by vomiting center

Esophagus dilates

Irritated stomach lining

Diaphragm contracts

Chemoreceptor area—receives chemical and hormonal messages

Stomach dilates

Vomiting center—receives messages via nervous system

Pylorus (exit from stomach) closes

Mike Courteney

Putting fingers down the back of the throat will also cause vomiting, and use is made of this reflex action in trying to make people empty their stomachs of certain poisonous substances. The function of this reflex is to protect the body from swallowing anything that is unsuitable. This method of induced vomiting is also used by people suffering from bulimia, when huge quantities of food are eaten and vomiting is induced shortly afterward. This is used as a form of weight control (see Anorexia and bulimia).

The ears and motion sickness
Motion sickness is another common cause of vomiting (see Motion sickness). This results from contrasting information that reaches the brain from the various organs of balance. At the center of this are the semicircular canals in the ear. If what we see conflicts with the information received from these canals, and the brain is not able to interpret the two, then it triggers off impulses to the vomiting center in the brain. This apparent warning action will result in nausea (see Nausea) and vomiting.

Some travelers are well aware of this problem, but it can also afflict sufferers of Ménière's disease (see Ménière's disease) in which the organs of both hearing and balance are affected.

The brain
A blow to the head, and it doesn't even have to be a hard blow, can be the cause of vomiting, and this usually indicates the likelihood of serious bleeding inside the skull. The desire to vomit usually occurs some time after the blow—often when one has completely forgotten about the injury, even as long as a couple of days later. It is an indication that a damaged blood vessel has allowed pressure to accumulate on the brain and around the vomiting center. This must be treated as soon as possible, because there is a very real danger that the person may slip into a coma (see Coma).

Morning sickness
Vomiting also frequently occurs in pregnancy. This is called morning sickness, a form of vomiting that is not fully understood but is believed to be related to the changing level of hormones in the blood during early pregnancy (see Hormones, and Pregnancy). In a few women it is persistent and severe and may necessitate a stay in the hospital (see Prenatal care).

Repeated vomiting
Repeated bouts of vomiting are often regarded as a symptom of a serious disorder and should be brought to your doctor's attention immediately.

Vomiting is a reflex action. Nerve impulses from around the body carry messages—of danger, irritation or even confusion—to the vomiting center in the brain stem. Toxic agents or hormonal changes act upon the chemoreceptor area nearby, and this also stimulates the vomiting center. At the same time, impulses passing to the cortex produce feelings of nausea. When the vomiting threshold is passed, the vomiting center initiates a number of physical changes that result in the ejection of the stomach's contents through the mouth.

What is brought up in the vomit is also important. It will usually consist of the last meal you had or may be almost entirely yellow-green, bitter bile. However, if it contains any sign of blood, then the implications are very serious and you should get medical advice immediately. The blood may look like dark coffee beans, since it will have congealed in the stomach well before the vomiting started.

Treatment
Where vomiting persists, or is accompanied by fever and general malaise, a doctor must be consulted, and the root cause treated. When someone has been vomiting, avoid giving solid foods; diluted milk and plenty of water is fine until the person feels able to return to a normal diet.

Vulva

Q Is soreness of the vulva always a sign of a sexually transmitted disease?

A No. There are many reasons for the vulva becoming inflamed and sore; but since it is the part of the body most intimately involved in sexual intercourse it is inevitable that sexually transmitted infection is a common cause. The important thing, especially if you may have been in contact with infection, is that you go to your doctor or a genitourinary clinic to make sure. Meanwhile, you should avoid further sexual intercourse.

Q I have developed a group of small growths on my vulva. What could be the trouble?

A This sounds very much like a condition called vulval or genital warts. This is a result of a viral infection and both men and women can be infected. It is often passed by sexual contact, though sometimes only one partner seems to be affected. Because there are as yet no effective antibiotics against viruses, treatment consists of regularly painting the warts with a caustic liquid. These preparations are very powerful and have to be applied carefully and accurately. Therefore the treatment has to be given by a doctor or nurse and cannot safely be self-administered.

Q Is it possible to get cancer of the vulva?

A Yes, cancer can develop on the vulva, but it is rare and almost entirely confined to women in the 50- to 70-year age group. It is often preceded by an area of thickening and itching on part of the labia, called leukoplakia. If you get any spots, lumps, or sores on your vulva, you should certainly seek medical advice.

Q My doctor has told me that I have *pruritis vulvae*. What does this mean?

A *Pruritis vulvae* is Latin for irritation of the vulva. This itching is associated with vulvitis, but you should consult your doctor to have the basic cause diagnosed.

The word vulva *describes the sexually sensitive outer region of the female reproductive system. The area is unfortunately susceptible to a variety of infections that are collectively known as vulvitis.*

Most prominent among the parts of the vulva are the two pairs of lips or labia. The outer and larger—*labia majora*—consist of thick folds of skin that cover and protect most of the other parts. They become thinner at the base and merge with the perineum (the skin over the area between the vulva and the anus). At the top the outer lips merge with the skin and hair on the pad of fatty tissue that covers the pubic bone, the *mons pubis* or *mons veneris*, which is often referred to as the Mound of Venus.

Within the labia majora are the *labia minora* or "lesser lips." They join at the top to form a protective hood over the sensitive clitoris, dividing into folds that surround it. They also protect the opening to the urethra. The area between the labia minora is largely taken up by a space called the vestibule. Before a woman is sexually active, the space is mostly covered by the hymen. This varies in shape, size, and toughness, and although it is usually either torn or stretched during the first sexual intercourse, it may either be strong enough to make intercourse diffi-

Situated at the entrance to the vagina, the vulva consists mainly of outer and inner lips called the labia. These folds of skin cover and protect the sensitive interior, including the main organ of sexual excitement—the clitoris.

The structure of the vulva

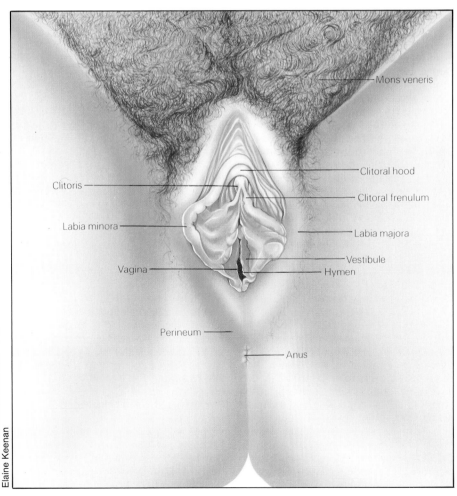

Mons veneris

Clitoral hood

Clitoris

Clitoral frenulum

Labia minora

Labia majora

Vestibule

Vagina

Hymen

Perineum

Anus

Elaine Keenan

Wearing tight-fitting, figure-hugging jeans and trousers occasionally is fine, but if they are worn every day they can trigger off inflammation of the vulva—vulvitis.

cult or, alternatively, have been previously ruptured by strenuous exercise, masturbation, or tampons. The tags of skin that many women have around the vestibule are the remains of the hymen, and are called the *carunculae myrtiformes*. At the back the labia minora join to form the fourchette, which is often ruptured during the first childbirth (see Birth).

The clitoris and glands

The clitoris is actually similar in structure to the penis, even to the extent of having a hood of labia, the equivalent of the foreskin, and a small connecting band of tissue called the frenulum. It is primarily an organ of sexual excitement. It is extremely sensitive, and when stimulated its spongy tissue fills with blood and becomes erect. Friction on the erect clitoris—either by movement of the penis during intercourse or by some other means—will usually lead to orgasm (see Orgasm). Other parts of the vulva also respond to sexual stimulation— the labia contain erectile tissue and often become enlarged during lovemaking; and the Bartholin's glands become active.

There are two pairs of glands associated with the vulva. The first are Skene's glands, which lie just below the clitoris and secrete an alkaline fluid that reduces the natural acidity of the vagina. The other, larger pair lies in the bottom of the vestibule. These are Bartholin's glands and they secrete fluid when a woman is sexually aroused so that the entrance to the vagina becomes moist and can more easily accommodate the penis. These glands are normally about the size of a pea and are not prominent. They are prone, however, to venereal and other infections, becoming swollen, red, and tender. This condition, called Bartholinitis, requires treatment with antibiotics. In some cases, an abscess forms in one of the glands—a Bartholin's abscess—and may need to be incised to release the pus (see Abcess, and Sexually transmitted diseases).

Vulvitis

This means inflammation of the vulva or of a part of it, the labia being the structures most often involved. Although vulvitis is mostly due to an infection, such as a yeast infection (monilia) or trichomoniasis ("trich"), it can also result from the friction of tight underwear or jeans, excessive rubbing or scratching, damage from stale urine or sweat, the chemical effects of vaginal deodorants, or allergy to some material or cosmetic preparation with which it comes in contact. Vulvitis

Ashted Dastor

is a likely complication of diabetes and obesity; senile vulvitis develops among the elderly as a result of decreased hormone levels (see Hormones). Currently on the increase is the form known as genital herpes, caused by infection from the herpes simplex virus (see Herpes).

Symptoms and treatment

Irrespective of cause, the symptoms of vulvitis are basically the same. The skin becomes red, sore, and itchy, and there may be some swelling. If there is a great deal of irritation—*pruritus vulvae*— scratching may make the problem worse,

causing the labia to become more sore and inflamed. In herpes, small blisters develop; these burst, leaving tender ulcers that allow bacteria to enter the vagina and cause further infection.

Treatment of vulvitis depends on the cause. It is therefore usually necessary to go to your doctor or to a genitourinary clinic for diagnosis and appropriate treatment. Meanwhile, you can get some relief from the symptoms by wearing only loose underwear or none at all, and scrupulously avoiding scratching. Also, avoid using fragranced talcum powder, which can exacerbate the condition.

Warts

Inhibiting and often embarrassing, warts are harmless growths that can make youth a time of misery. But they will go away, whether through medical treatment, so-called magic incantations, or simply when they are ready.

Q Why are warts more common among children than teenagers and adults?

A Warts are caused by a virus, to which it is possible to develop immunity so that reinfection is less likely. The strength of this acquired immunity is not as great for warts as for other common childhood viral infections, such as measles or chicken pox, but its development does mean that many people who had warts during childhood have a built-in defense against the infection as adults.

Q What is the difference between warts and verrucae?

A Verrucae are simply warts on the sole of the foot, although the virus that causes them is actually slightly different from the one that causes ordinary warts. They look different from warts elsewhere on the body because they are pressed into the foot and are usually surrounded or partly covered by a thick layer of skin.

Q Are warts ever dangerous and can they lead to further complications?

A The vast majority of warts are harmless. However, warts in the genital region can become a considerable nuisance if they obstruct the vagina, anus, or penile orifice, and wartlike growths in the throat may cause some obstruction to breathing.

Very rarely, however, a wart may develop from a benign growth into a malignant or cancerous one which requires urgent treatment, usually surgical removal.

Q I have been told that childhood warts should not be treated. Is this true?

A Childhood warts on the hands or knees are often best left alone, since they invariably disappear within three years, and often within months, whereas with treatment there is sometimes the risk of them spreading. Treatment with a salicylic acid paint may help speed up the warts' disappearance.

Warts are a very common, usually harmless, skin affliction that affect mainly children, and to a lesser extent adults and teenagers. They consist of small rounded growths that appear on the skin and can occur virtually anywhere on the skin surface, although they are most common on the hands, knees, face, and genitals.

Rarely any cause for concern, warts are usually painless and can disappear without trace within a few months or years. However, facial and genital warts may cause some embarrassment or discomfort, and these are best treated since they can

Although the virus that causes warts can be passed on by holding hands, this is no reason to put a stop to such a delightful gesture of mutual affection.

persist for years. A type of wart that appears on the sole of the foot, commonly known as a verruca, is often painful and also requires treatment (see Verruca).

Causes and transmission

Warts are caused by a virus called papillomavirus, which can infiltrate and multiply within the outermost layer of the skin cells. When the virus infects the skin, it causes the skin cells to proliferate in a disordered fashion, producing, in effect, a small, benign tumor. This is of interest to doctors since warts are the only type of growth found in humans that is definitely known to be caused by a virus (see Growths).

The wart virus is contagious and can thus be transmitted from one person to another or from one part of the body to

Sally and Richard Greenhill

another, either by direct skin contact or indirectly via an intermediate object such as a towel. A break in the skin, such as a scratch, may facilitate entry of the virus.

Hand warts are most probably transmitted by hand-holding and genital warts by sexual intercourse. The period between infection and the appearance of the warts may be weeks or months.

Warts on children are rarely transmitted to adults, probably because adults have acquired some immunity to the

and sometimes have a flat, plateaulike surface. Another variety, called filiform warts, consists of fine, elongated outgrowths from the face or neck.

Genital warts may occur in and around the folds of skin of the vulva in women or around the tip of the penis in men, or anywhere in the surrounding genital area. They often grow and spread profusely, creating clusters of cauliflowerlike growths that may cause little discomfort, despite their rather unsightly appearance.

Sometimes, however, they may obstruct normal sexual or excretory functions. Their presence should always be reported to your doctor since they often accompany more serious sexually transmitted infections (see Sexually transmitted diseases).

All warts have tiny blood capillaries, and if the surface of the wart is cut away, these appear as tiny bleeding points, or as black seeds, on the surface of the wart where the blood in the capillaries has coagulated. The presence or absence of these bleeding points or black filaments helps doctors to distinguish warts from other skin growths of similar appearance.

Treatment

Over the centuries a wide variety of folk remedies have been used in the treatment of warts, ranging from chants and incantations to rubbing the warts with plants.

A number of people have also claimed that they have special gifts or talents for charming warts away.

Although these unconventional cures may sometimes appear to work, a visit to the doctor will probably have a more rewarding result.

There are a number of different treatments for warts, but no specific drugs for combating the wart virus. However, the growths can be attacked with corrosive ointments, by freezing, or by electrically burning them off. All of these procedures are carried out by a doctor.

Common childhood warts on the hands and knees can be left to disappear in their own time, or they can be treated painlessly with an antiseptic acid paint. Applied twice a day, this usually causes the wart to disappear in two or three months.

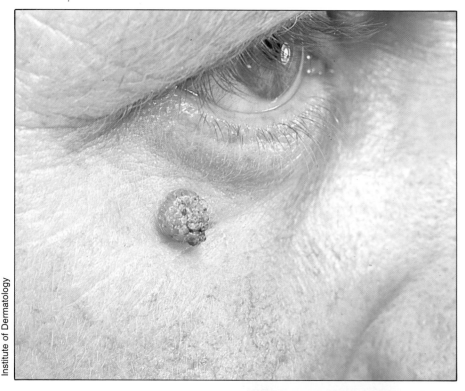

Institute of Dermatology

Troublesome adult warts on the face (above) or clusters of warts on the hands (right) can be unsightly and inhibiting. Either freezing or electrical burning techniques will remove them, in most cases, for good.

virus through infection during their own childhood. The viruses that cause common hand warts and genital warts are slightly different, so a person who was afflicted with hand warts during childhood is not immune to genital warts during adulthood.

Appearance

The appearance of warts varies a little according to where they occur on the body. Warts on the palms of the hands are usually solitary growths consisting of a hard, dome-shaped, raised area of skin with hundreds of tiny conical projections, which give the surface of the wart a velvetlike appearance. Their color also varies from pink to brown. Warts on the hands, knees, or face are often numerous

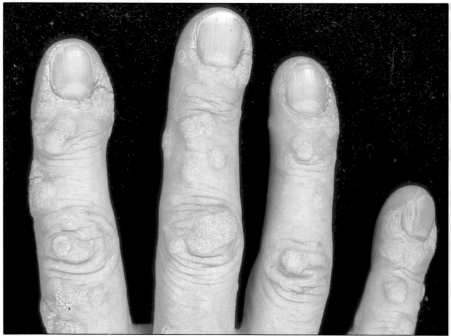

The famous Renaissance portrait of the Duke of Urbino by Piero Della Francesca is remarkable for its realism, showing hooked nose, warts and all.

Troublesome adult warts on the face or hands are sometimes treated by freezing with liquid nitrogen or solid carbon dioxide, which can be mildly painful but is very effective and causes little scarring. Electrically burning a wart off is more likely to cause a scar and is often followed by a recurrence of the infection, so this technique is less often used.

Genital warts are treated by painting them with a corrosive substance called podophyllum. This must be applied by a doctor or nurse, since careless application of the ointment can cause considerable soreness. It is important to wash the ointment off some four to six hours after it has been applied.

Podophyllum is never used to treat genital warts during pregnancy, since it may be absorbed into the body and can have harmful effects on the fetus (see Side effects).

However, even when a wart has disappeared or been removed, the wart virus sometimes lies dormant in the skin and may resume its activity some weeks or even months later.

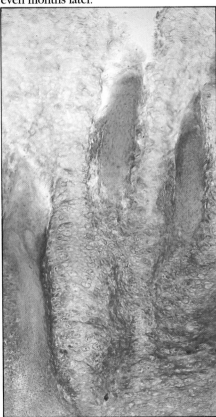

This photomicrograph of a slice of wart tissue shows the mass of active mutant cells (in purple) that are responsible for the growth of the wart.

"Magic" cures

The treatment of warts has a rich history of myth and magic, most of which probably originated in medieval days, when sufferers would have consulted the local healer for treatment. Herbs, chants, and incantations were the standard weapons against most ailments, and these treatments were effective in dealing with warts. Indeed, some of these methods are still used in rural districts. For no good medical reason, they sometimes appeared to have the desired result but it is probably more realistic to assume that the warts were about to disappear anyway.

However, some old wives' remedies may have some beneficial psychological effect, because if one is positively convinced that the remedy will work, then this may very possibly promote the wart's disappearance.

Here are some improbable cures:
- tape a cat's hair to each wart
- rub the leaves of a plant called wartwort over the growth
- bury a piece of meat in the yard
- leave a bag of pebbles with a silver coin inside by the wayside; if the finder keeps the silver coin, he or she will get a wart, while the sufferer is cured

Wax in ear

Q I've always used cotton swabs to clean my ears, but my doctor told me this could be harmful. Why is this?

A Cleaning the internal parts of the ear is unnecessary because the ear has its own self-cleaning mechanism. Cotton swabs can cause minute abrasions of the skin and expose the deeper layers to bacteria. By using a swab, you also interfere with the natural cleaning process by pushing wax deeper into the ear canal, causing blockage and deafness. Should it be necessary for a doctor to examine your ears, the impacted wax will block the view of the eardrum and delay diagnosis.

Q Is it possible to become deaf from earwax?

A Yes. Earwax can cause temporary deafness. A small amount of wax does no harm. However, if the canal is blocked completely over a period of time, or if the wax swells suddenly due to water entering the ear canal, a moderate degree of hearing loss, discomfort, and pain may result.

Q Do some people's ears have more wax than others?

A Yes. Some people, especially those who work in a very dusty environment, or who have eczema of the ear skin, profuse hair growth in the ears, or infections of the ear canal skin, are more likely to have a buildup of excess earwax.

Q Does having your ears syringed hurt at all?

A Ear syringing carried out by skilled medical personnel should be free from pain, but no one would say that it was an enjoyable experience.

Q Is it safe to attempt to syringe your own ears?

A No. If you find that your ears are blocked or you have some other complaint, consult your doctor. Hearing is very precious and any attempt to remove wax by yourself could be dangerous.

Although unsightly to look at, earwax does have a useful function: to provide a barrier against infection. The only time it needs to be dealt with is when it accumulates, and then medical help will be needed.

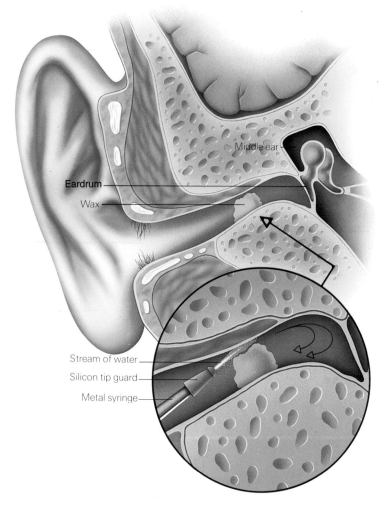

Richard Barry

Earwax, or cerumen, consists of a mixture of oily secretions of the modified sweat glands situated in the outer third of the ear canal, scales from the skin, and dust particles. It is sticky, water-resistant, and forms a natural barrier against infection.

Although earwax is harmless and is usually removed by the ear's self-cleansing mechanism, it may occasionally accumulate, causing temporary deafness (see Deafness). Medical treatment should be sought when this occurs.

Problems

In normal circumstances wax does not accumulate in the ears, because it is continually being moved outward by the movement of the jawbones and the natural shedding of the skin.

To remove wax that has become lodged in the ear, a syringe is carefully inserted into the ear canal and a jet of warm water is sprayed in, softening the wax. Then the ear is thoroughly cleansed and dried.

However, some people do produce more earwax than others. An accumulation is more likely to occur in people employed in dusty occupations, those who have excess hair in their ears, or those who have an inflammation of the skin or scalp.

Accumulated wax may cause a variety of symptoms, the chief one being temporary deafness. The wax may become impacted at the narrowest part of the ear canal by unskilled attempts to remove it with matches, hairpins, cotton swabs, or

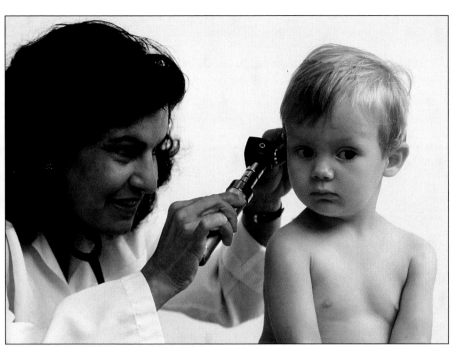

patient lies on his or her back on a couch, with the head turned to one side. Using a metal or plastic speculum, the otolaryngologist examines the ear with a microscope. Wax, any foreign body, or debris can then be removed with fine forceps. If there is a discharge of soft wax, then this can be aspirated (drawn out) using a suction tube attached to a vacuum pump.

Like most procedures, suction clearance is very safe in experienced hands and is a most satisfactory way of clearing accumulated wax from the ears.

The warning against trying to clear the wax out of your ears yourself should, however, be reiterated. Far too much damage is done by people poking about with hairpins, matchsticks, and cotton swabs. In particular, never use them on babies. If you cannot remove what you can see at the opening of the ear and wipe it away easily, leave it alone.

other implements. Accumulated wax may cause irritation and noises in the ear (see Tinnitus), but it is rarely painful.

Sudden deafness together with a feeling of pressure may occur after taking a swim or shower; this is due to water entering the ear and causing the wax to swell. Attempts to clear the ears will only push the wax deeper into the ear canal, causing pain, noises in the ear, or, more rarely, dizziness.

Treatment

Impacted earwax is one of the most common conditions seen in a doctor's office. A doctor can remove the wax safely by picking it out with very fine forceps or by a blunt hook under direct vision.

Alternatively the wax can be removed by syringing the ears. This is a safe procedure in experienced hands. Before syringing, the doctor may advise the patient to put drops, such as bicarbonate of soda in solution, warm olive oil, or a wax solvent, in the ears to soften the wax and make it easier to syringe.

Syringing is a painless procedure (see Syringing). A jet of warm water is forced into the ear canal, without touching the skin with the syringe's metal tip. The ear is then carefully cleansed and dried. Relief from deafness is immediate and dramatic. Special care and gentleness is required when syringing a child's ear. If the child is reluctant or uncooperative, it may be better for him or her to have the wax removed under anesthesia.

If the patient has a previous history of ear trouble or has had surgery on his or her ears, there may be perforation of the eardrum. The normal drum is not easily

A pediatrician examines a child's ear. Wax, a foreign body, or debris may either be removed with a fine forceps, or aspirated by a suction tube attached to a vacuum pump. The experience should be free from pain and discomfort.

ruptured, but where there has been a perforation that has healed, the scar tissue is vulnerable to injury and great care must be taken during syringing.

Where wax has accumulated in large amounts and has become solid, it should be removed by an otolaryngologist. The procedure is carried out by a suction machine, together with an operating microscope that provides high magnification and powerful illumination. The

---

General points
- Never insert hard objects like safety pins, matches, or paper clips into your ears to clean them
- If you have inflamed ears or sensitive skin, do not allow water to enter your ears. When showering, swimming, or washing your hair, protect your ears by placing a plug of cotton covered with Vaseline in the opening of the ear canal
- If you have dry skin that is causing itching in your ears, a few drops of warm olive oil once a week helps to keep the skin soft and moist and will ease the itching
- Always seek medical attention when you have an ear complaint

---

Care of the ears

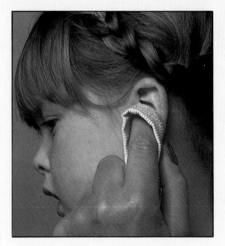

Daily care
- Wash the outer part of the ears with soap and water, and dry them gently with a soft towel. Do not rub the skin
- Should water enter your ears, hold the earlobe and shake it gently after turning your head sideways. Usually the water will run out
- If water is trapped in your ears and the wax expands and causes discomfort, do not try to remove it yourself. Consult your doctor
- If wax removal is necessary, your doctor is the expert. One specialist warned: "Never put anything smaller than your elbow in your ears"

Wellness

Q Do you have to be thin to be well?

A Excessive concentration on thinness is not healthy and may lead to a person needing help from a doctor, nutritional therapist, or psychotherapist. Over time, a well-balanced diet combined with moderate regular exercise will sort out most weight problems. Weight-loss dieting is bad because you lose healthy tissue as well as fat; your metabolism slows down, thereby counteracting the effect of reduced food intake. You must change your habits for good. Fashionable thinness is not the same as healthy thinness.

Q Do you have to cut out alcohol, coffee, and cigarettes completely to be well?

A Holistic practitioners advise cutting these substantially since they unbalance our systems. Doctors advise women to have under 14 units of alcohol a week and men under 21 units. One unit is a glass of wine, a measure of spirits, or a bottle of beer. A little wine may actually help to keep heart disease at bay. Up to three cups of coffee or tea a day are unlikely to do us harm. Researchers have found that if the occasional cigarette is your way of relaxing, it may do you more good than harm. However, there are better ways to relax.

Q Can you be well if you have a disability or have a chronic illness?

A Wellness is being as well as possible given our circumstances. A healthy diet is even more important for people whose systems are already struggling with illness. There are exercise programs designed for people with different impairments. Holistic medicine is ideal for improving the quality of life for people for whom doctors can do little: for example, massage for pain, hypnotherapy for depression. Conventional medicine is beginning to understand the role long-term mistreatment of the body has in the development of chronic disease.

Is wellness more than just absence of illness and, if so, how can we achieve it? Many of us go through life free from serious problems, but suffer symptoms such as headaches and sleeplessness that can cause misery over the years.

Karl Weatherly/Corbis

There is much advice about how to stay healthy, but often it can leave us feeling confused, and the pursuit of health itself can become just one more burden. We are led to believe that perfect health is within everyone's reach, so that, if we are sick, we find it all too easy to blame ourselves: we have not relaxed enough, we have not exercised enough, or we have eaten and drunk the wrong things. Modern medicine can achieve spectacular results in some areas but is defeated by the simplest of everyday complaints such as the common cold.

If we turn to alternative therapies (see Therapy) it is sometimes difficult to choose from the array of types offered,

A good diet and plenty of exercise are not just about health in its purely physiologic sense; health is also a joyous attitude to life.

and to know which will work for us. So how do we pick our way through all this, find the genuinely helpful advice, cope with the ups and downs of life, get the right sort of help when we need it, and still have time to be happy?

Illness and wellness
Conventional medicine (the sort provided by doctors and hospitals) takes a completely different view of illness and wellness from alternative medicine (see Holistic medicine). Doctors take the view

The healthy diet

Starchy foods—About half of what we eat should come from this group, which includes foods such as bread, rice, pasta, and potatoes. These are the foods that fill you up and keep you feeling full. Whole grain bread and brown rice and pasta are best from a nutritional point of view. This is because the outer layer of the grains contains all the vitamins and minerals and provides the fiber that keeps our digestion healthy. The inner white part is just starch.

Fruit and vegetables—These are the antiaging and antisickness agents in our diet, and are probably the most vital part of it. According to the World Health Organization (WHO) we should have at least five servings of fruit and vegetables a day. Freshness and variety are important, as is the method of preparation. Scrub, don't peel, and cook for the minimum of time; or, better still, eat them raw. Stir-fry, steam, or stew rather than boil because many vitamins are lost in the cooking water.

Protein and fat—Once we are adults it is not necessary to have protein at every meal. Only 10–15 percent of our diet needs to be made up of protein, and legumes, seeds, nuts, and grains (rice, wheat, and so on) can provide enough. Meat and dairy products should be treated with caution because they contain too much of the wrong sort of fat and are not easily digested. Fish should be eaten two or three times a week, if possible.

Sugary foods—Sugar and sugary foods such as carbonated drinks, candy, desserts, cookies, and cakes provide empty calories: lots of fattening power and no nutrients. Sugar is quickly digested and causes rapid fluctuations in our blood sugar levels that can lead to mood swings and a variety of physical problems such as diabetes and premenstrual syndrome (PMS). Sugar and sugary foods are best kept to a minimum or avoided.

limitations, to find a balanced way of life. Both doctors and holistic practitioners, however, agree that the basis of health is diet, exercise, and relaxation. Holistic practitioners go further and say that these are fundamental to our well-being on all levels. The following aims to give a flavor of both conventional and holistic wisdom.

Diet

The main constituents of a healthy diet are given in the adjacent box. However, these are only guidelines. Some people are more tolerant than others of animal products, sugar, alcohol, and so on. People who are very active or women who are pregnant or breast-feeding need more protein. We may have different dietary needs according to our body type, where we live, and the seasons. Even if we need to stick to the rules to start with, as we become healthier and more in tune with our bodies we should be able to choose intuitively what is best for us.

There may be practical, physical, or psychological reasons that make it difficult for us to eat in a balanced way. Lack

that if you have nothing seriously wrong with you, you are well. Illness is the presence of bodily symptoms (see Symptoms). These symptoms are usually caused by external factors such as germs (see Bacteria), and these germs affect everybody in the same way. Usually, treatment takes the form of drugs and surgery, although preventive health care, in the form of dietary and lifestyle advice, is becoming more of a feature.

Holistic medicine sees people as a whole—body, mind, emotions, and spirit. If all these parts of us are functioning properly and in harmony, we have a built-in ability to heal ourselves and cope with all external stresses (see Stress), whether they are caused by germs, the weather (see Seasonal affective disorder), bereavement (see Grief), and so on. Our natural state is health and happiness.

The function of holistic therapies is to give us the occasional boost when we become overwhelmed and to teach us to look after ourselves. The treatment is preventive as much as curative. With regard to maintaining our health day to day, doctors tend to lay down fixed rules that apply to everyone. Holistic practitioners, on the other hand, feel that, within certain guidelines, everyone has to find their own way of achieving health. The main goal is to work within our individual

Unhappiness and ill health, such as repeated headaches, appear to have a reciprocal bond. A holistic practitioner will address all aspects of a patient's life when dealing with his or her medical condition.

Oscar Burriel/Latin Stock/Science Photo Library

of money and time can make it difficult to eat fresh food and have regular meals. In this case, perhaps, we need to readjust our priorities.

Allergies (see Allergies) can make us crave the very food that is worst for us, and many physical illnesses (see, for example, Irritable bowel syndrome) and even psychological ones (see, for example, Anorexia and bulimia) may be caused by the wrong diet or nutritional deficiencies (see Vitamins). Emotional problems can lead to erratic eating, over- and undereating, or eating the wrong things for comfort (comfort eating).

Exercise

If we don't use our bodies, they deteriorate. We need to exercise (see Exercise) at least two or three times a week for 45 to 60 minutes to keep our bodies in good working order. Short, regular sessions are better and less risky than sporadic, prolonged ones. We don't have to be superfit, just fit enough. The box below describes the different types of exercise.

Not only does exercise keep us fit, it also makes us feel better emotionally and psychologically. Medical research in the United States in 1978 showed that it can be as effective as psychotherapy (see Psychotherapy) in treating depression (see Depression). The types of exercise that come to us from the East, such as yoga (see Yoga) and tai chi (see Tai chi), work on the body's subtle energy. This is energy said to flow around the body much like blood does.

Just as with blood circulation (see Circulatory system), the energy flow can become uneven and even blocked, and the exercise is designed to rebalance and free it. Acupuncture (see Acupuncture), acupressure, shiatsu (see Shiatsu), and reflexology (see Reflexology) work on the same energy. After this type of exercise you should feel both calmer and more full of vitality.

Eating plenty of fresh fruits and vegetables, rather than relying on convenience or processed foods, can contribute to our health and sense of well-being.

Exercise and what it can do for you

Exercise first and foremost helps us keep to the right weight. Aerobic exercise, which is activity that makes us out of breath, speeds up our metabolism, and makes us use up extra calories. It also improves the function of our lungs and heart so that the whole body is properly nourished by oxygen and blood. There are many different ways to do this—climbing stairs, fast walking, jogging, team sports, bicycling, and swimming are just a few examples. Exercise also makes us strong. Strong muscles keep our bones in the correct place so that the internal organs can function properly without being squashed or misaligned. Strong muscles are also less likely to be injured. Backache, for example, is often caused by a combination of strained muscles and poor posture, which causes the vertebrae to press on nerves. Keeping fit, gymnastic workouts, climbing, aikido, and some types of dance all increase our strength. Certain types of exercise keep us supple. Suppleness is having joints that work properly so that we can bend and stretch and move with ease and without pain. Decreasing suppleness is one of the first things we notice as we age. Dance and Far Eastern forms of exercise, such as yoga or tai chi, increase suppleness. These types of exercise are ideal for older people, or for people unused to exercise, because they are gentle and noncompetitive.

Relaxation and stress management

Stress (see Stress, and Stress management) is caused by a failure to deal with the problems that face us. Even happy events, such as going to college or the birth of a baby, can cause us stress if they mean making changes to our way of life.

Some doctors estimate that 75 percent of illness is stress related. Stress leads to a weakening of our immune system (see Immune system) so we become more vulnerable to certain illnesses. When we are stressed we are tense, and tension

A healthy way of life

How many of these statements are true for you?

My health is good. I am about the right weight for my build and height. I give and receive affection. I express my feelings when angry or worried. I have fewer than three caffeine-containing drinks (coffee, cocoa, or cola) a day. I take part in regular social activities. I eat at least one full, well-balanced meal a day. I do something just for pleasure at least once a week. There is at least one relative within 50 miles of home on whom I can rely. I have some time alone during the day. I get seven or eight hours of sleep at least four nights a week. I exercise hard enough to work up a sweat at least twice a week. I have a network of friends and acquaintances. I discuss problems such as work and money with other members of the household. I have at least one friend I can talk to about personal affairs. I smoke no more than ten cigarettes a day. I organize my time well. I have fewer than five alcoholic drinks a week.

leads to soreness and even serious problems in internal organs. Relaxation (see Relaxation) is one of the most important ways of coping with stress. It is not necessarily doing nothing. Rather it is finding time for ourselves away from the daily routine and bringing a sense of meaning into our lives. Everyone has his or her own way of relaxing, whether it is painting, listening to music, going for a walk, or doing something for someone else.

Physical relaxation helps prevent habitual bad posture (see Posture) such as hunched shoulders, which lead to aches and pains. Yoga classes always end with the corpse posture for physical and mental relaxation, and this is considered the most difficult posture of all. A therapy called the Alexander technique (see Alexander technique, and Therapy) can also help with physical relaxation. If you find it difficult to relax, try learning meditation techniques (see Meditation), autogenic training, or even self-hypnosis (see Hypnosis). Counseling and psychotherapy can teach us to react better to stressful situations or help us to find purpose in our lives. They can also help us with unresolved conflicts in our lives.

Seeking help

Sometimes we are unable to get healthy as quickly as we would like and so we turn to outside help. Holistic therapists maintain that conventional medical help should be a last resort because it upsets the natural balance of the body. However, emergencies, such as a serious infection or a severe injury, are best treated conventionally. It can be confusing choosing a holistic therapy. The simple answer is to go for one that appeals to you.

The older therapies (see Homeopathy) are better regulated and attested, but this does not mean that newer therapies, such as crystal therapy, will not work for you. Although these therapies aim to work on all levels (physical, mental, and spiritual), they tend to take a different line of attack. For example, hypnothera-

py, art therapy, and the psychotherapies work through the mind, emotions, and spirit; homeopathic remedies affect the physical and spiritual planes; and massage (see Massage), nutritional therapy, osteopathy (see Osteopathy) and herbal medicine (see Herbalism) work on the body.

A definition of wellness

The following definition of wellness comes from George Ohsawa, the founder of macrobiotics (see Macrobiotics), a dietary system based on traditional Japanese teachings. He lists the following seven conditions for true wellness:

Insomnia is a condition of perpetual tiredness that is caused by an inability to sleep for an adequate length of time. Although insomnia may be related to an illness, it is far more likely to be caused by mental unrest and unhappiness.

● **Never being tired**. If we feel tired it is because we are not resting properly, change our mind too much, or are not flexible enough to cope with our changing circumstances.

● **Having a good appetite**. For food, sex, work, knowledge, experience, happiness, health, and life. Oversatisfaction reduces our appetite so we should aim always to be slightly hungry and keep emptiness within ourselves.

● **Sleeping well**. This means sleeping deeply, not sleeping a long time, and is the result of energetic physical and mental activity while we are awake. Restless sleep is due to mental unrest.

● **Having a good memory**. This enables us to be wise. The healthier we become the more we remember, till we remember our true origins and become aware of our spiritual destiny.

● **Never being angry**. If we are truly healthy, we are in harmony with our environment. Health is the capacity to accept all circumstances with a smile and change difficulties into opportunities.

● **Being joyous and alert**. Joyousness is a natural result of good health and eating well day to day.

● **Having endless appreciation**. Even when we are physically sick, we are healthy if we are aware that we are the cause of our own sickness, thankful for the opportunity to learn, and surrender our destiny to nature in a spirit of endless appreciation. Conversely, we may be without physical or mental symptoms of disease, but, unless a deep gratitude permeates our whole life, we are not truly healthy and whole.

Alain Dex, Publiphoto Diffusion/Science Photo Library

Wheezing

The sound of wheezing is unmistakable—and sometimes frightening. Depending on the cause, it can be mild or severe, with or without recurrent episodes. However, treatment can do much to alleviate symptoms.

Q What actually causes the sound of wheezing?

A The wheezing sound is produced by air being forced through narrow tubes (bronchi) in the lungs. It can be high or low pitched, and works on the same principle as a wind instrument: the narrower the tube, the higher the note. If a single bronchus is narrowed, a single wheeze is produced, but many different-sized bronchi may be affected, giving rise to many simultaneous notes.

Q Should I give up smoking if I wheeze?

A Definitely yes! Cigarette smoke is an irritant and will make wheezing worse. Cigarette smoking itself can cause chronic bronchitis leading to permanent narrowing of the bronchi.

Q Is the wheezing caused by asthma permanent?

A No. A large number of asthmatics are entirely normal in between attacks, but they do require regular treatment to prevent further attacks.

Q Is wheezing always a symptom of some underlying condition, or can it also occur on its own?

A Under certain circumstances, wheezing can be a normal reflex. If an individual is exposed to toxic fumes or dust, a reflex bronchospasm may result: this is an attempt by the body to protect the lungs from further damage.

Q My husband had a bad heart attack recently, and lately he has been waking up at night wheezing and breathless. What could be the cause?

A With a history of heart disease, it is likely that he is suffering from episodes of pulmonary edema. When lying flat, fluid tends to accumulate in the lungs more easily. Sleeping with three or four pillows may alleviate the symptoms, but he should see his doctor to review his treatment.

Wheezing occurs when the normal flow of air in and out of the lungs during breathing is partially obstructed by a narrowing of the airways (bronchi). The noise produced is more marked during breathing out, when the air is being forced out of the lungs against the bronchial obstruction.

Mechanism

Narrowing of a bronchus may be caused by: spasm of the muscle that lines the bronchi (bronchospasm), for example, in asthma; excessive production of mucus by the glands in the bronchial wall (infection or chronic bronchitis); or edema (fluid produced by inflammation or by

Causes of wheezing

Interference with the passage of air in and out of the lungs produces wheezing. The lung section (bottom right) illustrates how, in pulmonary edema, excess fluid between *air sacs cuts down the amount of oxygen that passes into the bloodstream. The other diagrams show cross sections of bronchi with various causes of obstruction.*

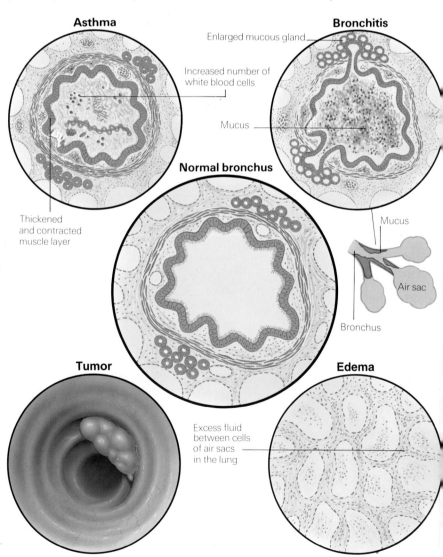

Asthma

Increased number of white blood cells

Thickened and contracted muscle layer

Bronchitis

Enlarged mucous gland

Mucus

Normal bronchus

Mucus

Air sac

Bronchus

Tumor

Edema

Excess fluid between cells of air sacs in the lung

Mike Courteney

heart failure). Often a combination of these is involved. In time this may lead to widespread narrowing of many bronchi, which can have serious effects on the function of the lungs. Occasionally a single bronchus may be narrowed, for example, by an inhaled foreign body or by a tumor growing into the bronchus.

Causes

Asthma, the most common cause, is characterized by recurrent attacks of breathlessness and wheezing, which can last from a few minutes to several hours or even days (see Asthma). These attacks are often precipitated by trigger factors such as allergy, infection, stress, or exercise.

Acute bronchitis (infection of the bronchi) can cause excessive amounts of mucus to be produced and may cause wheezing (see Bronchitis).

Although more common in babies and young children, acute bronchitis causes only mild wheezing in these cases.

Chronic bronchitis can also cause wheezing because the damaged airways are already narrowed. Once again factors such as infection, strenuous exercise, or cigarette smoking may precipitate or increase the wheezing.

Sudden attacks of breathlessness and wheezing can sometimes occur in a person suffering from heart disease or

A smoker knowingly inhales irritants each time he takes a drag, but all of us are unwittingly subjected to air pollutants unless, like this road sweeper in China, we take measures to protect ourselves.

following a heart attack, and are due to a different mechanism. If the heart is not functioning normally it may be unable to pump blood through the lungs efficiently, leading to the accumulation of fluid in the lungs (pulmonary edema).

In this case the wheezing may be accompanied by chest pain. Urgent medical treatment and usually hospitalization is required without delay.

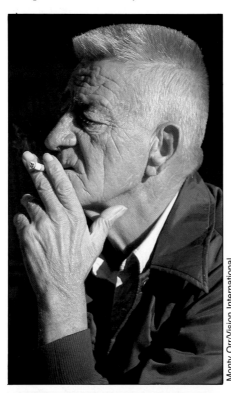

Monty Orr/Vision International

Treatment

Diagnosis is made by assessing the factors that have contributed to an attack, and the degree of airway obstruction. This is done by using a flow meter (which measures the speed at which the air can be blown out of the lungs) and a vitallograph (which measures the volume of air blown out over a given time). From this it will be decided how much of the airways' narrowing is reversible with treatment, and how much is irreversible due to permanent damage to the bronchi.

Treatment will depend on discovering the cause of the wheezing, and the severity and frequency of the attacks. An isolated attack due to acute bronchitis is usually mild and resolves itself quickly. Infection requires treatment with antibiotics and possibly a cough expectorant.

If the wheezing is marked, a bronchodilator such as ventolin may be given, either as an aerosol or in tablet form.

When there is recurrent wheezing from asthma or chronic bronchitis, regular treatment is necessary using bronchodilators and other drugs to insure that the airways are kept open.

Drugs are administered by inhalers or tablets, and the latter may be given as a long-acting preparation that need be taken only once or twice daily. For asthma sufferers, preventive treatment is also given via intal or becotide inhalers, and it is crucial that these are used regularly even when the patient feels well.

A sudden, severe attack of wheezing is usually due to acute asthma or acute pulmonary edema and requires urgent medical treatment.

If a known asthmatic becomes wheezy, two or three extra puffs of his inhaler may abort the attack. However, if it persists, medical help should be sought. Appropriate treatment is to administer injections to the patient of rapid-acting bronchodilators, and with inhaled bronchodilators via a respirator.

Acute pulmonary edema requires a similar treatment, but in this case diuretics (drugs that make the kidneys excrete large quantities of excess fluid) will also be administered, and may have to be continued for a while.

Outlook

In general, the treatment for wheezing is very effective. In the majority of asthmatics the narrowing of the bronchi can be reversed completely to normal between attacks; but where there is more severe asthma or chronic bronchitis, the narrowing may only be partially reversible. However, while wheezing and breathlessness can be very disabling, modern medical treatment has much to offer to alleviate uncomfortable symptoms.

Whiplash injury

Q Will wearing seat belts prevent a whiplash injury?

A This is one of the few injuries that seat belts cannot prevent. The injury occurs when the head snaps back suddenly if a vehicle is struck from behind. Head rests, if properly adjusted, can certainly prevent most of these injuries. Seat belts may lessen the severity of the injury by preventing the wearer from bouncing forward again once the initial blow is over, and may help to prevent other injuries where a driver or passenger could be flung against a windshield.

Q I heard that a whiplash injury can occur when a baby is abused. Is this true?

A It is possible for a whiplash injury to occur in these circumstances. It may, however, be much more difficult to diagnose than more obvious injuries caused by child abuse because there are usually no outward signs of injury at all. Therefore, since a baby cannot complain, especially of neck pain, such an injury might never be detected.

Q Are whiplash injuries as common today as they were, say, 20 years ago?

A Whiplash injuries have become increasingly common over the past 20 years. This may be partly due to the increased number of vehicles on the road. However, it may also be due to the increasing tendency for victims to file for damages, so that more cases come to the public attention.

Q Is it possible to break your neck in a whiplash injury?

A It is very rare for the bones of the neck to fracture in a true whiplash injury. In a whiplash injury the head is jerked back suddenly and the soft tissues of the neck are sprained. The type of neck injuries that cause broken bones are those in which the neck is actually loaded by an abnormal weight, for example, when diving into shallow water and cracking your head on the bottom.

With more vehicles on the road than ever before, the chances of a whiplash injury, or a sprained neck, have increased. How should a whiplash be treated, and are there any measures we can take to prevent it from occurring?

Joseph Sohm; ChromoSohm Inc./Corbis

The term *whiplash injury* conjures up images of devastating damage to the neck (see Neck). In fact, whiplash refers to a single type of neck injury that is essentially a sprain (see Sprains). Like any sprain, it can vary greatly in severity, ranging from a few days of mild discomfort to months of pain, or even to permanent disability. In the majority of cases, however, recovery is complete within about a month.

Causes

Whiplash injury is nearly always caused by traffic accidents, usually when a stationary automobile is struck from behind by another moving vehicle. When this happens, the occupants of the stationary automobile are suddenly propelled forward, causing their heads to be momentarily left behind. The neck is bent violently backward, and the muscles and ligaments at the front of the neck and throat are placed under a sudden strain. This results in minor hemorrhage (see Hemorrhage) into these muscles and ligaments, which resolves within a short period of time. In severe cases there may be momentary dislocation (see Dislocation) of one or more small joints in the neck, or even fractures (see Fractures) of the neck bones.

Properly adjusted head rests (below) are helpful in minimizing whiplash injury since they stop the head from jerking back in a rear-end collision. When a whiplash injury causes persistent pain and stiffness, a neck brace (right) can be worn to support and take over the function of the injured neck muscles and give them the rest they need to recover.

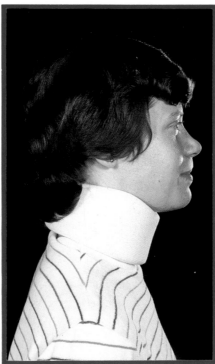

Biophoto Associates

achieved by lying flat so that the neck muscles do not have to work to hold the neck upright.

A more convenient method is to apply a collar or neck brace to support the neck: this takes over the function of the muscles and allows the individual to remain fairly active. At this stage, painkillers (see Pain management, and Painkillers) are useful to prevent sore muscles from going into spasm and worsening the symptoms.

Long-term treatment
If pain persists much beyond a couple of weeks, physical therapy (see Physical therapy) may be helpful. Gentle traction (see Traction) to the neck will relieve painful muscle spasm and reduce any pressure on the nerves that go into the shoulders and arms. Exercise (see Exercise) to mobilize the neck, often combined with heat treatment (see Heat treatment), may also help to relax tense muscles. Some patients fail to respond to any form of treatment and, in such cases, only time seems to result in any improvement.

The associated symptoms of dizziness, blurred vision, and headaches are often very difficult to treat. Again, drug treatment may be of some help, but often the patient simply has to learn to live with these irritating symptoms and wait patiently for them to subside. In the rare cases where a dislocation or fracture occurs, it may be necessary to stabilize the neck bones by means of surgery.

Outlook
Most patients recover completely within a month. With those whose symptoms become more persistent, it may take as much as one to two years for these to resolve, although again complete recovery is the rule.

vessels in the neck. X rays (see X rays) are usually unhelpful since the injuries are located in the soft tissues, which don't show on ordinary X rays.

In most cases the symptoms settle down within a few days. However, people may develop persistent pain and stiffness (see Stiffness), which may last for many months. Some of these pains may be due to underlying arthritis (see Arthritis) in the joints of the neck, which is triggered by the injury. In other cases, there is a vicious circle of pain and stiffness giving rise to muscle spasm, which in turn causes more pain and stiffness. In some cases there is a psychological element that keeps the pain going—often while an insurance claim is awaiting settlement. It has been observed that people rarely suffer from persistent problems from whiplash injuries suffered in sports, domestic accidents, or motor sport competitions, where the question of compensation does not arise (see Psychosomatic problems).

The main danger of whiplash is that symptoms will become persistent. Serious injury to the neck is rare: fractures of the neck bones, slipped disk (see Slipped disk), dislocations of the joints, spinal cord (see Spinal Cord), and nerve root (see Nervous system) injuries are more commonly caused by bending the neck forward or by direct force applied to the top of the head. Other complications may include pain so acute as to be immobilizing. Constant headaches and dizziness may require heavy medication.

Initial treatment
Initial treatment consists of resting the neck so that the neck muscles can relax and avoid going into spasm. This may be

Symptoms and dangers
Often there is little pain immediately after the accident. The following day, however, there is an indistinct pain in the neck that may be difficult to pinpoint, and this may spread into the shoulders (see Shoulder) or upper arms. Neck movements may become restricted by muscle spasm (see Muscles). Those with more severe injuries may complain of blurred eyesight (see Eyes and eyesight), headaches (see Headache), dizziness (see Dizziness), or difficulty in swallowing (see Throat) because of bruising (see Bruises) around the nerves and blood

---

Preventing whiplash injuries

- Use properly adjusted head rests: this will prevent the head from jerking back to an extreme degree in rear-end collisions
- Apply the hand or foot-brake when the vehicle is stationary: if it is hit from behind, it won't accelerate rapidly, thereby avoiding any sudden jerking of the head
- Insure that rear lights and brake lights are functioning, and that the rear fog spotlights are used in conditions of poor visibility. This will reduce the chances of a rear-end collision occurring

Whitlow

Q Is it possible that a whitlow might require surgery?

A Yes, but only minor surgery. If pus forms, letting it out by a simple incision after the skin has been numbed by an ethyl chloride spray will hasten healing and reduce pain. The old complication of an infection festering under the nail, which would require its removal, rarely happens because of effective antibiotics. Milder infections are usually treated with antiseptic paints.

Q I am a housewife and have had a nail infection for months. What can I do to make it clear up completely?

A If the skin around the nail base is normal and firmly attached to the nail, this is not a whitlow, but either a fungal infection of the nail itself (usually starting with yellowish brown discoloration at a corner of the free edge), psoriasis of the nails, or the result of previous damage to the nail bed.

However, if the nail fold is constantly inflamed and swollen, and occasionally discharging pus from a broken nail seal, this is a chronic whitlow, either bacterial or fungal. A bluish green discoloration suggests a bacterial cause. Keep the finger as dry as possible. Use cotton gloves under rubber or plastic gloves for tasks where the hands are immersed in water. Use a spirit-based paint that will kill bacteria and fungi two or three times daily on the nail folds. Treatment may take several weeks. If the whitlow is very painful or does not improve after a month, consult your doctor.

Q Can a whitlow ever mean losing a nail and, if so, would the nail grow again?

A Yes. If antibiotics are not effective, surgery may be necessary to remove the nail. This will regrow in about three months. It may not be as smoothly curved as the old one. Slight damage to the nail bed might occur during removal resulting in flattening and grooving of the new nail.

Infections at the side and base of the nail are commonly referred to as whitlows. They occur frequently, but there are several effective methods of treatment.

The area where the skin meets the nail is firmly covered by the cuticle or nail seal. But through damage to the cuticle, this seal can be broken, thereby allowing infectious agents to enter. Paronychia is the medical term for infections that result, but commonly they have acquired the distinctive name of whitlow.

Causes

Wetness, soap, and injury are the main causes of cuticle damage. Excessive immersion in water softens and weakens the cuticle while prolonged contact with soaps and detergents removes oil from the skin, leaving it less supple and more likely to split. For this reason, whitlows most often affect housewives and others whose hands are repeatedly in water.

Minor injuries may also damage cuticles. Fingers are particularly prone to injury since they are used so much in work and play. A baby's whitlow may be caused by injury and by the wet environment produced by thumbsucking. Careless manicuring may damage cuticles, but,

A whitlow at the base of a nail can be very unsightly. Excessive immersion of the hand in water, washing dishes without gloves, for example, can cause the infection.

equally, neglect may result in the cuticle at the base of the nail growing out over the half-moon and splitting and curling up so it is caught and damaged.

Symptoms and treatment

Chronic whitlows usually occur in fingers damaged by immersion in water. The infection is slower to develop, but is persistent or recurrent. Pus may ooze out from under the swollen nail fold (see Pus). The nail may be ridged and furrowed due to infection having damaged it as it was formed, and it may become infected and discolored at the edges. Before treatment the bacterium or fungus must be identified by swabbing and culture. Local treatment with antibiotics or antifungal paint is needed and may take many months. The fingers must be kept dry.

Acute whitlows are sudden, severe infections, usually due to injury. The nail fold becomes inflamed, hot, swollen, and painful. Pus may form and grow close to the nail plate and will require incision.

Oral antibiotics are a quick and effective treatment, and sulfate paste applied to the whitlow for a day or two relieves the pain and swelling. Milder infections respond to antiseptic paints such as one percent gentian violet in spirit.

Institute of Dermatology

Whooping cough

Highly infectious and very distressing for its sufferers, whooping cough can be one of childhood's most dangerous illnesses. However, it can be effectively prevented by immunization in infancy.

Q Do most doctors now advise immunization against whooping cough?

A Yes, providing there is no history of convulsions or brain damage in you or your children. It has been shown that the risks of severe illness from whooping cough are greater than from the vaccine.

Q Why is whooping cough such a dangerous illness in babies and small children?

A Children who have whooping cough produce very thick, sticky mucus in the air passages to the lungs and this can prevent air from getting to the lungs unless it is coughed away. Small children are sometimes too weak to cough up this sticky plug and their lungs get blocked. Babies can suffer lack of oxygen, which causes brain damage, and are also vulnerable to pneumonia.

Q Does a baby get natural immunity to whooping cough from its mother?

A No. Pertussis antibodies, or the cells in the blood that fight the whooping cough infection, do not seem to pass across the placenta. Consequently babies are born without any protection against whooping cough. They can get some immunity from the colostrum (the breast milk in the first days after birth) if they are breast-fed. However, because it is such a dangerous illness in small babies, they should be given antibiotics immediately if they come into contact with the virus.

Q My three-year-old son recently recovered from whooping cough but still has the whoop. How long will this last?

A It can be as long as three or four months before it goes. Also, every time he has a cold the whoop may get worse. Don't worry, however, it's not another attack of whooping cough. Some of the whoops may even be just a habit. Incidentally, the Chinese call the illness the hundred-day cough because it can last that long.

Whooping cough, or pertussis as it is medically known, is a highly infectious bacterial disease caused by *Bordetella pertussis*. Anybody who has neither had, nor been immunized against, whooping cough can catch it. The disease is spread by droplets of bacteria (see Bacteria) that are in the air. The bacteria settle in the mucous lining of the respiratory tract (see Lung and lung diseases, and Throat), causing inflammation (see Inflammation) and production of a thick sticky mucus (see Mucus).

Incidence of whooping cough

Whooping cough in the unprotected may be severe and even dangerous, especially in very young children, and often requires admission to the hospital (see Hospitals). Nearly half of infants under one year who develop whooping cough suffer periods of failure of breathing (see Breathing),

and about a quarter of those under six months of age show pneumonia (see Pneumonia) on X-ray examination. About 2 percent of all people with whooping cough suffer seizures. These are most common in infants under six months. Overall, the death rate in whooping cough is about 1 in 200. Most of the deaths occur in babies younger than six months, and the principal causes of death are brain damage (see Brain damage and disease) from lack of oxygen (see Oxygen), toxin from the *Bordetella* organism, and secondary bacterial infection (see Bacteria, and Infection and infectious diseases). Many babies are infected with

Whooping cough immunization carries a minimal risk of complications. A parent may be asked to sign a form consenting to the vaccination and exonerating the doctor who gives it from responsibility.

Mike Abrahams/Network

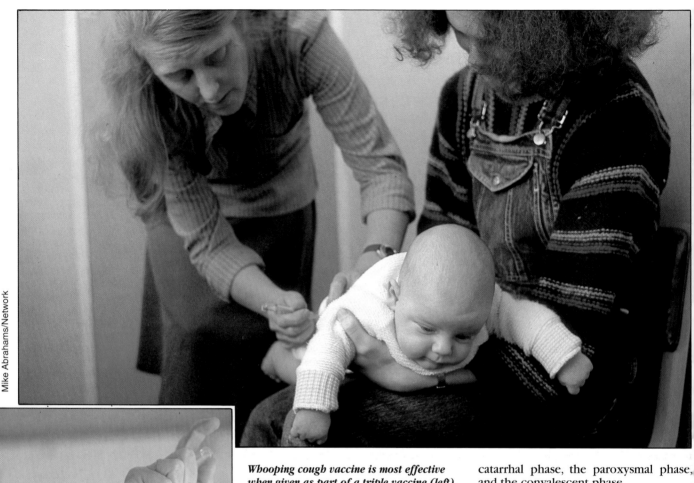

Mike Abrahams/Network

Whooping cough vaccine is most effective when given as part of a triple vaccine (left), the other two being diphtheria and tetanus. This three-month-old baby (above) is having the first of three doses. In the 48 hours following a vaccination a baby may suffer a slight reaction and become feverish or irritable. Redness or swelling often occurs at the site of the injection but will soon settle down, leaving a small lump that disappears in a month or two.

whooping cough by adults who are suffering from a mild form of the disease, and whose earlier immunity has waned.

Course of the illness

The incubation period (see Incubation) lasts 6 to 20 days from contact, with 7 days as an average. The patient is infectious from the catarrhal phase and for about four weeks, and he or she should be isolated for a month or until the cough has stopped (see Quarantine). Children under the age of one year in particular should be kept away from those who have the condition. The illness can be divided into three distinct stages: the

The organism Bordetella pertussis causes whooping cough and is used to make the vaccine, which works by stimulating the body to produce antibodies to the infection.

catarrhal phase, the paroxysmal phase, and the convalescent phase.

The catarrhal phase lasts one or two weeks. Initially the symptoms are rather like a cold (see Common cold): runny nose, red runny eyes, a slight cough, and temperature (see Fever). The paroxysmal phase lasts from two to four or more weeks, and in this stage there are episodes of coughing, becoming increasingly worse and more frequent, often up

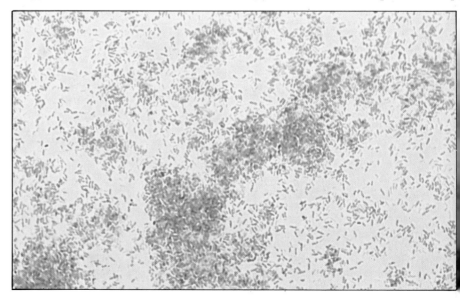

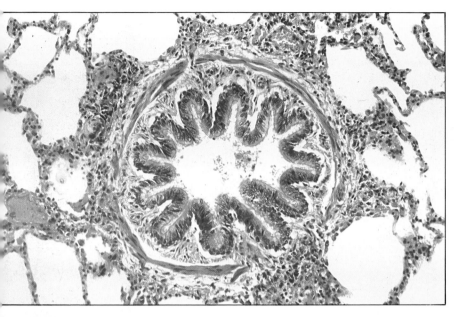

Whooping cough particularly affects the bronchioles—the tubes that carry air to the lungs (seen here in cross section).

to around 40 bouts a day. The bouts consist of 5 to 10 repetitive coughs while breathing out, followed by a sudden effort to breathe in, which in older children produces the characteristic whoop (see Coughs). The face goes red or blue, the eyes bulge, the tongue sticks out, both eyes and nose run, and the veins in the neck become more obvious. Episodes of this coughing occur until the patient manages to dislodge the plug of mucus. During this time, in severe attacks, young children may lack oxygen (see Oxygen) and stop breathing or have a convulsion (see Convulsions).

At the end of the coughing bout the child will vomit (see Vomiting). The vomiting is really more characteristic of whooping cough than the whoop. These episodes are extremely exhausting, and infants become tired and lose weight. Attacks can be triggered by movement, yawning, sneezing, eating, drinking, or even by thinking about them. In between attacks, the patient appears relatively well.

During convalescence (see Convalescence) the paroxysmal cough, whoop, and vomit gradually subside, although the cough and whoop may last for many weeks or months, and often recur if the child catches a cold or throat infection (see Throat).

Diagnosis

The diagnosis (see Diagnosis) is usually made on the clinical symptoms, but in older children and adults who suffer a milder attack this can be difficult. The best method is to take a swab (see Specimens) from the back of the nose (see Nose) and do a culture. Blood tests are not very helpful, though the number of lymphocytes (a type of defensive blood cell) may be very high, which aids diagnosis. Otherwise, two samples of blood are needed, at the beginning and end of the illness, to show a rise in pertussis antibodies during that time. If the sample is not taken early enough, it won't show a large enough rise to make the diagnosis.

Complications

Most deaths from whooping cough are caused by complications such as pneumonia (see Pneumonia). Usually pneumonia is not due to pertussis bacteria, but to other invading bacteria that enter the affected lungs. Plugs of mucus may block off the bronchi (the tubes leading the air from the throat to the lungs), and cause the lung to collapse. It may then become infected by bacteria. Sometimes the lung collapse is permanent.

The most serious complications of the established disease in children who have not been protected by immunization are those affecting the brain. It must be remembered that the type of cough produced by this organism makes it almost impossible for the child to take a breath in the course of a paroxysm of coughing. One cough follows another so rapidly that there is not time to breathe in. It is only when the long paroxysm has passed that the child can inspire, and even then, obstruction to inspiration—the cause of the whoop—further impedes air intake. The thick mucus that forms in the bronchial tubes in whooping cough tends to obstruct the bronchi.

All this adds up to the risk that the child will fail to get enough oxygen. Since the brain has much higher oxygen requirements than any other organ of the body, this situation can lead to brain deprivation and damage. Although this is very rare, the effects can be disastrous. They include convulsions, blindness, deafness, movement disorders, paralysis, coma, and death.

Treatment

Antibiotics (see Antibiotics) are not helpful once the illness has begun, but if the antibiotic erythromycin is given to a child who has been in contact with the disease before any symptoms appear, the severity of the illness may be reduced. The drug is given to children who have whooping cough because it makes these children less infectious to others.

Other treatment is symptomatic: avoiding stimuli that cause coughing; a warm room, especially at night; small and frequent drinks and meals; and no rushing about. Children who go blue during coughing bouts, or who cannot keep fluid down, need hospital admission for oxygen therapy, suction to remove mucus plugs, and replacement of fluids either by a tube

A child with whooping cough should be kept warm at all times. Your doctor may prescribe antibiotics, which will make the child less infectious to others. The most trying period is the paroxysmal phase, when coughing is most severe. This can last up to four weeks and usually subsides over the following months until recovery is complete.

Q My daughter had whooping cough last winter and since then has had a series of coughs and colds. Does this mean that the illness has weakened her resistance to infection?

A No. It's probably just bad luck. However, you should ask your doctor to check her over because sometimes part of the lung collapses after whooping cough and this may be her problem.

Q Is croup the same as whooping cough?

A No. Croup arises from a viral infection that causes swelling of the larynx so that when a child breathes in there is rather a harsh bark. It's not usually associated with a paroxysmal cough or vomiting, and generally gets better in a few days.

Q My granddaughter has a bad cough that sounds very much like a whoop, and she sometimes vomits at the end of a coughing fit. Could this be whooping cough?

A Yes, it might be. Although sometimes the phlegm in a bad cough can cause vomiting, it rarely causes a whoop. Take her to your doctor and keep her away from other children, particularly babies.

Q Is it possible to get whooping cough even after immunization?

A Yes, it is, though it's a much milder disease. It's more likely to reoccur in teenagers and adults who were immunized as babies, rather than in children.

Q My child has had convulsions and the doctor won't give her whooping cough vaccine. Should she also not have had the tetanus and diphtheria vaccine?

A No, there is no evidence at all that the tetanus and diphtheria vaccine causes any neurological problems, and it is very important that she should have these and the polio vaccine that is usually given at the same time.

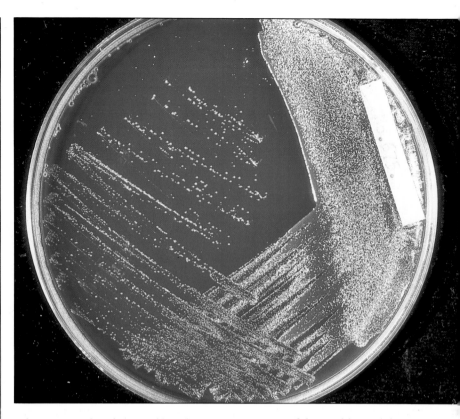

Whooping cough is diagnosed by taking a swab from the patient's nose and using it to prepare a bacterial culture. The organism can thus be accurately identified.

through the nose into the stomach, or by injection into a vein. Some doctors give a mild sedative (see Sedatives) to reduce coughing spells.

Prevention

Lifelong prevention only occurs after an attack of whooping cough, so that pertussis can only be prevented by active immunization with the pertussis vaccine. The vaccine consists of a suspension of killed organisms of *Bordetella pertussis*. They stimulate the body to produce antibodies without actually giving rise to an attack of whooping cough.

The vaccine has to be given in three doses to give about 95 percent protection against the disease. The vaccine is more effective if given at the same time as diphtheria and tetanus vaccine (hence the triple vaccine of diphtheria, tetanus, and pertussis given to most infants).

The American Academy of Pediatrics recommends that a course of five whooping cough vaccinations be given to children at two months, four months, six months, 15 to 18 months, and four to six years. Immunity from whooping cough wanes steadily after immunization and an additional booster dose is necessary for adolescents (15 to 17 years of age) and young adults (25 to 30 years of age). The purpose of these additional doses is to get rid of a reservoir of *Bordetella* organisms in older people, which is known to be a source of infection for young children.

The immunization controversy

Whooping cough was once common in the United States, but, following widespread immunization, its incidence declined and for the past ten years has remained at a steady level in communities in which immunization uptake has been high. There have, however, been sporadic epidemics from time to time as a result of failure of immunization programs, usually because of the fear of side effects (see Side effects). The death rate from whooping cough has been reduced by immunization to very low figures indeed.

In view of these facts it is no longer acceptable that parents should be influenced by out-of-date information about the risks of immunization. In the mid-1970s, when vaccination against whooping cough had been widely used for about 16 years, reports began to appear about cases in which children had suffered convulsions and permanent brain damage attributed to such immunization. Because the same effects are a feature of the disease, there was no clear evidence that these cases were due to the immunization. However, severe anxiety among parents led to a widespread rejection of whooping cough immunization. The result was major whooping cough epidemics with the deaths of many young children.

Risks of immunization

The common adverse reactions from whooping cough vaccination consist mainly of swelling and redness at the site of the injection. A small, painless lump may form. This is of no consequence and will disappear in due course. Occasionally the reaction takes the form of crying, screaming, and fever. Very occasionally a child will become pale for a time and go limp. Convulsions sometimes occur, but these are not uncommon in children in the first year of life, whether they have been immunized or not.

In one major research study in Britain, the conclusion was that the number of cases was too small to provide conclusive evidence that the vaccine could cause permanent brain damage. Studies in the United States produced similar findings. In one of these a group of children who had seizures or floppy episodes within 38 hours of vaccination were checked six or seven years later. None of them showed serious brain damage or intellectual impairment.

When not to vaccinate

Because of the risk of complications, pertussis vaccine should not be given to any child who has a temperature or feverish illness; who has had convulsions, or whose parents or siblings have had convulsions; who has late development; or who has a known disorder of the central nervous system (see Nervous system). If there is any severe local or general reaction such as a very high temperature (see Temperature), confusion, odd behavior, or a convulsion after the first immunization, pertussis vaccine should be left out of subsequent vaccinations.

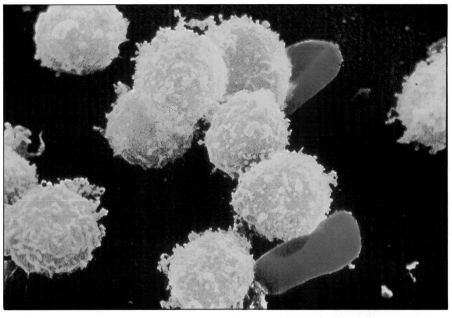

Science Photo Library

New vaccines

As we have seen, immunization against whooping cough is given in a combined form with a triple vaccine that also protects against diphtheria and tetanus. Immunization is highly effective. Traditionally, the whooping cough vaccine has contained the *Bordetella* organism that has been killed by heat so that it cannot cause the disease. This is called whole cell vaccine, and it fairly often causes minor to moderate local reactions. A few unusually sensitive individuals have had seizures.

Because of concerns over these side effects new whooping cough vaccines have been developed and tested since the late 1970s and early 1980s. These contain

A mild attack of whooping cough may be difficult to diagnose. In this case, raised levels of lymphocytes (the round, colored yellow cells) in a blood sample may be a useful aid in identifying the illness.

purified extracts of the *Bordetella* organism and thus are called acellular vaccines. Several of these have been licensed for use in the United States. When combined with diphtheria and tetanus toxoids they are called DtaP vaccines.

At present acellular whooping cough vaccines are recommended only for children between 15 months and seven years of age, and for children believed to be at risk of seizures if given whole cell vaccine (see Vaccination).

Incidence of whooping cough in the United States

The effect of pertussis vaccine on the incidence and mortality of whooping cough in the United States. The straight black lines superimposed on the graph indicate the trends prior to the vaccine and as projected if vaccine had not been introduced.

Incidence
Mortality

year

Withdrawal symptoms

Q I've heard that people can become habituated rather than addicted to certain drugs. Will they have the same withdrawal symptoms once they quit the drug?

A When a doctor refers to drugs to which patients can become habituated, he or she probably means those drugs that are habit-forming. These would include mild painkillers, and laxatives. With addictive drugs, patients experience quite severe withdrawal symptoms. However, when a patient comes off a habit-forming drug, he or she may only have a vague sense of unease and loss. Nevertheless, it can be almost as difficult to persuade someone to stop using a habit-forming drug as it is to persuade someone to stop a true addiction.

Q Why do people go back on drugs once they've quit, especially after they have suffered such terrible withdrawal symptoms?

A There are probably two main reasons for this. In the case of heroin withdrawal, there is a phase during which the acute symptoms of withdrawal are over but there are still bodily changes that result from long-term use of the drug. Breathing control is not quite normal, and there may even be such symptoms as premature orgasm or ejaculation. This phase may go on for some time, and addicts who are particularly distressed may be tempted to have immediate relief of these low-level symptoms by taking some of the drug. Second, it is important to remember that the drug and the habit were once the central part of the addict's life. If this keystone is removed, then something else must be put in its place. Otherwise, the social and psychological pressures that helped to foster the addiction in the first place will simply push the addict back to his or her old habit. The success of some community projects in getting people off drugs is probably explained by their ability to replace the drug with something more meaningful in the addict's life.

Most of us have seen vivid portrayals of the agonies of withdrawal from drugs or alcohol on our television and movie screens. But what actually happens during withdrawal, and what are the dangers to the addict?

Transworld Features

Addictive drugs, however undesirable they may be, are deeply embedded in modern culture (see Drug abuse). Addictive drugs include not only so-called hard substances like heroin (see Heroin), morphine (see Morphine), and cocaine and crack (see Cocaine and crack), but also such everyday and socially acceptable drugs as alcohol (see Alcoholism) and cigarettes (see Smoking). Once the addict attempts to end his or her addiction, he or she will suffer from withdrawal symptoms. Most of these symptoms can be very unpleasant and, in some cases, even fatal.

The confirmed heroin addict will beg, borrow, steal—and worse—to feed his habit and keep the specter of withdrawal at bay.

Above all, the addict will have to have great strength of character, combined with medical treatment, to be able to survive the withdrawal from the addictive drug (see Rehabilitation).

What is addiction?
Drug addiction has a number of characteristics. When there is true physical dependence, an addict will experience a

Withdrawal from an addiction is only the first stage in an addict's long and arduous journey toward well-being. Therapy sessions can prove vital in enabling former addicts to get to the root of their addiction and to gain strength from others who are undergoing similar experiences.

John Greim/Science Photo Library

physical illness that can be recognized as withdrawal symptoms when the drug is stopped. Further, addicts will develop what is known as tolerance to their addictive drug. This means that they gradually end up taking huge amounts without suffering from the effects that could quite possibly kill a nonaddict.

One peculiar aspect of this tolerance serves to underline how addiction may be regarded as a state of mind in the drug user (see Psychology). Most addicts admit that they found the first experience of their drug rather unpleasant. This is particularly so with morphine and heroin, but it is also true of cigarettes: few smokers can honestly say they enjoyed their first cigarette. Something in the addict's state of mind or social circumstances causes the addict to persist with a habit despite the side effects (see Side effects) and until tolerance is built up.

Morphine and heroin

There are two separate aspects to the withdrawal of these drugs. First, the patient will go to extreme lengths to try to get a further dose of his or her drug, while the level of his or her anxiety will increase as the time for a fix approaches. Second, the addict will experience very specific physical symptoms once the drug is withdrawn. These include tears, a runny nose, and sweating (occurring about eight hours after the last dose),

Withdrawal symptoms

Drug	Symptoms	Duration of symptoms	Treatment
Morphine and related drugs such as heroin	Symptoms start at the time that the next dose is due and include increasing anxiety. Other symptoms include sweating, goose bumps, trembling, and disturbed sleep. Later, muscle spasms, abdominal pains, and diarrhea may set in	Symptoms last for a varying length of time depending on the duration of action of the drug. With heroin, the symptoms start after a few hours and they are at their height between 36 and 72 hours later. This is followed by a period which may last for weeks or months when there may be disturbances of bodily functions	Symptoms can be stopped at any time with a dose of an opiate drug. Many treatment centers like to change from heroin to methadone before withdrawal is attempted
Barbiturates	Restlessness, anxiety, trembling, confusion, vomiting, and disturbed sleep. Convulsions often occur. Roughly half of patients go on to develop a full-blown delirium	Duration depends on which drug is used: symptoms last longer in long-acting drugs. If delirium occurs, it is usually on the third day. Four or five days may be required for full recovery	The addictive drug will stop the attack at any time, which is why a gradual lowering of the dose is used. Once the delirium occurs, no drug is able to stop it
Alcohol	Mild: trembling relieved by another drink. Moderate: anxiety and hallucinations. Severe: fits and delirium tremens (DTs) with severe hallucinations. Collapse and death are not uncommon	Minor withdrawal shaking can be seen after a drinking bout and resolves within a few hours. Moderate symptoms take a day or so to get better but the DTs may take up to a week	Like other drugs, alcohol itself will stop the symptoms. Minor symptoms can be relieved with a drug called chlormethiazole: this has replaced the practice of giving small doses of alcohol during withdrawal. The DTs must be allowed to run their course
Cocaine and crack	Irritability and tiredness. Long-term users can suffer with depression.	Uncertain. Depression can be long-lasting	None
Amphetamines and other stimulants	Sleepiness, lassitude, overeating, agitation, and depression	Similar to cocaine and crack	None
Tobacco	Irritability, anxiety, and overeating	May last for weeks	Nicotine chewing gum may help people over the withdrawal symptoms

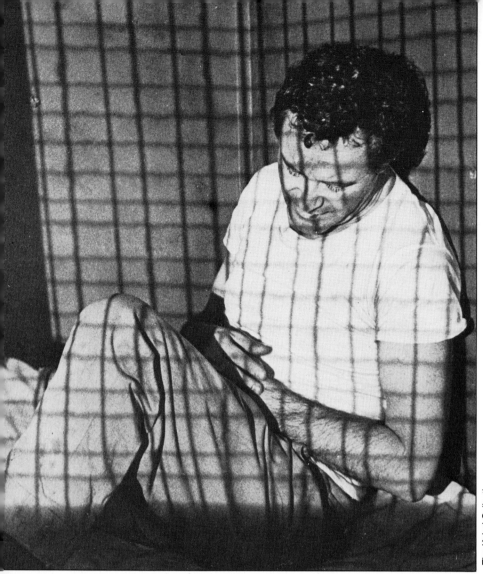

The addict will begin to have hallucinations (see Hallucinations), which can be very frightening.

On the third day, the patient will have full-blown delirium tremens (DTs). During this time the patient is delirious and often hyperthermic (overheated). As with heroin withdrawal, collapse of the circulation can occur and this can be fatal. Fits often result from the withdrawal of alcohol and are almost inevitable if barbiturates are suddenly stopped.

Crack and cocaine
Occasional users of cocaine suffer few and minor withdrawal symptoms. These commonly amount to no more than a degree of irritability and lassitude and a desire to indulge again in the drug. Long-term users may suffer more marked withdrawal effects. There may be severe depression. The withdrawal effects of cocaine are virtually the same as those of amphetamine.

Treatment
During withdrawal from morphine and heroin, symptoms are made less unpleasant by giving the addicts a morphinelike drug called methadone, which is given by mouth. Because this drug persists longer in the body, the symptoms do not come on so suddenly or so severely, although they will actually last longer. Gradual reduction of the dose over weeks or months also helps to reduce the severity of the symptoms.

In alcohol withdrawal, a drug called chlormethiazole may help to reduce or even abolish the symptoms. The drug can also be used in barbiturate withdrawal. However, it is unable to stop the DTs once they have developed.

Perhaps the most common withdrawal symptoms occur on quitting smoking. These include irritability and anxiety, and a tendency to eat more and put on weight. Smokers can be helped by nicotine chewing gum. Nicotine seems to be one of the main addictive factors, although it is only one of about 3000 compounds in cigarette smoke. Once a smoker has stopped cigarettes and changed over to the gum, he or she may find it very easy to go on reducing the amount of gum until he or she is using none at all.

In cases of addiction to drugs, alcohol, or barbiturates, however, even after withdrawal symptoms have abated, there is often a need to continue treatment, usually in the form of rehabilitation. Willpower on its own may not be enough, especially if addiction has involved a hard drug such as morphine or heroin.

Most developed countries have social machinery to combat both drug addiction and alcoholic problems, and a backup program that provides reinforcement and support is a vital adjunct of this.

followed by a period of restlessness and disturbed sleep (see Sleep and sleep problems). Upon waking, the addict will have more severe symptoms such as uncontrollable trembling, goose bumps, and irritability that can often result in violent behavior.

The real crisis of withdrawal, however, occurs after about 48 hours. The addict will suffer a runny nose as during a severe cold, sweating, goose bumps, uncontrollable yawning, muscle spasms that cause sudden and uncontrollable kicking, abdominal pains (see Abdomen), and diarrhea (see Diarrhea). Although the addict is extremely weak and depressed at this stage, there may be uncontrolled activity of the nervous system (see Nervous system), with ejaculation in men and orgasm in women (see Orgasm). Occasionally the blood pressure (see Blood pressure) falls sharply, causing collapse and sometimes even death.

The symptoms recede after a week or 10 days. After this, though, it is still possible to detect the effect of the drug on the body: for example, breathing control is disturbed (see Breathing), and there is an exaggerated increase in breathing as the amount of carbon dioxide in the blood

Withdrawal symptoms from alcohol, as seen in this still from the movie **The Days of Wine and Roses**, *can be similar to those of heroin.*

rises. The addict is very likely to go back to drugs during this second phase. In fact, this vulnerability represents continuing bodily dependence on the drug, and it is during this phase that the addict trying to break the habit needs most support.

Alcohol and barbiturates
The symptoms of barbiturate withdrawal are very similar to those of alcohol withdrawal. The first stage of alcohol withdrawal may occur in people who only drink moderately, but who have had one or two heavy drinking sessions in the course of the previous few days. There is often a pronounced shaking of the hands, which is relieved by taking another drink. This alcoholic tremor is a definite sign that drinking is getting beyond control and should be stopped or, at the very least, cut down.

The next stage is one of anxiety (see Anxiety) and agitation. This only occurs in chronically heavy drinkers and happens about 24 hours after the last drink.

The Kobal Collection

Worms

Q How can you avoid getting worms in the tropics?

A Hygiene is very important, since many roundworms are spread by taking in food or water contaminated with human feces. Hookworm can be avoided by wearing shoes. Many filarial worms are spread by bloodsucking insects, so try to avoid insect bites.

Q Can you avoid worms by cooking food thoroughly?

A Yes, there are some worms that can be avoided by cooking food thoroughly. Both the common tapeworms are spread by undercooked beef and pork. The larvae die at 144°F (62°C), so very high temperatures are not necessary. A tapeworm that is found in fish (*Diphyllobothrium latum*) occurs in Scandinavia; it is caught by eating raw fish. *Anisakis marina* is another parasite that can be ingested with raw fish; it is a parasite of herrings and infects humans in Holland and Japan, where raw herring and sushi are eaten. There are also two forms of liver fluke in Asia that can only be caught by eating raw or undercooked fish.

Q I was horrified to find that my child had roundworms. Are they common in the States?

A Although most common in the tropics, the United States has up to 4 million cases of ascariasis each year. Drugs are used to kill the roundworms in the intestines.

Q What worms are you likely to get in the US?

A Pinworms (enterobiasis) are the only really common problem, particularly among young children. They live in the intestines and the female deposits eggs near the anus. Severe anal itching is the most obvious sign and the eggs are transmitted when they are embedded under the fingernails and later deposited on bedding, clothing, food, or in the air. Treatment is by two doses of pyrantel pamoate, and usually involves the entire family.

Throughout the world worms constitute a major health problem. Although few serious types of infestation are likely to occur in temperate climates, in the tropics worms cause a wide range of debilitating diseases.

Worms are referred to as helminths. They are many-celled animals as opposed to the single-celled bacteria (see Bacteria) and protozoa that are the other main parasites (see Parasites) of man. Of the parasitic worms, each species has a specific life cycle that allows infestation to continue and to pass through another animal before infesting a human host. For example, schistosomes, which cause schistosomiasis, pass through a phase of development in the water snail before infesting humans.

Some of the worms that cause trouble in humans actually have another animal as their primary host. The host is the animal in which the worm reaches its adult form, and any animal that it infects during the egg or larval stage is called the intermediate host. In this way, the larvae of the echinococcus worm, which infests dogs, may be passed in the larval stage to humans, forming a hydatid cyst that develops in the human liver.

Helminths that cause trouble in humans are divided into three major groups. The first of these are the nematodes, the roundworms producing such diseases as elephantiasis. Next are the cestodes or tapeworms; and last the trematodes, or flatworms, which give rise to schistosomiasis and liver fluke infestation. The cestodes and trematodes have similar life cycles.

Nematodes

The nematodes have a wide range of shapes and sizes and great variability in the way their life cycles work. Those of medical importance to humans include various types of roundworm.

Filariae are a very important group of worms that cause such diseases as elephantiasis (see Elephantiasis), and river blindness. The adult worms are round, and both males and females need to be present in the primary host so that reproduction can take place. These worms are carried from person to person by a bloodsucking insect, with a different insect species for each species of worm.

In general, the pattern is that the adult worms mate and the female produces a large number of larvae, or microfilariae, which swarm into the human host's bloodstream. If an insect bites the infected human, microfilariae are taken in with the blood. These develop in the mosquito, and are injected back into another human, setting up a new infestation and thus spreading the infection.

Young children are most at risk from picking up common roundworm larvae from kittens and dogs; parents should therefore insure that strict rules of hygiene are applied to both children and pets.

How worms infest humans

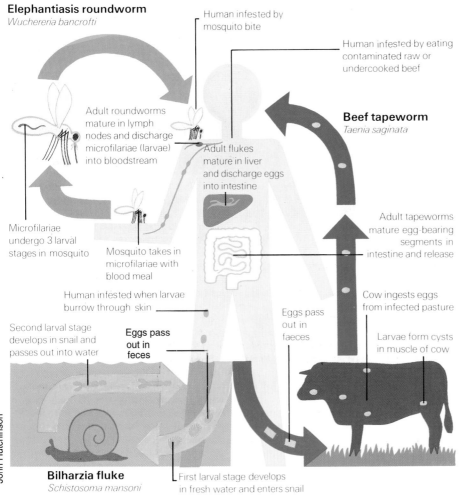

Elephantiasis roundworm
Wuchereria bancrofti

Human infested by mosquito bite

Human infested by eating contaminated raw or undercooked beef

Beef tapeworm
Taenia saginata

Adult roundworms mature in lymph nodes and discharge microfilariae (larvae) into bloodstream

Adult flukes mature in liver and discharge eggs into intestine

Adult tapeworms mature egg-bearing segments in intestine and release

Microfilariae undergo 3 larval stages in mosquito

Mosquito takes in microfilariae with blood meal

Human infested when larvae burrow through skin

Cow ingests eggs from infected pasture

Eggs pass out in faeces

Second larval stage develops in snail and passes out into water

Eggs pass out in feces

Larvae form cysts in muscle of cow

Bilharzia fluke
Schistosoma mansoni

First larval stage develops in fresh water and enters snail

John Hutchinson

Hookworms are very common throughout the tropics and subtropics. They all have a similar life cycle, where the adult worm lives in the duodenum (part of the small intestine). Here it feeds on blood and lays its eggs, which then pass out in feces. In warm soil the eggs change into larvae, and these make their way through human skin should they come in contact with it.

Once in the bloodstream, the larvae are carried to the lungs. They then travel up the windpipe to be swallowed and find their way to the intestine. There is often severe itching (see Itches) at the entry point. Hookworm larvae of other species, such as the dog hookworm, may find their way through the skin and at the point of entry cause a rash called a larva migrans (see Rashes).

Ascaris cause a large number of infestations, and it has been estimated that up to a quarter of the world's population may be infected with ascaris. The worms live in the intestine, the eggs being ingested directly from food that is contaminated with feces (see Feces). Once the larva hatches in the duodenum, it gets into the bloodstream and imbeds itself in the lungs. From here it is coughed up the windpipe and swallowed.

Transmission of worms to humans occurs in three ways (above): from an insect carrier, such as a mosquito; from the infested meat or feces of an animal; or directly via the skin, as in the case of the bilharzia fluke.

A number of roundworms live in human intestines at some stage in their life cycle. They include the ascaris adult (below), and larva (inset), whipworms (below right) and the hookworm (right), whose larva enters via the skin.

London Scientific Fotos

C. James Webb

Ascaris causes few symptoms in most people, but there may be inflammation of the lungs as the larvae pass through. Large numbers of ascaris in the intestine can certainly cause abdominal symptoms and lead to blockage of the intestine.

Threadworms, common all over the world, also live in the intestines. The adult female worm emerges from the anus to lay eggs that then cause irritation. The infested person has probably picked up the eggs on the fingers when scratching and inadvertently swallowed them. This may lead to reinfection of the same person and to infection of others, which is a situation most common in children. The main symptom that the patient notices is anal itching.

Trematodes (flatworms or flukes)

Bilharzia (schistosomiasis) is one of the diseases caused by a trematode. The Egyptian form affects the bladder (see Bladder and bladder control) because that is where the eggs of the organism hatch into adult worms and cause inflammation.

The two other forms of the disease infest the large intestine. Eggs are passed out in the feces and develop in water snails before the larvae find their way back into the human body by burrowing into the skin. The liver fluke is another trematode (see Liver fluke) that causes

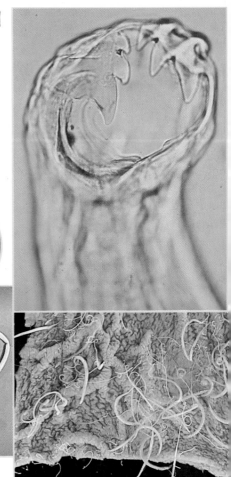

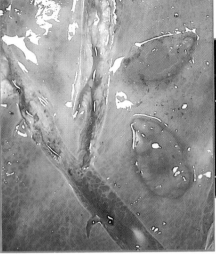

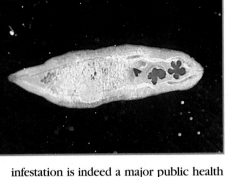

The infamous bilharzia fluke (above) lays its eggs in the human intestine, but humans are only rarely hosts of liver flukes, which are carried by other animals. Fasciola hepatica (right) infests cattle; Opisthrocus viverina (far right) lives in fish.

Heather Angel

London Scientific Fotos

problems, especially in Southeast Asia where raw fish (called sushi in Japan) is a popular delicacy.

Cestodes (tapeworms)

Tapeworms affect only meat-eaters. The typical tapeworm is the beef tapeworm, *Taenia saginata.* Humans are the primary host, and the worm anchors itself to the wall of the upper intestine, producing a great string of egg-bearing segments (the tape). Eggs pass out in the feces, and for the infestation to be passed on they must be eaten by some suitable intermediate host such as a cow. Inside the intermediate host they batch into larvae, which spread to invade all the muscles. The life cycle continues if a human eats the infested uncooked flesh.

Despite the enormous size they may reach, sometimes up to 30 ft (9 m), tapeworms produce few symptoms. The eggs of the pig tapeworm, *Taenia solium*, may, however, pass into the bloodstream.

Treatment and control

Drugs are available to kill practically all the worms that infect humans, but some of these drugs are toxic in themselves. Worm infestation is indeed a major public health problem, but it must be control rather than cure that is the answer. Many sorts of infestation could be avoided by better sanitation (see Infection and infectious diseases, Public health, and Sanitary protection) and by reducing the risk of food and water being contaminated with human feces. In other cases the intermediate host could be controlled, thus cutting down the risk of disease. For example, the Chinese have made great strides in the elimination of schistosomiasis by vastly reducing the population of water snails.

The dog tapeworm (left) can be transmitted to humans; prevention lies in worming all dogs regularly (bottom left). In most cases, however, human tapeworms (below) are the result of eating partly cooked or raw meat and fish. The eggs of Taenia solium *(bottom), a pig tapeworm, can cause the serious disease known as cysticerosis.*

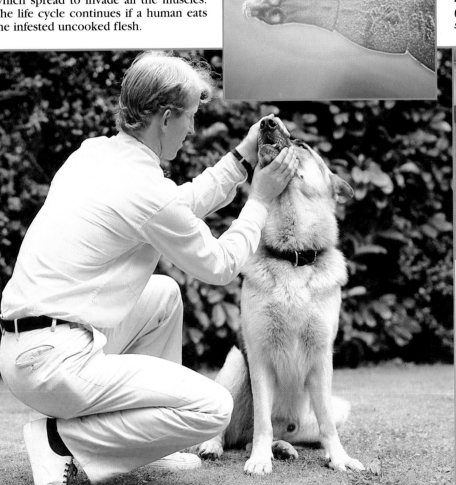

C. James Webb

London Scientific Fotos

Wounds

Q I seem to bruise very easily. Is there anything that I can do about this?

A Some people do bruise more easily than others. This is probably because the small blood vessels in the skin are more fragile. Most people who have this problem are perfectly healthy, and the condition is just a nuisance that has to be lived with. Only in rare cases is bruising a sign of blood clotting disorders or vitamin deficiency.

Q What is the best way to control bleeding?

A The best way is to apply pressure directly onto the bleeding area. This stops the bleeding and allows clotting of blood in the wound within a few minutes. In a leg or an arm wound it is also helpful to elevate the part as high as possible (this reduces the blood pressure in the limb). Tourniquets should be avoided since they can do great damage if applied by someone inexperienced.

Q When I had a deep cut, the doctor sutured it with dissolving stitches. How do these work?

A Dissolving stitches are strong when they are put in, but gradually they begin to soften up in the body. As they dissolve, the body's cells remove the small pieces of debris, and the stitch eventually disappears. This type of stitch is commonly used inside the body. Skin wounds stitched with dissolving stitches tend to make slightly more scar tissue, so these are not usually used on the parts of skin where a fine scar is preferable.

Q Do you only get scars with deep cuts?

A Yes. A cut has to go through all the layers of skin to cause scarring. The outer layer of skin (epidermis) is largely made up of dead cells that come up from the deeper layer of the skin. If only the outer layer is damaged, as in a shallow cut or graze, the damage is repaired by cells moving up from the dermis, and no scarring occurs.

Everyone suffers from a wound from time to time. Usually most of these are simple injuries that heal without any difficulty, but others can result in some kind of permanent impairment or disfigurement.

M. A. Bennett/Colorific!

The seriousness of a wound depends on what structures in the body are injured rather than on the wound's actual size. A small puncture to a vital organ like the heart (see Heart) or brain (see Brain) may cause death, while a large wound involving only skin (see Skin and skin diseases) may have no lasting effects.

Types of wounds

Wounds fall into several categories: abrasions, contusions, lacerations, incisions, and punctures. Gunshot wounds can have one or more features of these, but are included here because they very often require specialist treatment.

Abrasion: An abrasion is a graze (see Abrasions and cuts). An abrasion occurs when the skin is rubbed forcibly against something rough. The outer layer of the skin, or epidermis, is rubbed away, exposing the deeper layer, or dermis. This deeper layer contains small blood vessels, so a little bleeding occurs. It also contains many nerve endings and these are left exposed by the graze, resulting in the intense stinging pain that accompanies such wounds.

Contusion: A contusion is a bruise (see Bruises). It occurs when a part of the body is struck by something blunt, leaving the skin unbroken. The tissues beneath the skin—the fat, muscles, and internal organs—receive the force of the blow. Small blood vessels in these tissues burst, and blood (see Blood) leaks into the tissues. This causes the tissues to swell and become tight. When this happens, further bleeding stops, but the tightening tissue causes pain. The blood

We can be injured in the most ordinary situations, such as enjoying an adventure playground (below), or while gardening (below right). Some situations will, of course, lead to greater injuries than others, as this Guatemalan (right) found: he was shot twice in the abdomen during a gunfight.

that seeps into the tissues in a contusion gradually loses most of the oxygen that it is carrying and, as it does so, turns a bluish black color. This is why bruises are dark blue to black at first. Later the blood is broken down and reabsorbed by the body, and the bruise gradually becomes greenish yellow or light yellow. Occasionally the blood collects in a pool among the tissues rather than weeping out into the tissues. This is called a hematoma.

Gunshot wounds: These, and wounds caused by bomb blast shrapnel, cause extensive damage to tissue, and are particularly likely to become infected.

The amount of damage a bullet causes obviously depends on the type of tissues through which the bullet passes. The speed of the bullet is important. Low-velocity bullets (for example, those fired by handguns) tend to damage only those tissues through which the bullet actually passes. High-velocity bullets (most rifle bullets, for example), on the other hand, create a shock wave as they pass, and can cause serious damage to tissues lying at some distance from the bullet track itself.

Laceration: A laceration means a tear, but it is commonly used to refer to any sort of cut (see Lacerations). Lacerations can vary from a trivial wound that just goes through the skin to very deep wounds involving such important structures as nerves, blood vessels, and tendons (see Tendons). Lacerations can occur through contact with something sharp, such as a knife or a piece of glass, or they can occur with a blunt blow; for example, striking the forehead on the floor may split open the skin.

Incision: This word is commonly used to mean a cut made with a clean sharp instrument as in surgery. Therefore the only difference between an incision and a laceration is that an incision is intentional, as in a surgical operation, and the damage is limited to those actual tissues that were intended to be cut.

2165

Puncture: A puncture is a wound made by a pointed object such as a needle or a thorn. Punctures are deeper than they are wide, and serious damage can be done to deep structures without much obvious damage on the surface. Because these wounds are often made by long, thin objects, it is common for a little piece of the object to break off inside, leaving a foreign body.

Wound healing

Wounds heal in one of two ways: they either resolve completely, leaving no trace, or they heal by scarring (see Scars, and Healing).

A wound can heal without leaving a trace only if the wounded tissue has not been completely disrupted. Grazes heal in this way because only the top layer of the skin is rubbed away, leaving intact the deeper layer. This deeper layer contains the cells that multiply to form the top layer, and when the top layer has been damaged this process continues until normal skin has been restored. Occasionally the site of a deep graze is visible years later as a slightly pale area of skin.

Contusions also heal completely since the wound consists mainly of blood seeping into the tissues. This blood is broken down and absorbed by the body, so bruises gradually soften and disappear. Since the structures in the bruised area are not damaged, no scarring results.

Other types of wound heal by scarring. When the injury occurs, there is a gap in the tissue that becomes filled with blood. This blood becomes clotted and, soon after, the blood clot is invaded by cells called fibroblasts. These cells produce a simple type of fibrous tissue that helps to tie the sides of the wound together. At the same time the fibrous tissue is penetrated by small blood vessels from the surrounding tissues. This blood supply brings with it more fiber-producing cells, as well as a good supply of raw materials: oxygen, protein, sugar, and so on. The healing wound is a very busy area at this early stage of healing, and this is shown by the fact that a healing wound is slightly swollen and firm, and the scar is a bright red to pink. Over the next few months the early fibrous tissue becomes more highly organized, with the protein

Popperphoto

We are always at risk of receiving a wound, even if it is only trivial. Many wounds are disastrous, not least those deliberately inflicted. Witness the killing of Lee Harvey Oswald, President Kennedy's assassin, by Jack Ruby (above), or the gravity of combat wounds (left). Bullfighting is a sport deliberately undertaken for its danger (right): the matador runs the risk of being gored, or even killed, by the bull every time he goes into the ring.

fibers lined up to resist the stresses in the wound. The scar becomes more mature and is seen to become softer and whiter. In some areas, scars become almost invisible and blend in very well with the surrounding tissue (a good example is a scar on the palm of the hand). In other areas such as the abdomen and chest, the scar tends to widen as it heals, leaving a permanent, obvious scar.

In relatively simple tissues such as skin or fat, a small scar has little or no effect. In more specialized tissues scarring may stop their function altogether. For example, if a nerve is cut then stitched back together, impulses passing along it from the brain can still flow, but if the area fills with scar tissue the nerve will not work. Special techniques for repairing nerves can minimize this problem.

Treatment

Nature is a great healer of wounds. Any treatment given does not affect this healing process, but it sets the stage for healing without complications, and with a minimum of side effects.

Abrasions: These generally heal quickly and completely. The only treatment that

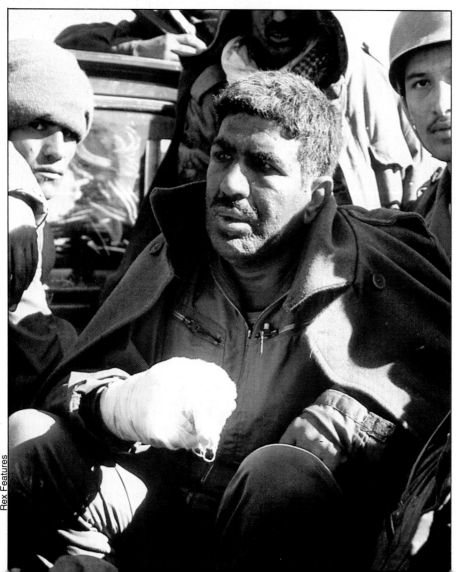

Rex Features

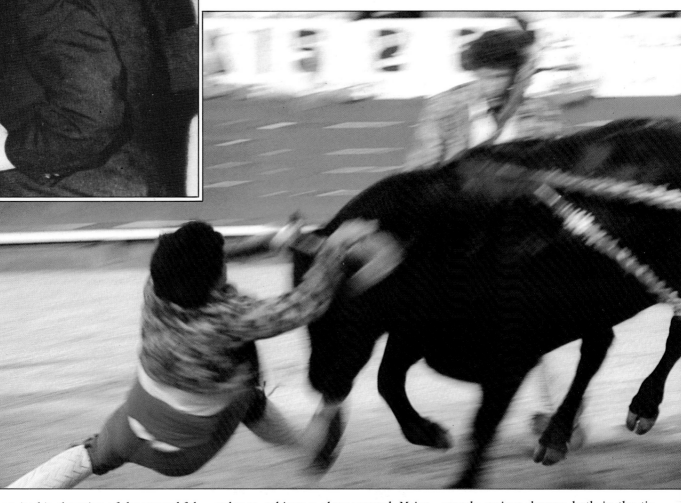

example, a black eye. Bruises resolve at their own speed and there is little that can be done to hasten this process.

Gunshot wounds: Treatment consists of early surgery to explore the path of the bullet. All tissue that has been so badly damaged that it cannot survive must be removed at this first operation. It is often necessary to remove large amounts of tissue, or even to amputate a limb, in order to achieve a clean wound. Major bleeding must be stopped, and damaged vessels repaired to insure a blood supply to the surrounding tissues. Damaged intestine must be removed to prevent leakage and serious infection, and broken bones must be cleansed, splinted (see Splints), or put in traction (see Traction). Complicated surgery to reconstruct damaged tissue is left to a later date. Initial surgery is performed to save life and to set the stage for a clean, healthy wound.

Techniques for treating major gunshot wounds have improved greatly in recent years, so that most people who reach the hospital alive now survive and recover.

Lacerations: Lacerations often need treatment. Bleeding is best controlled by direct pressure over the cut, using clean gauze or cloth. Elevation of the lacerated part helps to reduce bleeding. Firm pressure applied for several minutes generally stops bleeding from small vessels. If a larger vessel is cut, continuous pressure may be necessary until the victim reaches the hospital. Even if a large artery is cut it is better to apply the pressure directly to the wound rather than to use a tourniquet. This is because a tourniquet can do serious damage both in the tissues that are being squeezed and in the rest of the limb that is having its blood supply stopped.

Because all tissues have a certain degree of elasticity, any cut tends to retract or become larger. For example, a straight cut of 6 in (15 cm) to the skin becomes a 6 in by 1 in (15 cm by 2.5 cm) wide wound. This is why many lacerations need to be stitched together to allow the cut edges to heal in the shortest time and with the smallest possible scar. The stitches need to be left in place for a long enough time for healing to make the wound strong enough to hold itself together. In a wound that has merely gone through the skin, only the skin itself is stitched. In deeper wounds sev-

is required is cleansing of the wound followed, in some cases, by a dressing (see Dressings). Cleansing can be done with a mild soap and water (cold water is more soothing). Ideally the graze should then be left exposed to the air. Within a few hours a tough scab forms over it, acting as a natural protective dressing. In practice it may be better to cover the graze with a dressing to prevent it from rubbing on clothes or becoming dirty. Plastic materials tend to keep the graze moist and dark, favoring infection, so a material that breathes is better.

Contusions: These require little attention. The application of a cold compress or ice pack as soon as possible after the injury helps to prevent swelling (see Swellings), and this may be very worthwhile in, for

Q I bruised my hip very badly in a fall and now it is very painful. Is it possible that I have broken my hip?

A Yes. Bruising is a feature of broken bones because the bone actually bleeds into the surrounding tissues. This shows on the surface as bruising. If the break in the bone has not actually come apart it is possible to use the limb, although it will continue to be painful until the fracture heals. The danger is that the fracture may come apart, so it would be best to see your doctor.

Q I stepped on a nail in the yard. Should I have a tetanus injection?

A Tetanus or lockjaw is a very serious type of infection caused by bacteria that live in soil and animal excrement. The infection can be prevented by a vaccine that is usually given in childhood. It is necessary to have a booster shot every 10 years to keep up your resistance, so if you have not had a booster it would be wise to have it now.

Q Why does an eye turn black when it is injured?

A A black eye is really a bruise. When bruising occurs, blood leaks out of the small blood vessels in the injured area. This blood rapidly gives off the oxygen it is carrying, and as it does so it changes from bright red to dark blue-black. It is this color that shows through the skin as a bruise. The tissues around the eye are very loose and the overlying skin is thin, so a black eye swells up dramatically and may become very dark in color.

Q When I grazed my arm recently my mother said I should not cover the wound. Was she right?

A Yes. It is usually best to let a graze breathe. Over the first few hours it will form a dry scab that serves as a very effective dressing. Covering a graze makes the area moist, favoring the development of infection.

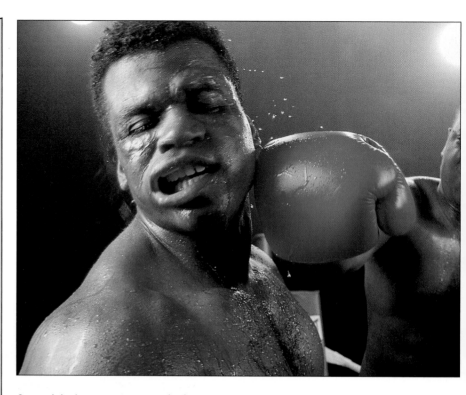

Sports injuries are common and take a variety of forms. A blow to the head, for example, causes bruises and swelling, so a cold compress is a soothing remedy.

eral layers of tissue may be divided, and each layer is stitched separately.

There are two principal types of stitches: that is, absorbable and nonabsorbable. Absorbable stitches are made from materials that dissolve slowly and that can be removed by the body, the most common being catgut, which is in fact made from sheep's intestines. Nonabsorbable sutures are made from silk, nylon, or steel. The type of suture (see Sutures) that is used depends on the judgment of the doctor. As a general rule, nonabsorbable sutures are stronger and are less likely to react in the tissues, while absorbable sutures are convenient in that they don't need to be removed.

Dressings for lacerations may be the only treatment needed (see Dressings), or they may be used after stitching. A firm dressing will help stop bleeding and make the wound more comfortable. Adhesive strips may be used instead of stitches to pull the wound together. In general, dressings are used as a protection against rubbing or knocking the wound while it is healing. There are many types of dressing materials, but none has any magical effect on wound healing. Often leaving the wound open to the air is as good a treatment as any.

Puncture: A puncture wound needs treatment if the puncturing object is large or dirty. Because the wound is deep it is easy to underestimate the amount of damage just by looking at the surface. It may be necessary for the track of the puncture to be opened by means of surgery and any damaged tissue cleansed and repaired.

Complications

Whenever the skin is broken, bacteria (see Bacteria) enter the wound from outside. Whether these bacteria actually cause an infection (see Infection and infectious diseases) depends on their strength and number, and on the ability of the tissues to resist the bacteria. Of

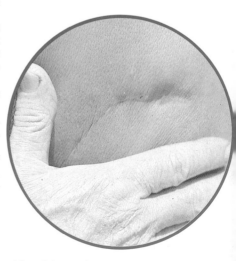

This abdominal scar is the result of a spear wound that turned septic. The patient (a native Brazilian) had medical treatment to clean the wound so that it could heal.

these two factors the most important is the resistance. For example, a young healthy person who gets a cut on a fingertip rarely gets an infection in the wound since the tissues have a good blood supply and the individual's defenses take care of any bacteria that get into the cut.

If a wound contains a lot of badly damaged tissue, infection is much more likely to occur. The damaged tissue will have a poor blood supply so the body's cells may have difficulty in reaching the area where infection is beginning. The bacteria actually feed and multiply on the dead tissue, and as they multiply they will begin to break down and destroy previously normal tissue.

Symptoms of a wound infection take 24 to 48 hours to develop after the injury. The victim notices increasing pain in the wound as the infection causes swelling and tightness in the tissues. The pain becomes constant and throbbing, while the wound itself swells and becomes red and hot. Later, fluid may begin to escape from the wound. Initially this is clear

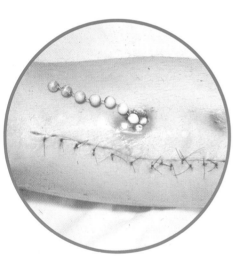

fluid, but later it may become pus (see Pus). The victim will feel unwell and may have a fever (see Fevers).

The best treatment of an infected wound is prevention (see Preventive medicine). Any wound should be thoroughly cleansed. Superficial wounds need only be washed with mild soap or an antiseptic. Deeper wounds should be examined by a doctor. If there is dirt ground into the tissues, or if there is a lot of bruised, crushed tissue, all this will need to be removed, leaving clean healthy tissue. If the wound is very dirty, antibiotics (see Antibiotics) may be given.

In established wound infections, the wound must be opened up so that any fluid or pus can drain away, and the dead and damaged tissue can be removed. If the wound has previously been sutured, the stitches are generally removed. It may be helpful to elevate the infected area since this helps to get rid of the swelling. Antibiotics should be taken until the wound has calmed down (a minimum of five days).

One particular type of infection that must be guarded against is lockjaw or tetanus (see Tetanus). The tetanus bacteria give off tiny spores that are very hardy and live in soil and animal excrement. If the spores become established in a wound, they give off toxins that attack the nervous system, causing severe muscle spasms. Muscle spasm attacking the jaw muscles causes a forcible biting action, hence the term *lockjaw*. Once this condition starts, treatment is difficult and many

A bad fracture can cause a serious external wound (left). This leg was operated on, stitched up, and antibiotic beads were placed in the open wound to combat infection. This victim of the bombings in Lebanon (below) is receiving emergency surgery: shrapnel wounds are often lethal, depending on where they occur.

victims die. Lockjaw is prevented by cleaning wounds thoroughly and giving vaccine (see Vaccinations) against tetanus. Most people receive the vaccine as children, and booster shots are needed every 10 years to maintain resistance. In practice, most people only receive a booster when they actually suffer a wound, rather than being vaccinated regularly.

Another complication is foreign bodies. This includes any piece of foreign material that is left behind in a wound. Foreign bodies cause two problems: they may press on important structures, causing pain and damage, and they cause inflammation (see Inflammation) in the tissues. The cells of the body are able to recognize when a piece of foreign material is present, and then try to get rid of the intruding body. This process results in inflammation, which continues until the foreign body is removed. Some foreign material is inert, that is, it does not cause much of this type of reaction. Stainless steel and glass can remain in the body for years with little or no reaction. Biological materials such as cloth or wood cause very intense reactions, and must be removed for this reason.

It is a common belief that foreign bodies such as needles move around in the body, and may end up lodged in a vital organ. In fact, this does not happen. A needle or a piece of glass in the hand or foot (see Splinters) usually needs to be removed because it hurts when standing or gripping, but the same foreign body in a large muscle such as the thigh is best left alone since it will never cause any harm. There are many war veterans who have shrapnel embedded in various parts of their bodies for decades without suffering any ill effects. It is important to remove foreign bodies if infection is present, since they tend to maintain an infection despite treatment, thus impeding wound healing.

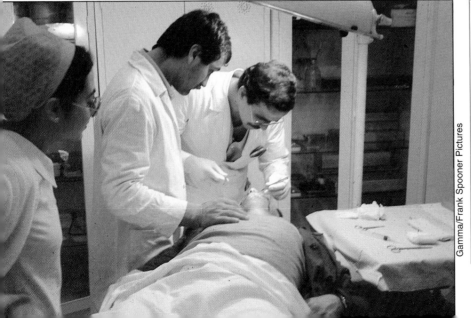

Gamma/Frank Spooner Pictures

Wrinkles

Q Why do some people get wrinkles earlier than others?

A Prolonged exposure to the sun's radiation is one of the main causes of wrinkling, so people who work outdoors tend to get wrinkles earlier than those who spend most of their time indoors. Skin pigmentation provides some protection, so people with colored or sallow skins are less prone to wrinkling than fair-skinned people. Other factors that play a part in the early development of wrinkles include a poor diet, ill health, smoking, and poor skin care.

Q Is it true that doing facial exercises will delay the onset of wrinkles?

A This is debatable. Some people believe that facial exercises stimulate the muscles to grow and thus tighten the overlying skin and so prevent wrinkles. Others claim that the overuse of facial expressions will accelerate wrinkling since a characteristic pattern of facial lines will be fixed earlier. Attention to diet, weight, and exercise will probably maintain skin tone far better than making faces in front of the mirror!

Q Does skin cream containing collagen prevent wrinkles?

A Collagen is certainly an important component of healthy skin, but wrinkling is believed to be caused not by the lack of it but by changes in its structure. Thus there is little scientific basis for the claim that the use of collagen will rejuvenate skin. This is not to say that creams containing collagen will not delay the appearance of wrinkles, but such an effect is probably due to the moisturizing properties of the cream rather than its collagen.

Q Is it possible to have heavy bags under the eyes surgically removed?

A Yes. This operation is called a blepharoplasty and is like a face lift. The excess skin and fat are removed, and the remaining skin stretched and restitched.

Like graying hair, the appearance of a few wrinkles is a classic sign of aging. How do they come about, and can anything be done to avoid or put off this universal, and seemingly inevitable, phenomenon?

Skin wrinkling is usually apparent in anyone over 40, and often first occurs much earlier. Although wrinkles can give the face character, many people feel they are something to be avoided or postponed (see Skin and skin diseases).

Causes

The most important underlying change that brings about wrinkling involves the connective tissues just under the outer layer of the skin, which are made up of two types of protein fiber: collagen and elastin. The collagen provides the matrix for the tissue, and the smaller number of elastin fibers give elasticity and suppleness. With time, however, the amount of elastin diminishes and the collagen fibers become disorganized, cross-linking and enmeshing with each other. Consequently the tissue gradually loses elasticity. A general thinning and drying out of the skin is part of the process of aging (see Aging), and this also predisposes to wrinkling.

Sunlight affects the skin (see Sunburn), and accounts for the predominance of wrinkling on exposed areas of the body, particularly the face, neck, and backs of the hands. The ultraviolet component of

This Algerian woman is deeply wrinkled, not only from age but also because she has spent her life in a country where the sun is intensely strong for most of the year.

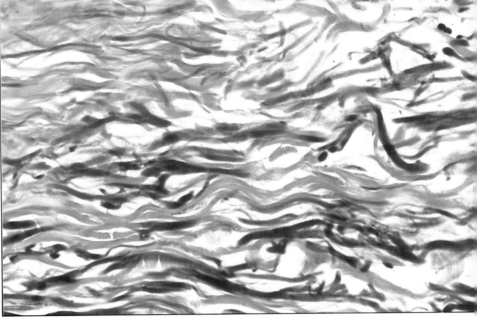

You shouldn't worry about growing older. The striking looks of film star Jane Fonda are undimmed, despite a few wrinkles.

sunlight accelerates the chemical changes in skin that cause wrinkling, and its effects are pronounced in fair-skinned people who have little natural protection against the sun's rays (see Melanin).

The difference, in the same environment, between skin exposed to solar radiation and that protected from it is strikingly illustrated in cloistered nuns living in tropical countries. Doctors have been struck by the absence of wrinkling and other effects of sunlight on the skins of women whose dress and way of life have provided lifelong avoidance of direct sunlight.

Ultraviolet radiation has a direct effect on the DNA in the skin cells. The damage to DNA is normally repaired by the natural processes of DNA repair and replication, but these are not capable of repairing all the damage, and some DNA remains abnormal. This effect is cumulative, and eventually abnormal skin results. This abnormality is mainly manifested in wrinkles, but it can also appear as several forms of skin cancer, including rodent ulcers (see Ulcers).

Facial expression also plays a role. Whenever we smile, grimace, or frown, furrows are formed in the skin according to which facial muscles are being contracted. Over the years these facial lines become ingrained so that they are visible all the time.

A further influence on the pattern of wrinkling is the amount and distribution of subcutaneous fat deposits in and around the face. Excess fat deposits tend to be drawn downward by gravity to form bags under the eyes, double chins, and heavy jowls. In older people, jowl creases may extend up to the cheeks, and tend to run perpendicular to the lines of facial expression, producing a crosshatch pattern of wrinkles.

Finally smoking (see Smoking), particularly cigarette smoking, seems to speed up the process of wrinkling. The reason for this is not known, but one theory is that smokers screw up their faces more often to prevent smoke irritating their eyes and this accentuates the lines of expression. Also cigarette smoke contains at least 3000 different chemical substances, many of which are absorbed into the bloodstream and carried to every part of the body, including the skin, where they may damage the proteins of the skin.

Avoidance and camouflage
The effects of aging cannot be put off forever, but the onset and development of wrinkles can be delayed. Perhaps the most important protective measure is to avoid prolonged exposure to hot sunshine and to use sunscreens with a high sun protection factor, which help to prevent the type of skin damage that promotes wrinkling.

Dry skin has a greater tendency to wrinkle than oily skin, so using a moisturizing cream is another worthwhile preventive measure. Avoiding or cutting down on smoking may also have a beneficial effect.

For many women, wrinkles become a particular problem around menopause, and this may be due to hormonal changes. Hormone replacement therapy may slow down wrinkling, but this is not yet proven (see Hormone replacement therapy).

There are a number of types of anti-wrinkle cream available that vary in effec-

The breakdown that occurs in the skin's supportive tissue is a fundamental cause of wrinkling. With time, the elastin fibers (blue) diminish and the collagen fibers (pink) become loose and disorganized, resulting in loss of firmness and elasticity.

tiveness. They cannot remove wrinkles but can give temporary camouflage. Some work by moisturizing and plumping up the skin, while others simply fill in the wrinkles. The implication that healthy collagen can be restored by skin creams should be viewed with skepticism.

Surgical treatment
Once wrinkles are established, surgical treatment is probably the only effective way of removing or reducing them, either by a face lift or chemical abrasion.

Face lifts (see Cosmetic surgery) involve making incisions at the borders of the face, stretching the skin upward and outward and restitching. The initial results are often impressive, but wrinkling may recommence a year or two after surgery.

Cosmetic procedures to remove redundant stretched skin are not without risk. There have been cases in which too much redundant eyelid skin has been removed with the result that the eyes have been unable to be closed. This quickly leads to severe exposure damage to the peripheral parts of the corneas.

In chemical abrasion a caustic gel is spread over the face and neck to break down the outer layers of skin, which are then removed with the gel. The new skin that grows in its place is usually considerably less wrinkled, but the procedure is rather painful. Healing (see Healing) may take several weeks, and sometimes the skin is left looking patchily discolored.

Skin that has been treated in this way is extremely sensitive to sunlight for several weeks and it is imperative to protect it from ambient sunlight during this time.

Wrist

Q Doctors seem to find it difficult to find the pulse in my wrist. Why should this be?

A The pulse at your wrist (the radial pulse) belongs to the radial artery. The artery is likely to be in a slightly different position in all wrists. Your pulse may be a bit deeper than usual or it may lie slightly to the right or left. In either case, it does not signify anything of importance, although your doctor might appreciate a warning that your pulse is difficult to find.

Q My wrists have always seemed rather weak. What can I do to strengthen them?

A Why not try taking up some sport such as tennis or squash. Any activity in which you have to grip a racket or club is likely to strengthen the wrists and make them more flexible. Of course it will have the added advantage of improving your general fitness and health at the same time.

Q My eight-year-old daughter is an avid gymnast and is always doing handstands. Is there any risk of her damaging her wrists?

A Wrist injuries are always a risk in sports such as gymnastics, but in fact your daughter's wrists are more likely to be strengthened than hurt. Deformities of the wrist do occur as a result of exercise on rare occasions, but generally this is only if the bones are already diseased or weakened.

Q Recently I broke a small bone in my wrist and I now have a plaster cast on my arm. Is it all right for me to drive?

A The simple answer is no. If you drive during the first few weeks you are likely to stop the bones from mending properly. More importantly, you should also remember that with a cast on your arm you are a potential hazard on the road. The flexibility of your wrist will be drastically reduced and you could be a danger both to yourself and others.

Composed of eight bones and surrounded by tendons, the wrist is very flexible and surprisingly trouble-free. Like all bones, the wrist can break, but the most painful problems occur when the tendons become inflamed.

Each wrist is actually a complex of numerous joints between lots of little bones. This gives the joint great flexibility but makes it a potential weak spot. It is strengthened by a web of ligaments and tendons that link the bones and make lifting possible.

The structure of the wrist

The wrist is made up from eight separate bones called carpals. They are like small pebbles arranged in two rows and bound together by about twenty ligaments and tendons (see Ligaments, and Tendons). The carpals sit between the metacarpals of the hand and the long bones of the arm.

The bones in the row nearest the arm, which run from the thumb to the little finger, are the scaphoid, lunate, triquetral, and pisiform. The second row consists of the trapezium, trapezoid, capitate, and hamate. The only one of these bones that is visible on the skin surface is the pisiform, which can be seen as the bumpy wrist bone.

The tendons that almost completely surround the wrist joint are enclosed in a tunnel called the carpal tunnel. This protects the tendons from rubbing against the moving wrist bones.

Movement of the wrist

The carpal joints are relatively immobile, although as a unit the wrist is very flexible indeed. The exception is the joint between the trapezium and the thumb bone. This type of joint makes it possible to grasp an object between the finger and thumb. An opposable thumb makes humans particularly adept at using tools.

Anatomically, the wrist joint is described as ellipsoid. This means that, although it enables up and down actions, side to side and some circular movement, it cannot rotate like the hip and shoulder joints. This

Swift and cunning movements are essential in first-class table tennis and depend largely on the wrist's great flexibility.

All-Sport

Structure of the wrist

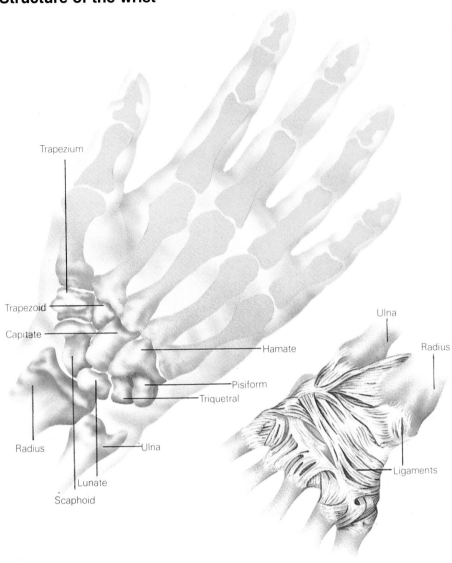

Trapezium

Trapezoid

Capitate

Radius

Ulna

Lunate

Scaphoid

Hamate

Pisiform

Triquetral

Ulna

Radius

Ligaments

The eight wrist bones are strengthened by ligaments and tendons (above) and are at their most vulnerable when having to bear the brunt of the body's weight (left).

Sally and Richard Greenhill

limitation helps to insure the stability of the joint. However, it is thought that the wrist joint is only properly stable when the tendons, ligaments, and muscles are acting to keep all the components of the joint in the right place (see Joints). This tension is necessary, even when the body is completely at rest.

Such a fragile joint is clearly easy to damage. Lots of people will have experienced a slight sprain (see Sprains) or strain and noticed how much it affects manual manipulation—every tiny action hurts the damaged joints.

Fractures and dislocations

Of all the injuries that involve the wrist, the most common is a break at the lower end of the radius—one of the two long

bones in the forearm. This is called a Colles fracture, and is treated by manipulation to reset the bones and immobilization in a cast (see Fractures, and Manipulation).

The small carpal bones can also suffer hairline cracks. Sometimes there is a swelling on the back of the hand, just below the thumb, but often there are no external signs, only pain and stiffness (see Stiffness) in the joint. Often even X rays do not show up these small cracks (see X rays), but they can still be a problem. A hairline crack can separate a small portion of bone from its blood supply and this can result in bone death. If there is any suspicion that this is happening the doctor will immediately immobilize the wrist joint to prevent any more damage.

The bones of the wrist can also become dislocated if banged or moved awkwardly, especially the lunate bone in the center of the wrist and the triquetral below the little finger. The dislocation shows up as a bulge on the outside of the wrist and should be manipulated into position by a doctor as soon as possible.

Problems with the tendons

The most common problem to afflict the wrist is called carpal tunnel syndrome (see Carpal tunnel syndrome). The fibrous carpal tunnel encloses all the wrist tendons and one of the main nerves supplying the hand, the median nerve (see Nervous system). If the fibers in the tunnel become swollen or compressed they press the nerve against the wrist bones, causing pain.

The syndrome can be caused by simple overuse of the thumb and fingers. It is also common in late pregnancy when edema (swelling) can put pressure on the median nerve (see Pregnancy). It is generally more common in women than in men.

Whatever the cause, carpal tunnel syndrome begins with a sensation of pins and needles or numbness, especially in the thumb and next two fingers. The wrist may swell up by the thumb, and the forearm and thumb are often very painful. Usually the symptoms will gradually ease as the swelling or pressure is reduced. Occasionally, however, the syndrome may be persistent or recurrent, in which case surgery may be required to effect a permanent cure.

Another problem is called tenosynovitis. The lubricated tendon sheaths become inflamed as a result of a bacterial infection or rheumatoid arthritis. It becomes difficult and painful to uncurl the fingers, and sometimes movement may result in audible grating noises. The fingers and thumb may also feel numb as if they have permanent pins and needles (see Pins and needles). A doctor will usually prescribe antibiotics for bacterial infection and aspirin to relieve pain.

X rays

Q If X rays are really so dangerous, why is it that they are still so widely used?

A Modern X-ray equipment and strict safety precautions keep the doses of X rays used in the vast majority of X-ray examinations down to an absolute minimum. In theory, even the smallest X-ray dose carries a slight hazard, so it is the doctor's responsibility to make sure that the X rays are only taken when the information obtained will be of clear benefit to the patient.

Q In the last week of my first pregnancy, my obstetrician said that she needed an X ray of my pelvis. Although I agreed, I have since worried that the X ray could have harmed my baby?

A Your obstetrician was probably worried that your pelvis might have been too small for the baby to pass through safely, and was right to resolve her doubts by taking an X ray rather than risk waiting for problems to develop during labor. In this situation, an X ray was the best way of obtaining a definite answer, and was well worth any slight risk taken. In any case, it is during the first trimester that the fetus is at greatest risk of damage from X rays, and having an X ray in late pregnancy is generally considered to be relatively safe.

Q My brother-in-law has already had a number of tests, and is now about to have a special X ray of the brain called a carotid angiogram. What will this involve?

A A carotid angiogram is an examination in which a contrast medium is injected into the carotid artery, filling the blood vessels of the brain and outlining them clearly when X rays are taken. As in other types of angiography, the most comfortable and convenient way of injecting the contrast is through a long, very fine plastic catheter or tube, which is inserted into the femoral artery in the groin. This is manipulated under X-ray control until its tip lies in the artery to be studied.

A freak discovery gave medicine one of its most valuable diagnostic tools: a window into the inside of the body. Known simply as X rays, their use enables early and accurate detection of internal injury and disease.

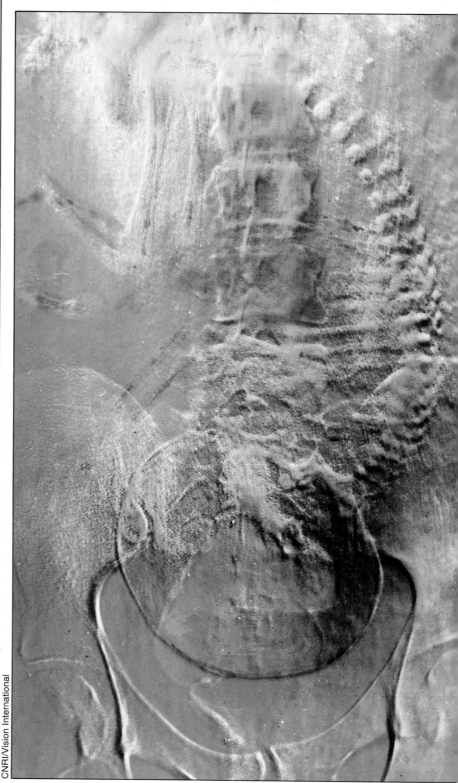

CNRI/Vision International

On November 8, 1895, Professor Wilhelm Conrad Röntgen, while conducting an experiment at the University of Würzburg, Germany, made a chance discovery that became a legend. For the purposes of the experiment his laboratory was in total darkness, and the electrical apparatus that he was studying had been enclosed in a lightproof black cardboard cover. Yet, as he passed an electric current through his apparatus, he became aware of a faint glow coming from a piece of chemically treated paper that was lying on a nearby workbench.

Professor Röntgen had discovered how to produce invisible, mysterious rays (he named them X rays), which had not only penetrated the opaque cardboard cover, but which had caused the fluorescent paper to glow. Later he discovered that the rays from his apparatus could also blacken a photographic plate and produce a permanent image using the fluorescent paper. He immediately began to investigate other properties of the rays and found that they could penetrate all kinds of solid objects. Imagine his surprise when he then placed his hand in the path of the X rays and saw for the first time an image of his own bones suddenly appear on the fluorescent paper.

Today, some 80 years later, X rays are an indispensable aid to modern diagnostic medicine (see Diagnosis), and indeed most hospitals now spend more money on their X-ray department than on any other. With less discomfort or inconvenience to the patient than ever before, the latest sophisticated technology provides a safe and reliable means of detecting disease at an early stage, and of monitoring treatment efficiently and effectively.

What are X rays?

X rays belong to the same family as light waves and radio waves, and, like radio waves, they are invisible. They are produced artificially by bombarding a small tungsten target with electricity in a device called an X-ray tube. X rays travel in straight lines and radiate outward from a point on the target in all directions. In an X-ray machine, the X-ray tube is surrounded by a lead casing, except for a small aperture through which the X-ray beam emerges.

Each of the body's tissues absorbs X rays in a predictable way, and this is the particular property of X rays that enables them to be used in medicine to form images of the body. Bones (see Bones)

Computer color enhancement techniques add detail to X rays. Here (facing page) an eight-month fetus can be seen in an ideal position, ready for birth. X rays during the last part of pregnancy are relatively safe.

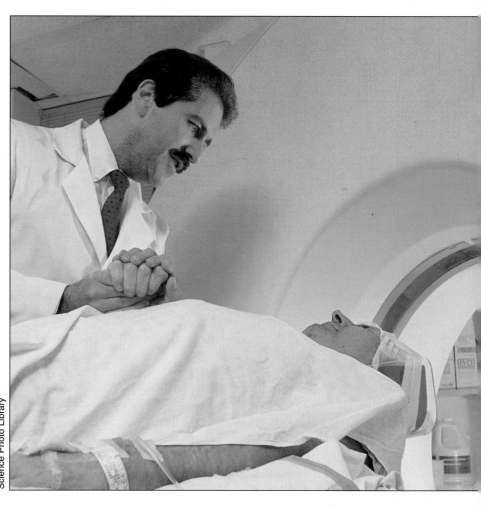

Science Photo Library

are dense and contain calcium, which absorbs X rays well. Soft tissues, such as skin (see Skin and skin diseases), fat, blood (see Blood), and muscle (see Muscles), absorb X rays much less efficiently. So when, for example, an arm is placed in the path of an X-ray beam, the X rays pass readily through the soft tissues but penetrate the bones less easily; the arm casts a shadow. X rays blacken photographic film, so the shadow cast by the bones appears white, while the shadow of the soft tissues is a dark shade of gray.

The X-ray examination

The X-ray image, or radiograph, is really a demonstration of the anatomy of the part of the body under examination, and it is now possible to make a detailed inspection of almost any part of the body with X rays. X rays are therefore of greatest use in the diagnosis and follow-up of disease and disorders that alter the structure of the body. Sometimes such changes in structure are so dramatic that they are immediately obvious even to the untrained observer; this is often the case with broken bones (see Fractures), for example. Frequently, however, the changes are more subtle, and may only

A radiographer reassures a patient who is about to undergo a computed tomography (CT) brain scan. The patient's head is secured in a brace in order to keep it still when he passes into the circular scanner.

be apparent to the trained eye of a radiologist (the doctor who specializes in the interpretation of X-ray images).

Prior to an X-ray examination, instructions about any special preparations that may be necessary are given to the patient when the appointment for the examination is made. In the case of examinations of the abdominal region (see Abdomen), for example, it is often preferable for the patient to take laxatives (see Laxatives) and a special diet (see Diet) for two days beforehand, since emptying the intestines results in radiographs of much improved quality.

When the patient arrives at the X-ray department, the radiographer who will be taking the X rays explains the procedure. The patient undresses to expose the area concerned, and must remove any objects, such as jewelry or dentures, that might produce an image on the radiograph. The position of the patient when the X ray is taken is carefully and accurately chosen

The use of X rays

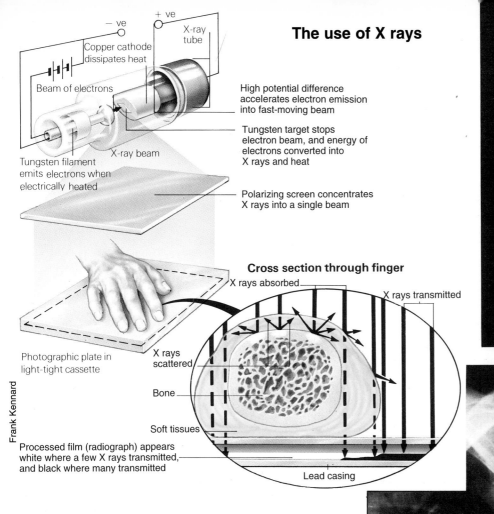

− ve **+ ve**

Copper cathode
dissipates heat

X-ray
tube

Beam of electrons

High potential difference
accelerates electron emission
into fast-moving beam

Tungsten target stops
electron beam, and energy of
electrons converted into
X rays and heat

Tungsten filament
emits electrons when
electrically heated

X-ray beam

Polarizing screen concentrates
X rays into a single beam

Cross section through finger

X rays absorbed

X rays transmitted

Photographic plate in
light-tight cassette

X rays
scattered

Bone

Soft tissues

Processed film (radiograph) appears
white where a few X rays transmitted,
and black where many transmitted

Lead casing

Frank Kennard

Biophoto Associates

so as to provide the best possible demonstration of the part under examination, though this position may have to be modified if the patient is sick or in severe pain. Positioning the patient is one of the radiographer's most important tasks.

Each X-ray film is usually carried in a flat cassette, and the patient lies, sits, or stands with the region of interest in contact with the cassette. It is essential to avoid movement while the X ray is taken, since this results in a blurred image. Every effort is made, therefore, to keep the patient comfortable, to use the shortest feasible exposure time (usually a mere fraction of a second) and, if necessary, to support or immobilize the region of interest with foam pads or a cloth bandage.

When everything is ready, the radiographer leaves the room and presses the exposure button on the control panel to execute the X ray. Although the control panel is situated behind a protective screen, the radiographer is still able to see and talk to the patient at all times. If, for any reason, it is necessary for someone to remain in the room while X rays are taken, unnecessary exposure to X rays is prevented by wearing a lead apron.

Special techniques

For most purposes, a standard X-ray examination is all that is required. Special techniques are available, however, that

X rays radiate outward from a tungsten target. They pass through the soft tissues of the body, but are absorbed by the bones. The shadow cast by the bones is caught by the photographic plate (above).

enable areas not adequately seen on standard radiographs to be studied in greater detail. In general, these more sophisticated techniques necessitate the use of what are known as contrast media. These are substances that cause the tissue concerned to become opaque.

The use of contrast media (which are then eliminated from the body by the kidneys) can enhance views of the gallbladder (see Gallbladder and stones) and bile ducts (see Bile), and the urinary and digestive tracts (see Digestive system). When a contrast medium is injected directly into blood vessels (known as an angiograph), the arteries (see Arteries and artery disease) and veins (see Veins) are clearly outlined, and any abnormalities revealed. Likewise, using a contrast medium to highlight the fluid that surrounds the spinal cord (see Spinal cord)

is frequently useful in detecting a nerve compressed by a disk (see Slipped disk) or a tumor (see Tumors).

By using a suspension of barium sulphate (an inert, chalky mixture that is opaque to X rays), it is possible to visualize the alimentary tract throughout its length. During a barium swallow examination, the patient is given a glass of flavored barium to drink (it tastes a bit like a milk shake; see Barium liquids). The patient's swallowing mechanism can be studied, abnormalities of the esophagus (see Esophagus) can be detected, and the stomach (see Stomach) is clearly outlined.

During the examination the image is monitored continuously on a television screen, and the patient lies on a tilt table so that, with careful maneuvering, each part of the stomach and duodenum can be studied in turn.

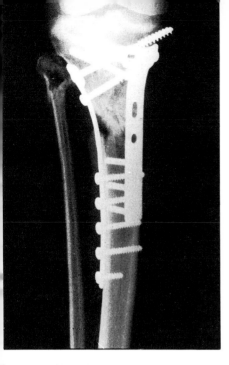

means of a rectal tube (this is called a barium enema), and this is one of the most important methods of detecting cancer of the intestine.

Opacification of the urinary tract is achieved by intravenous injection of a solution that contains iodine; this is rapidly eliminated by the kidneys. Like barium, iodine is opaque to X rays, and if X-ray films are taken at various intervals after the injection, the kidneys, ureters, and bladder are clearly shown. The technique is called intravenous urography (IVU or IVP) and is of great importance in the diagnosis of many types of kidney disease (see Kidney and kidney diseases).

Dental X rays

X-ray techniques simplify the diagnosis of a wide range of important dental problems, and are now in everyday use (see Teeth and teething).

Tooth decay can sometimes be surprisingly difficult to detect, especially when it lurks in the space between the back teeth and in other inaccessible recesses. Decay, root disease, abscesses, and infections can all be visibly demonstrated with X rays, which will confirm the diagnosis at an early stage, document the extent of any disease, and help determine the most suitable form of treatment. A basic X-ray examination has become a routine part of the dental checkup.

The equipment used is not normally very complicated. A low-powered X-ray unit is used, and is often linked up to the dentist's chair. Small films (called bitewing films) are gripped in the patient's mouth next to the teeth to be examined.

More complex conditions, such as abnormalities of growth and development of teeth, jaw fractures, cysts, and tumors, require a more detailed examination. One particularly valuable technique is orthopantomography, in which the X-ray machine moves around the jaw of the patient while the X ray is taken, producing a panorama of the teeth and jaws. This technique shows both upper and lower jaws, any unerupted teeth, and the position and relationship of all the teeth on a single X-ray film.

When the two jaws do not fit together well, a side view of the face and jaws may be taken, showing the relationship of the teeth, jaws, and soft tissue. The pictures help the orthodontist to plan treatment, which may involve plates, braces, or corrective surgery (see Orthodontics).

CAT scanning

The most sophisticated application of X rays is computerized axial tomography, commonly known as CAT scanning or CT scanning. This is a highly sophisticated X-ray procedure developed independently by American physicist Allan Cormack

After badly breaking both legs in a motorcycle accident, this victim had to have his bones literally pinned and bolted together (above). This dramatic X ray (left) shows a bullet lodged in someone's upper chest: luckily the X ray shows no severe injury such as a punctured lung or damaged heart. By injecting contrast media into the carotid artery, the blood vessels of the brain show up on X-ray film. The rather mysterious yellow band is the outline of the skull (below).

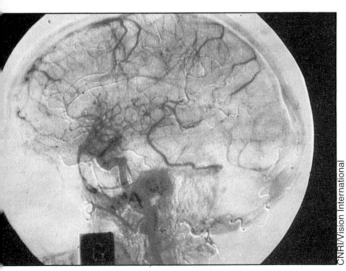

CNRI/Vision International

The lining of the stomach is seen more clearly when the stomach is distended with gas (the patient has to swallow fizzy tablets) since it then becomes coated with a thin film of barium. The examination is conducted by a radiologist, and usually takes around 20 minutes. A series of X-ray films are taken during the examination, to give a permanent record. This is one of the best methods of detecting peptic ulcers (see Ulcers). Barium can also be introduced into the large intestine by

As X-ray technology advances, so the uses of X rays multiply. Special photographic techniques mean that both the body outline and internal features can be captured. Here the voice box is being examined.

Charles Day

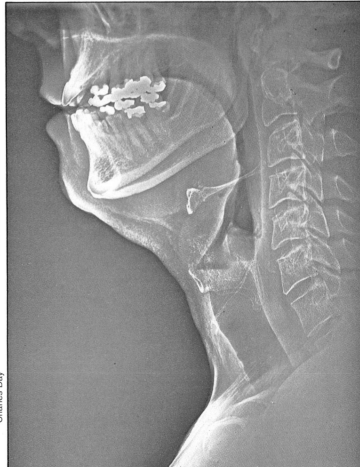

Q I twisted my knee about two months ago playing baseball. It has been troubling me ever since, and keeps locking. I'm having an arthrogram next week. What could this show?

A Air and a contrast medium are injected into the knee joint under local anesthesia, giving a clear view of the joint. It sounds as though you might have torn a cartilage, and the arthrogram will confirm whether or not this is so.

Q My doctor examined me recently and suggested that I have a mammogram. What does this mean, and is it painful?

A A mammogram is an X ray of the breast, and may be slightly uncomfortable. It may be performed if a lump is found in the breast, or if there is anything to suggest that a breast cancer might be present. Following a baseline mammogram you will have regular periodic X rays. The radiation dose in this type of X ray is low, so any very slight risk is offset by the advantages: early diagnosis of the disease, and, consequently, peace of mind.

Q My five-year-old daughter is having a kidney X ray next week. Will this be painful, and can the dye injection be risky?

A In an IVU examination, an injection of a contrast medium containing iodine is given, usually into a vein in the arm. Young children understandably dislike injections, even when it's for their own good. However, the procedure itself will be entirely painless. Do tell the radiologist if your child has asthma, or any allergies that you know about, since an allergy to the contrast sometimes occurs.

Q How is it that X rays can be used to fight cancer?

A Unfortunately, X radiation can be dangerous. It damages all living cells, but particularly those cells that grow and divide profusely, as in cancer. Careful use of X rays has made it possible to destroy cancerous cells, or retard their development, while exposing healthy cells to as little radiation as possible.

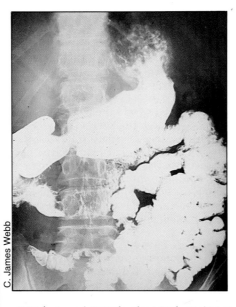

C. James Webb

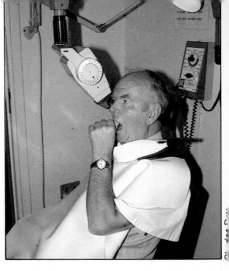

Dental X rays are now commonplace (above). The X-ray plate is held against the teeth while the X-ray machine takes the picture. The apron protects the body from radiation. A technique called orthopantomography *takes a panoramic view of the teeth (right): a child's second set of teeth can be seen coming through quite clearly. Twenty minutes after swallowing barium liquid, the digestive tract can be clearly seen on an X ray (above left). The stomach, duodenum, and the rest of the small intestines are all shown.*

(1924–) and British electrical engineer Godfrey Hounsfield (1919–), a development that won them jointly the 1979 Nobel Prize for physiology or medicine. The invention of the CAT scanner was one of the half-dozen most important medical advances of the 20th century.

X-ray tomography was in use long before the CAT scanner was invented. It was a method of using a swinging X-ray tube and film holder to record an image of a thin slice of the body. The results were crude and many consecutive exposures, each involving a full dose of radiation, had to be made to provide useful information about the location and size of radiopaque objects and tissues.

The major advance that made the modern CAT scanner possible was the realization that a computer could be used to store data from a large number of the separate X-ray slices and then to correlate these data to synthesize a detailed image of a cross section of the inside of the body. The CAT scanner uses low-energy X-ray sources to send narrow beams of X radiation through the body to small detectors on the opposite side. These detectors are highly sensitive, and output an electrical signal that varies with the total density of the tissue through which the X rays pass. With each pulse of X ray, the resulting output from the detector is stored in the computer along with the orientation of the corresponding beam. The total radiation dose to the patient, in the course of a CT scan, is about the same as that of a conventional chest X ray.

The computer is thus supplied with large numbers of pairs of data, the exact orientation of each of the numerous axes of X-ray projection and, for each axis, the exact amount of attenuation caused by the bodily tissues. By solving large numbers of differential equations, the computer is able to determine the precise density of the tissue at every point at which the axes intersect, that is, at virtually every point within the plane under examination.

CAT scanning provides a level of resolution and detail that were unobtainable by previous forms of X ray, and was a major breakthrough in the noninvasive diagnosis of disease. It enables images to be made of structures, such as the brain, that are surrounded by bone. Conventional X rays are unable to show any detail in such structures. In addition, the CAT scanner has the advantage that it can show body planes in any desired orientation. The mass of data stored in the computer can be used to build up images in any required plane. Images can be viewed on a monitor screen, and records of these can be made on transparent photographic film.

The basic idea behind CAT scanning has been seminal in allowing the development of a family of scanners using sources other than X rays. These include the MRI scanner (see Magnetic resonance imaging), the ultrasound scanner (see Ultrasound), and the positron emission scanner (see PET scanning).

Radiotherapy

Not only is the X-ray technique one of the most valuable diagnostic tools available to doctors, but it is also an invaluable weapon against cancer. X rays can damage all living cells, but cells that are growing and dividing profusely, like cancer cells, are damaged more easily than normal cells, and are slow to recover.

Radiotherapy is thus an important method of treatment in many types of cancer. Sometimes it is used on its own, as, for example, in the treatment of cervical cancer (see Cervix and cervical smears) or leukemia (see Leukemia), in order to take out all the abnormal cells. At other times it is used in conjunction with other methods. For example, during the treatment of breast cancer (see Breasts), where the malignant tumor is surgically removed, radiography will often be used to destroy any remaining tumor cells. Finally, it is used as a palliative measure (see Pain management) in order to relieve symptoms of cancers

took no precautions at all when working with X rays. They discovered to their cost that large doses of radiation (see Radiation sickness) cause skin burns (see Burns, and Skin and skin diseases) and dermatitis (see Dermatitis), cataract formation in the eyes (see Cataracts, and Eyes and eyesight), the appearance of various types of cancer, and damage to the reproductive organs (see Ovaries, Penis, Testes, Vagina, and Vulva) resulting in genetic abnormalities in their children (see Genetics, and Mutation).

Today we are in a rather more fortunate position, not only because we have a much more complete understanding of

the nature of the hazards, but are better able to reduce them to an absolute minimum. Modern X-ray film, equipment, and techniques are designed specifically to produce high-quality images at the lowest possible radiation dose to the patient.

The possible hazard of genetic damage is usually minimized by shielding the patient's reproductive organs from the X-ray beam whenever possible with a sheet of lead. Furthermore, any non-urgent X-ray examinations of women of childbearing age are usually carried out only during the first 10 days of the menstrual cycle (this is called the ten-day rule), during which the possibility of pregnancy is unlikely.

Outlook

There are occasional scares in the media about the risk involved in X rays. From an ethical point of view, it is, of course, important for a patient to be fully informed of possible side effects of diagnostic, therapeutic, and palliative uses of X rays. However, with the increasing refinement, in terms of safety and effectiveness, of both X-ray scans and radiotherapeutic equipment, patients should be reassured that in every instance benefits will far outweigh any risk of serious side effects. X rays will continue to be an invaluable tool in modern medicine.

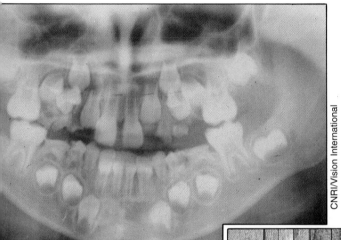

This print (below) shows the type of equipment used during the early years of radiography. The X-ray tube was simply placed over the area of interest, with the photographic plate behind. This sort of exposure inevitably caused numerous side effects.

CNRI/Vision International

that are too far advanced to be cured. For example, in the case of cancer of the esophagus (see Esophagus), radiography may be used to facilitate swallowing, or, in the case of a brain tumor (see Brain damage and disease), to relieve the severity of the patient's headaches.

The fact that radiation can also damage normal healthy cells sets the parameters for both the dosage and the length of exposure. Side effects (see Side effects) can be extremely unpleasant: fatigue (see Tiredness), vomiting (see Vomiting), and loss of hair (see Hair) in the irradiated areas are well-known side effects, although all these can be alleviated by treatment with drugs.

A few types of cancer are highly sensitive to radiotherapy, particularly tumors of the lymph glands (see Lymphatic system) and testes (see Testes), and a complete cure is often possible. The cure rate for other types of cancer is also high, although this, of course, depends on how early treatment is started.

Hazards of X rays

The early pioneers of radiology had no idea how dangerous excessive exposure to X rays could be, and they therefore

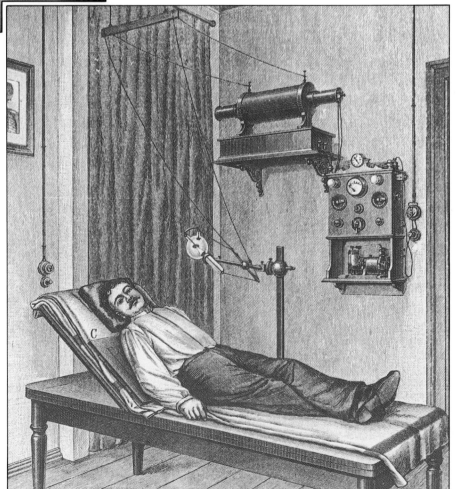

Ann Ronan Picture Library

Yeast infections

Q I am being treated for a vaginal yeast infection. Can I carry on using the pessaries when I have my period?

A Yes. It is generally thought best to continue with this treatment throughout a period, and there are even tampons available that are impregnated with antiyeast preparations.

Q I have athlete's foot, which I am told is caused by a fungus. But how do I know it isn't thrush?

A Athlete's foot is nearly always caused by one of the filamentous fungi that are best known for causing the various forms of ringworm. Thrush, on the other hand, is caused by *Candida albicans*, which is one of the yeast fungi. Athlete's foot can occasionally be due to Candida, and this is an important factor to bear in mind if the infection is not clearing up satisfactorily.

Q Is it possible to prevent severe yeast infections in those very ill people who are at high risk?

A There is a new practice of giving anti-Candida agents by mouth. The idea is to clear the gut of the infecting organisms. The gut is thought to be the source of the yeast in bloodstream infection, except in those cases where it is introduced through the skin by some medical procedure.

Q I have had two episodes of vaginal yeast. Does this mean that my boyfriend keeps reinfecting me?

A Candida exists everywhere that humans are. People may have repeated infections, but it is impossible to tell if they are continually reinfecting themselves or if they are getting the infections from the environment. It may be worthwhile for your boyfriend to be prescribed ointment to treat his penis while you treat yourself. Many doctors advise treating a woman's partner simultaneously as a matter of course.

Many people will suffer from a yeast infection at some time in their lives. It is usually no more than a nuisance, and only presents serious problems when associated with a severe generalized illness.

A yeast infection is caused by a fungus called Candida (Monilia). It can affect many parts of the body, but it is particularly likely to affect the vagina. It can also occur at any time of life, from the first few weeks to old age. Normally the infection causes little more than serious irritation, but it can spread through the bloodstream causing a severe general infection.

Causes
Compared with the number of bacteria that infect humans, there are very few fungi that cause problems, and these fall into two groups: yeasts, the most common of which is Candida, and filamentous fungi.

The yeasts are very similar in form to the type of yeast that is used to make bread rise. When examined under the

A yeast infection can occur at any time of life, even in tiny babies, although it is very unusual in breast-fed babies. Babies are most likely to get it in their mouths. An antifungal medicine will clear it up quickly.

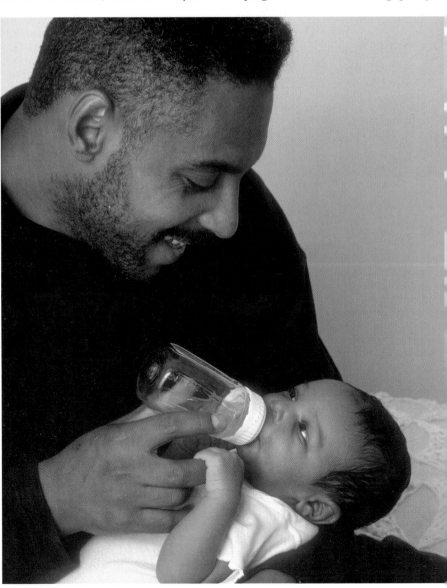

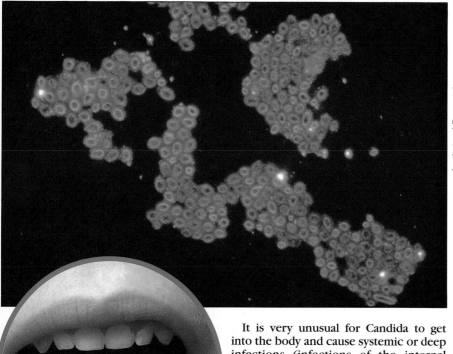

Institute of Dermatology

When viewed under the microscope (left), Candida fungi appear as small, round organisms, very similar to the yeast used in making bread. They can cause a painful infection inside the mouth (inset) and in the nail folds (above)—this is most likely to happen in people who constantly immerse their hands in water, thereby weakening the protective cuticle.

microscope they are seen as small, round organisms. It may be difficult to identify a particular Candida organism. The filamentous fungi produce long threads, which are made up of a series of single-celled organisms joined together like the sections of a drainpipe.

A number of different types of Candida cause disease; the most common of these is *Candida albicans* (which means white). Candida is an organism that is present on the skin or in the digestive tract of most people. If it starts to cause symptoms, this is usually because some other problem has allowed the Candida organisms to multiply to a greater extent than usual. For example, elderly people often develop thrush in their mouths, and the precipitating factor is usually a cut or abrasion, perhaps where an ill-fitting denture rubs the gums or lips (see Thrush).

A vaginal yeast infection is the exception—it is very common for the Candida organism to breed in the vagina, even if the vaginal mucosa (lining) is normal and healthy (see Vaginal discharge).

It is very unusual for Candida to get into the body and cause systemic or deep infections (infections of the internal organs and tissues). This is most likely to happen in people who already have some illness that lowers their resistance to infection. Systemic infections may occur when patients are on drugs that suppress the immune system, or when they have a disease, such as leukemia, that has this effect.

In rare cases, there may be a chronic infection of the mouth or vagina, or elsewhere on the surface of the body. This is called chronic mucocutaneous candidiasis. The exact cause is not certain, but it is an inherited defect in the immune system's response to disease and the problem starts in infancy or childhood.

Babies can also get thrush in their mouths any time after about the age of three weeks. This usually only happens in those babies who are bottle-fed rather than breast-fed, but it does not mean that there is anything wrong with the baby's immune system.

Symptoms

The two most common sites of Candida infection are the mouth and the vulva and vagina (see Vagina, and Vulva), where infection is called vulvovaginitis. Infection in the mouth is often found in people who wear dentures, and takes the form of small white patches on the gums, lips, and inside the cheeks. These may be very sore, particularly on eating, and they are usually worse in people who have a serious illness of any kind.

The yeast infection may affect large parts of the mouth and spread down into the esophagus, making eating virtually impossible. This can be a definite setback

for someone who is recovering from a serious operation or illness.

Vulvovaginitis as a result of yeast causes a white discharge with irritation. It can affect women of almost any age, but it seems to be most common in pregnant women and it is rare in children. Women who are diabetic are also prone to vaginal yeast infections, and it is often this symptom that initially alerts doctors to the disease before other symptoms develop.

Men can also suffer from genital Candida infections. For example, inflammation of the tip of the penis (balanitis) is often caused by Candida, and it is even more common for genital infection to be associated with diabetes in men than it is in women. Overall, however, candidal balanitis is less common than candidal vulvovaginitis.

Some women get repeated vaginal yeast infections without any predisposing condition. This problem seems to be occurring more frequently, and the conventional explanation is that these women are being repeatedly infected, perhaps by their sexual partners. However, this is not a satisfactory theory since Candida is an organism that is present in most people most of the time, but is only occasionally the cause of symptoms. It has also been suggested that the increase in incidence of chronic vaginal yeast infections is due to the wider use of the Pill, and there is some evidence to support this view.

Other parts of the skin, including the nail folds, may also be infected. Infection of the nail folds is called paronychia, and Candida paronychia is common in people who constantly immerse their hands in water (see Whitlow). Infection of damp sweaty skinfolds also occurs.

Q Is sex out of the question while you are being treated for a vaginal yeast infection?

A Sex can be painful if you have a yeast infection so you may prefer to abstain. However, there is no reason why you shouldn't start having sex again toward the end of a course of treatment, especially if your partner uses a condom. It is probably wise to make sure your partner is being treated too.

Q My baby got a yeast infection in her mouth at the age of two months. I thought it was a sexually transmitted infection and I couldn't understand where it came from since I was not having sexual relations at the time. What was the cause?

A It is common for babies to get yeast infections, although they tend to occur only in those who are bottle-fed. Don't reproach yourself that it was due to a lapse in your care; Candida fungi are so common that it is inevitable that a baby will come into contact with one at some stage. Babies often react to their first contact with Candida by getting a mouth infection.

Q When my baby had a yeast infection in his mouth I found it difficult to give him the medication my doctor prescribed. Is there an easy way he could have taken it?

A It can be very difficult to give medicine to small babies, particularly if they lose interest in their food, as they often do with a yeast infection. You could ask your doctor for some pessaries. These can easily be fitted into the split end of a pacifier and the baby may be happy sucking on this. Pessaries are perfectly safe taken by mouth in such a case.

Q Can babies get a yeast infection anywhere else apart from their mouths?

A Yes. It is common for young babies can get an infection on top of a diaper rash, since Candida tends to grow in warm, moist places such as this.

To help prevent yeast infections, buy underwear with a cotton inset (above). A suggested alternative remedy is plain yogurt, introduced into the vagina on a tampon or applicator. Yogurt is also said to restore the good vaginal bacteria that can be destroyed by antibiotics.

Candida causes infections of the internal organs in people who already have some other disease. For instance, the kidneys and urinary system may be involved in people with diabetes. Surgery can also predispose to infection, and invasive techniques, such as the use of an IV, may inadvertently introduce infection into the bloodstream; the only symptom of this may be a swinging temperature. It tends to occur in people who are already being treated for infections in the bloodstream.

Dangers

The main danger with Candida is in people who are very ill, and the more ill they are, the more likely they are to suffer from systemic infection. The most serious infections are those that affect the heart, brain, and eyes. Endocarditis (infection of the heart valves) often requires surgery to replace the affected valve, although it may also follow a valve replacement operation, and it occurs in drug addicts.

Treatment

The treatment of simple yeast infections is effective, and differs greatly from that of systemic disease. The medications that work on surface infection—nystatin and amphotericin B—are not absorbed when taken orally. In vaginal infections the medication is given in the form of pessaries and creams. People with recurrent mouth infections, or where the infection has spread into the esophagus, are given oral treatment.

Once systemic infection has been diagnosed it is essential to use a treatment that reaches the bloodstream. The problem with amphotericin B is that when given by injection it becomes toxic and its effects have to be carefully monitored. Other new drugs are also effective and may ultimately prove more satisfactory.

Chronic mucocutaneous candidiasis is difficult to treat since the defect lies with the body's ability to combat infection. The drug ketoconazole seems to be effective.

Yellow fever

Q I have heard that you only get yellow fever from monkeys. Is this true?

A No. One of the interesting things about the disease is that it has two different cycles of infection. Yellow fever is caused by one of the arboviruses, and this means that it is carried from person to person by an insect, which in the case of yellow fever is the mosquito. In cities, man is the reservoir of infection, so that an infected person has only to be bitten by a mosquito for the disease to be transmitted. On the other hand, in tropical forest areas the disease primarily affects monkeys, and the cycle of infection takes place high in the forest canopy where both the monkeys and mosquitoes live. It is certainly possible for people to catch the disease from monkeys, but only indirectly: they would have to be bitten by a forest mosquito.

Q If you have had yellow fever are you likely to get it again?

A No. One infection provides very good immunity. People who are brought up in tropical rain forest areas do not often suffer the effects of the disease, although examination of their blood shows a high level of immunity.

Q Could you catch yellow fever in the United States?

A Yellow fever may certainly be brought to the United States by travelers incubating the disease. However, it is very unlikely to spread here, since the infection has to be carried from person to person by mosquitoes, and the species of mosquito that the virus infects does not exist in the United States.

Q Can you be vaccinated against yellow fever?

A Yes. There is an effective vaccine available that is used worldwide. Vaccination is therefore not only sometimes a legal requirement for anyone visiting many parts of the tropics, it is also a sensible precaution.

So called because it attacks the liver and causes severe jaundice, yellow fever is one of the most dangerous tropical virus diseases. It is, however, a disease that can be effectively prevented by immunization.

Yellow fever originated in West Africa but is now found in the whole of tropical Africa. It also occurs in Central and South America and the Caribbean, and it is thought that the infection was first carried across the Atlantic at the time of the slave trade. Fortunately it does not occur in tropical parts of Asia, in North America, or Europe, and there are strict controls to prevent the accidental spread of the infecting type of mosquito by airplane.

Cause

Yellow fever is one of the diseases caused by the family of viruses known as the arboviruses, which have in common the fact that they are transmitted by blood-sucking insects (see Viruses). The arboviruses tend either to produce symptoms of meningitis (see Meningitis), or to cause one of the hemorrhagic fevers, in which bleeding into the skin and the internal organs occurs (see Hemorrhage).

The arboviruses typically infect animals as well as humans. In the case of yellow fever, monkeys and humans are the main hosts of the virus. In tropical forests it is a major disease of monkeys, and is difficult to eliminate. Mosquitoes carry the disease from monkey to monkey, and anyone bitten by an infected mosquito can get it.

Apart from the cycle of infection that occurs high in the canopy of a tropical rain forest, there is also the urban cycle of infection. Thus infection may be carried directly from person to person by the infecting mosquito.

Symptoms

After the bite of an infecting mosquito there is an incubation period of several days while the virus is multiplying in the body. Severe cases start characteristically with a sudden onset of fever (see Fevers), headaches, and pain in the abdomen, back, and limbs. The patient may hemorrhage and vomit blood (see Vomiting), and because the virus injures and destroys liver cells jaundice is common (see Jaundice). The kidneys may start to transfer blood and protein into the urine.

Recovery can start at any stage and is remarkably complete, conferring lifelong immunity. However, in about 5 to 10 percent of recognized cases there is a relentless deterioration ending in death, and in some outbreaks this figure is much higher. At the same time, there seems little doubt that yellow fever can pass almost unnoticed, especially in people brought up in areas where it is endemic.

Treatment

Once the disease has developed there is no curative treatment, but good nursing care is important in maintaining the patient's comfort and aiding eventual recovery. The outlook for patients is generally good if a fair standard of medical care is available. In the case of failing kidneys, for example, an intensive care unit is crucial. Relapses do not occur, and the disease confers immunity (see Immune system).

Prevention

The only preventive measure formerly available was the control of the infecting mosquito. Now the major preventive measure is vaccination. An effective vaccine is available and is recommended for anyone traveling to, or through, the tropics. A certificate of vaccination is required for many countries. The vaccine provides protection from 10 days after the shot, and this lasts for about 10 years. Babies under 12 months should not be vaccinated against this disease.

Yellow fever is impossible to eradicate from the huge rain forests of the tropics, where monkeys are the hosts and mosquitoes the carriers of the virus. Vaccination is therefore essential for anyone traveling in these regions.

John Wright

Yoga

Q I feel tense all the time. Could yoga help me relax?

A Yoga could most certainly help you since it is aimed at relaxing both body and mind. The asanas, or postures, are meant to be performed slowly and gracefully, so that the mind is soothed while the body is exercised. The breathing exercises and the Relaxation or Corpse postures are particularly helpful for relieving tension. You could benefit after only one or two sessions.

Q The yoga postures I've seen illustrated in books look like impossible contortions. I'm sure I couldn't do them. Is this what yoga is all about?

A No. What you have seen are the postures for advanced students. There is a wide range of simple and graceful exercises for beginners to perform. With practice you will find your body becoming more supple and you will be able to get into postures you would once have thought impossible.

Q My husband says that I am too old at 61 to take up yoga. Is his opinion correct?

A No. There are many people in their seventies who practice yoga exercises. However, check with your doctor before you start. Then join a class and practice daily. Yoga exercises are ideal for older people because they are carried out slowly: you ease your body into a position rather than forcing or jerking it. I am sure that you will feel lighter on your feet, more alert, and more relaxed.

Q Can I lose weight by taking up yoga exercise?

A Yoga on its own will probably not cause you to shed many pounds, but you should look and feel more trim because yoga exercises firm and tone the muscles. The best way to lose weight is to go on a diet and take up yoga as well. Yoga postures will firm up areas like the abdomen, upper arms, and thighs, which are prone to flabbiness if you are dieting.

To the uninitiated, yoga conjures up images of visionary-eyed mystics performing impossible contortions. In fact, the basis of yoga is harmonious exercise that is immensely beneficial, both physically and mentally.

Yoga is a system of physical and mental control based on a philosophy that originated in India. It grew out of the belief that a human being should strive to merge his or her spirit with the universal spirit, or a transcendental consciousness. The philosophers believe that this union (the word *yoga* means union or fusion) could be achieved through discipline, both physical and mental, and that this would eventually lead to the total identification of the individual with that higher consciousness.

In the form most often practiced in the West, however, yoga is basically a series of exercises or postures that relax the mind and body, and emphasize harmonious coordination of movement, stretching, and breathing. Along the way yoga exercises help to tone up muscles, stimulate blood circulation, regulate digestive processes, and improve mental equilibrium. Equally important, yoga can be mastered by anyone with the right motivation.

Yoga and health

Yoga exercises comprise a series of body-stretching postures that are intended to work on the whole body. The postures are performed slowly, gracefully, and thoughtfully to achieve serenity of mind as well as physical health and flexibility. Regulated breathing exercises are usually part of the program.

The discipline requires practice, but the rewards are quickly apparent. Even a beginner will get a feeling of well-being from postures intended to exercise every tendon, muscle, and ligament. Because there are no quick or jerky movements, yoga is ideal for students from age seven to 70. A word of caution, however: if you suffer from any kind of medical condition

Ron Sutherland

Yoga breathing exercises

Ideally, yoga breathing exercises should be performed before starting the postures. They are not hard to master and are of great value in calming the mind, relaxing the system, and combating fatigue. The complete breath can be practiced in any spare moments. All the exercises can be performed either sitting or standing.

Abdominal breath: 1. Place your hands lightly on your abdomen. 2. Inhale slowly and deeply through the nostrils, pushing your stomach out like a balloon. 3. Exhale slowly through the nose, contracting the abdomen. 4. Repeat three times.

Bellows breath: 1. Place your hands on your rib cage. 2. Inhale slowly and deeply, expanding the ribs sideways. 3. Exhale slowly, contracting the rib cage. 4. Repeat three times.

Clavicular breath: 1. Place your fingers on the clavicular area above the chest. 2. Inhale slowly and deeply, and feel the back of your throat fill with air. 3. Exhale slowly. 4. Repeat three times.

Complete breath: 1. This combines the three previous exercises. 2. Exhale, then, while counting up to eight, inhale deeply, raising your shoulders, pushing out your abdomen and expanding your rib cage. 3. Hold your breath while counting up to eight. 4. Exhale slowly counting up to eight. 5. Pause 10 seconds, then repeat.

Alternate nostril breathing: 1. Close your right nostril with your right thumb. 2. Inhale slowly and deeply through your left nostril. 3. Now close your left nostril with two fingers. 4. Hold your breath for two seconds. 4. Take away your right thumb, opening your right nostril and exhaling through it. 6. Repeat by inhaling through the left nostril and exhaling through the right. 7. Repeat the whole exercise three times.

To perform these exercises correctly, there are a few points you should remember. Always exhale as slowly as you inhale—don't let your breath out in a rush. Always take as deep a breath as you can, and always empty the lungs fully. This is designed to bring as much oxygen as possible into the system.

---

you should consult your doctor before taking up the discipline.

Each exercise, whether it is simple or complicated, is designed to benefit a different area of the body. The postures are executed slowly and then held for a period of time to give the muscles a chance to derive the maximum benefit from the position. The contortions that many people associate with yoga are for advanced students only.

Not only are the muscles toned and firmed by yoga, but the internal organs also benefit. For example, abdominal exercises produce taut muscles and stimulate and relax the abdominal organs. Similarly, inverted positions benefit the heart and the lungs while increasing the supply of blood to the brain. The result is that many people find that they are less fatigued and more alert after a session of yoga than they were before.

Special breathing techniques are often used in conjunction with the physical yoga exercises. The basis of yoga breathing is a deeply drawn-in breath, filling the lungs and pushing the stomach out like a balloon. This is held for a few seconds and then released slowly, contracting the stomach. Breathing is done through the nose, and slow, deep breaths of this kind also help to release stress and tension (see Stress, and Tension).

Yoga and dieting

Many people associate yoga with particular types of diet, such as vegetarianism. It is not necessary to change your diet to perform yoga, although serious students do not usually eat much heavy, rich food because it can interfere with performing the more complicated exercises.

Yoga on its own will probably not induce any great weight loss, but there may be a dramatic improvement in appearance since the exercises firm up the muscles and improve posture. For overweight people yoga should, ideally, be combined with a diet since it will

Because of their greater agility and elasticity, children can make fairly difficult yoga exercises look simple. Yoga will also help a child to develop grace, poise, and the powers of concentration.

The Soorya Namaskar or Sun exercise is a preparation. The set of movements is performed at the start of each session of yoga. It consists of a cycle of gentle, almost langorous, postures, which loosen up all the muscles that will come into use, and promote a serene state of mind.

Ron Sutherland

A selection of yoga exercises, each of which has a specific aim or benefit. Some are easy; others are more difficult, and should be attempted only when the yoga teacher feels that his or her pupil is ready. Clockwise, from top to bottom: the Cobra, an effective abdominal exercise; the Locust, which works on the spine; the Bridge, which benefits the back; the Wheel, a spectacular posture that attacks the areas where fat tends to accumulate; the Plough, a fine exercise for relieving backache; the Bow, which is a posture especially suited to the dieter's needs; and, finally, the Headstand with legs extended, which strengthens the heart and improves blood circulation.

Q I've just had a baby and feel very flabby. Could yoga help me to get my figure back?

A Yes. Yoga exercises are excellent because they tone up all the muscles of the body. Check with your doctor first and, as long as he or she has no objection, join a yoga class and practice daily. If you feel particularly flabby around the abdominal region, ask your yoga teacher to show you the specific exercises for this area. You can then practice them as often as you like. Don't overstrain your body in your eagerness to get your figure back; yoga is a gentle art, and you will soon see results.

Q My eight-year-old daughter wants to take up yoga. Do you think she is too young?

A No. Her youthful flexibility will give her a great advantage. The exercises will teach her body control, concentration, gracefulness, and the ability to relax. She will probably progress fast and soon be able to master complicated postures.

Q I suffer from backaches. Do you think that yoga will do me any good at all?

A Quite possibly, but check with your doctor before joining a class. There are yoga postures that are particularly helpful to sufferers from backache, lower-back pain, and rheumatism. Explain the problem to your teacher and ask him or her to teach you those postures that might help you most.

Q My friend swears by yoga; she says that since taking up the exercises she feels better, eats less, and sleeps more soundly. Are her claims correct?

A Almost everybody who takes up yoga exercises and practices them regularly reports an improvement in physical and mental well-being, so your friend could be correct in attributing her good health to yoga. Why not put it to the test? Ask your friend if you can accompany her to the classes and find out for yourself what the benefits are.

Yoga relaxation

Always end a session of exercises with the Relaxation or Corpse posture. It can also be performed on its own whenever you have the free time or opportunity. Carried out correctly—and it does take practice—it relaxes mind and body, easing tension, reducing fatigue, and producing a feeling of revitalization.

Lie on your back on the floor, arms by your side, legs straight out and together. Try to let go completely, imagining that your body has great weight and is sinking through the floor. Try to empty your mind of all thoughts except the weight of your body. Now relax every part of your body in turn in this order:

1. The scalp and the forehead; 2. Eyes and eyeballs; 3. Mouth and jaw; 4. Throat; 5. Neck; 6. Shoulders; 7. Thorax; 8. Upper arms; 9. Forearms; 10. Hands and fingers; 11. Abdomen; 12. Buttocks; 13. Thighs; 14. Calves; 15. Feet and toes.

Lie for one minute, then repeat, starting with feet and toes. Lie flat out again for one minute. Sit up slowly. Rise slowly.

keep the body firm even as the individual loses weight. Diet without exercise can result in folds of flabby skin (see Slimming). Yoga exercises are particularly useful in that they work on every part of the body, including the abdominal area, the upper arms, and the thighs—areas that are prone to flabbiness.

While it is true that the Indian yogi would be a vegetarian, yoga as a philosophy stresses moderation. The Indian yogi abstains from meat because it is hard to digest, but this is not necessary for everyone. For good health a diet low in refined sugars and starch, a minimum of canned or frozen foods, and an emphasis on whole wheat bread, milk, dairy products, fresh vegetables, and fresh fruit will combine well with yoga exercises (see Diet).

Yoga practice demands that food should be well-chewed as an aid to digestion and that, ideally, the stomach should be only half full at the end of each meal; this allows the digestive juices to function efficiently. This is obviously a good precept for anyone who suffers from digestive disorders.

Medical conditions

Many people have reported gaining relief from a wide range of medical conditions by practicing yoga and, while it is difficult to verify these claims with any accuracy, there are certain exercises that do

Yoga is ideal exercise in middle and old age, since the postures are effected smoothly and do not force the body at all.

seem to benefit people suffering from specific complaints.

The abdominal exercises, like the Cobra and the Bow, help all the organs of the digestive system to function without the aid of laxatives. These exercises are claimed to alleviate conditions such as indigestion, constipation, heartburn, and even colitis. The positions that exercise the spine, like the Locust, Plough, Tree, Bow, or Back stretching, help to relieve backache, menstrual or other cramps, lower-back pain, and rheumatism. Inverted positions, such as the Headstand and Shoulderstand, strengthen the heart and allow blood to flow freely to the organs in the upper parts of the body; they can also help sufferers from ailments such as asthma or bronchitis. In addition, these inverted positions also result in increased circulation to the thyroid gland, stimulating its function in regulating the body's metabolism and increasing an overall feeling of vitality (see Thyroid).

For people who are obese, exercises that may be helpful include Bow, Knee

Yehudi Menuhin, violinist and conductor, is a fervent disciple of yoga. Here he conducts the centenary concert of the Berlin Philharmonic standing on his head!

and Head, Back stretching, Twist, and Triangle. These attack the areas where fat tends to accumulate and, when combined with a sensible diet, can bring marked improvement (see Obesity).

Some yoga exercises can be continued through the first months of pregnancy, though a doctor's opinion should be sought. Obviously some postures—the Headstand, for example—are forbidden, but some of the simpler exercises can be very beneficial. After pregnancy, again on doctor's advice, yoga can be resumed and can be effective in firming up abdominal muscles and toning up the body. Many of the breathing exercises used in natural childbirth were derived from yoga breathing techniques.

The mental tranquility that is another benefit of yoga helps to give sound sleep, and many people report that it cures their insomnia (see Insomnia). Increased mental

alertness and clarity of mind are also claimed. Converts to yoga argue that they can carry out daily tasks with less fatigue than before they took up the discipline.

Rejuvenation

In India many yogis live to an advanced age, and while this may be due in part to their diet, yoga exercises are probably also very influential. Yoga cannot arrest the process of aging, but it can keep a person looking younger for longer.

Yoga can be taken up by people in their sixties and seventies—though it would be a good idea to discuss this with the doctor before doing so—since the exercises do not force the body in any way. With practice, the stiffness that is common in later life can be replaced by a degree of suppleness. It has also been claimed that yoga helps to relieve arthritis that for many people is the bane of old

The Lotus is probably the best known yoga pose. It is a meditation posture that helps to create serenity of mind and a feeling of well-being in the student.

age (see Arthritis). Certainly more elderly people should feel all the benefits of increased flexibility of muscles, better posture, increased vigor, and alertness.

Many older people suffer from insomnia, and this can be alleviated by yoga. Many will also benefit from postures that ease backache and rheumatism.

Taking up yoga

Yoga classes are held all over the United States. Your local library or community center may be able to give you details. It is better to learn in a class since a teacher will be able to monitor your progress better than you will yourself, and will be able to introduce you to new exercises as you become ready.

Once you have started your classes, however, you need to practice daily for best results. You should not exercise within two hours of eating a meal, and don't wear constricting clothing. You do not need a large space, but it helps if you can practice in front of a mirror. Do the exercises that you have learned in class, remembering to go into and come out of each pose slowly. For best results try to exercise for at least 15 minutes daily; the time of day is unimportant.

When you first start yoga exercises you will probably find that your body is very stiff and does not respond well to your commands. The stiffness will disappear with practice and you will soon find that you can take up postures that looked impossible to begin with. One of the main benefits of yoga is that even attempting an exercise, even though you may not be able to complete it, can benefit the body. Do not feel discouraged after one or two failures—if you persevere you will soon feel the benefits.

Zest

Q I don't sleep as well as I used to. This leaves me tired and irritable during the day, and I don't have the zest for life that I once had. What can I do about it?

A Try to work out what it is that is interfering with your sleep. Perhaps you are subconsciously depressed or anxious about something. Perhaps you are not getting enough leisure time, so that you take work worries to bed with you. If you can't resolve the problem yourself within two weeks, ask for your doctor's help in unraveling it. Whatever you do, don't start taking sleeping drugs, which may only end up by making the situation worse.

Q I seem very sluggish these days. Do you think vitamin pills or a tonic would help me?

A No, almost certainly not. You must first find out why you are less full of life than you used to be. It could be something physical, such as anemia. However, it might equally be something mental, like some nagging worry or unresolved problem. If necessary don't hesitate to get your doctor to help in sorting it out with you.

Q Since my husband died I have become a real misery. I used to be such a lively person, and wonder whether I will ever get my zest for living back?

A Yes, you will eventually. Grief and bereavement are very draining, and you are unlikely to feel much zest for anything while it remains with you. Although grief is a very natural thing, it sometimes is allowed to go on longer than is really necessary—it becomes a kind of habit. Perhaps you need to give yourself a better chance to get out of it by mixing more with other people, going to parties again, and so on, even if you don't feel much like it at first. Treat yourself to some new clothes; try doing something different or going somewhere completely new. It's surprising how quickly things can change once you make the first all-important move.

An eager relish to get the most from life, a lively will to tackle its problems—zest is an aspect of personality that fluctuates with our health and state of mind.

Strictly speaking, *zest* is not a medical term. But it is a word used by both doctor and patient when discussing lethargy, depression, illness, or even behavior or attitude (see Depression, and Lethargy).

The term *zest* means great interest, keen enjoyment, a lively and enthusiastic relish for life. It is an attitude of mind that is largely determined by personality type and genetic inheritance. Zest is not something we all have or even should have, but when it is missing from a normally lively person it may be cause for concern.

Physical well-being

A loss of zest may be symptomatic of impending sickness, anxiety (see Anxiety), depression, or even poor eating habits or excessive living. If you feel that your zest for life has disappeared, then sit back and take stock of your circumstances.

Are you enjoying a balanced diet, or have you become sluggish through overindulgence and lack of exercise? What about alcohol? It is almost too easy to get into a state of subintoxication where the brain is seldom free from the numbing effects of alcohol. Even sleeping pills and tranquilizers can dampen one's energy and, if taken on a regular basis, the most lively of people may find their *joie de vivre* waning. A temporary course of drugs such as antibiotics may have a similar effect.

Regular sleep and exercise, plenty of play, and a vacation (at least once a year) involving a complete change of scene are important if one is going to keep one's energy levels high.

All in the mind

Of course, sickness and bereavement do drain an individual's resources, and it often takes considerable time and adjustment before a normal zest for life returns.

Zest, however, is not just a matter of physical condition and enthusiasm; it is very much a state of mind. If your lifestyle is rather flat, excitement is missing, or you find your work boring and undemanding, then this may affect you mentally and emotionally, producing an attitude of bored indifference to what goes on around you. Only by objectively assessing all aspects of your life can you determine those aspects of it that need changing, and, once the first steps have been made, you will be surprised how quickly your zest returns.

If you feel, however, that there is a medical cause behind your loss of zest, do discuss it with your doctor. Simply talking it through may be all that is needed.

Zest for living, the attitude that allows us to draw vitality from nature and those around us, need never desert us. Grandchildren can be a source of inspiration for the elderly.

CLARKSTON